5

£2.50

THE PURSUIT OF
GREECE

THE PURSUIT OF
GREECE

AN ANTHOLOGY SELECTED BY
PHILIP SHERRARD
PHOTOGRAPHS BY
DIMITRI

JOHN MURRAY

© Philip Sherrard 1964

Printed in Great Britain by
William Clowes and Sons Ltd, London and Beccles
for John Murray
Fifty Albemarle Street London

To
MAURICE BOWRA

CONTENTS

Introduction 1

The Approach 17

Athens and Attica 31

The Way, the Mysteries, and Salamis 45

Kithaeron, Corinth, and the Argolid 59

Eurotas, Taygetus, Helen, and Mistra 87

The Mani, Charos, Rivers, Olympia 105

The Seven Isles 127

Missolonghi, Delphi, St Luke 141

Arta, Epiros, Suli, Meteora, Thessaly 165

Athos 195

The Aegean and the Islands 213

Crete 255

Envoi 267

Acknowledgements 277

List of Sources 279

List of Authors 285

Index 287

INTRODUCTION

'AS the sapphire and the aquamarine from the turquoise, so differ the waters of the Aegean from the flat blue of the Mediterranean whole.' Thus, some years before World War II, wrote Robert Byron. And he continues: 'Sail from Italy or Egypt. And as the rose-tinted shores of islands and promontories rise incarnate from the sea, a door shuts the world behind. Earth's emotion diffuses a new essence.... What magnet to our stifled love hold this blue, these tawny cliffs and always the mountains framing the distance? Why does the breeze blow with a scent of baking herbs which the misty shores echo in their colours? What is this element, hybrid of air and water, physical as a kiss, with which the night enfolds us?'

Some fifty or sixty years ago, such questions as these would have been entirely rhetorical. It would have been quite clear what magnet held our stifled love, why the wind blew thus and not otherwise, and what element enfolded us at night. For Greece was that most sacred of all countries, the land of gods and heroes, the land which had given birth to our civilization, to liberty, enlightenment, democracy, the arts, the sciences, rationalism, and to everything else of value:

> Where'er we tread, 'tis haunted, holy ground;
> No earth of thine is lost in vulgar mould,
> But one vast realm of Wonder spreads around,
> And all the Muse's tales seem truly told,
> Till the sense aches with gazing to behold
> The scenes our earliest dreams have dwelt upon.

Such dreams are very powerful. And this one of the glory that was Greece, the dream of the classical Greece, has been one of the most powerful in the minds of cultured Europeans during the late humanist, Renaissance and post-Renaissance phase of our history. At about the beginning of this century, another English traveller, H. W.

I

Nevinson, fair specimen of the cultured European, came to Greece. He arrived one afternoon and straight away made for the Acropolis of Athens, the centre of this antique glory. Unfortunately he was a bit late, the gates were closed, and though he rattled and called, no one came to let him in. So, with the sun going down behind 'Parnes and Kithaeron', he seated himself on one of the marble steps before the entrance, and: 'I tried to realize', he wrote, 'that I was present at the very centre and supreme height of human greatness. Around this very rock the mind of man once rose to a degree of wisdom, conduct, and beauty unsurpassed in any other part of the world. . . .'

For such people as these the dream of the Greece of the golden age was absolute. It filled the whole field of vision. It excluded everything but itself. That is why those questions would have been rhetorical. Greece was 'the very centre and supreme height of human greatness', and it would have been impossible for its atmosphere not to be charged with miracle and magic.

But during the last few decades those questions have ceased to be entirely rhetorical. The classical dream has ceased to be absolute. The mirage has broken. Indeed, some have begun to wonder what precise connection the Greece of the classical studies has with any historical reality: 'It is vain and foolish to talk of knowing Greek,' wrote Virginia Woolf, 'since in our ignorance we should be at the bottom of any class of schoolboys, since we do not know how the words sounded, or where precisely we ought to laugh, or how the actors acted. . . . When we read a stanza in a chorus, the end or opening of a dialogue of Plato's, a fragment of Sappho, when we bruise our minds upon some tremendous metaphor in the *Agamemnon* instead of stripping the branch of its flowers instantly as we do in reading *Lear*, are we not reading wrongly, losing our sharp sight in the haze of associations? Reading into Greek poetry not what they have but what we lack? Does not the whole of Greece heap itself behind every line of its literature? They admit us to a vision of the earth unravaged, the sea unpolluted, the maturity, tried but unbroken, of mankind. . . . Back and back we are drawn to steep ourselves in what, perhaps, is only an image of the reality, not the reality itself, a summer's day imagined in the heart of a northern winter.' And Robert Byron is even more critical of this unreal image and its author, the classical scholar, this 'student, ultimately interpreter, of Greek texts; endowed with a kindred love of exact reasoning and exact representation, together with a kindred absence of historical perspective and emotional outlet; he has fabricated from literature and stones an ideal of humanity, which he and his followers have pronounced applicable to eternity. It is the singular odium of this eternal comparison, for centuries the bane of European culture, which necessitates, once and for all, the relegation of classicism to its just place in the tale of human development.'

What is evident from this is that somewhere during the last fifty-odd years the dream of the classical Greece has lost its hold; that a shift has taken place in the attitude with which Greece is regarded, with which the traveller approaches her shores. What is this shift and how has it come about? This is quite a long story, and means going back to the beginning, to show how the classical dream was built up in the first place, so that it acquired the hold it did. And if this seems a somewhat roundabout way of introducing an anthology on Greece, it must be said in defence that unless such a digression is made it may be difficult to understand why an anthology whose aim is to present an image of Greece that more truly reflects the complexity, range, and spontaneity of the 'Greek experience' should seem to be so studiously non-classical in tone: for only when it is clear how this dream developed will it also be clear why it has so little to do with any Greek reality, ancient or modern; and why therefore the attempt 'to track (the Greek) spirit to its home, to capture it and wrest from it its magical secrets' has led to the choice of the pieces in this book.

One of the things which become clear when one reads the poets or dramatists of ancient Greece—and I have in mind particularly Homer, Aeschylus, and Sophocles—is that the world they deal with is for them immensely real and living. The gods, the supernatural beings that so frequently appear and direct man's life and thought, were not for them, as they may be for us, mere figments of the imagination, poetic invention, and so on. They are living dynamic forces, terrible, often terrifying realities. When Homer's heroes appeal to the gods, and Orestes, seeing the Furies unleashed and on his trail, cries: 'You do not see these beings, but I see them. They are hunting me down', they are not speaking of mere allegorical figures. They are revealing and expressing the inner movement and operation of cosmic powers in certain concrete situations. And this sense of the activity of such powers seems to pervade the whole of life. The gods are active in nature itself, in natural and human relationships: they are a way of life, an attestation of life—not effigies, illusions, or inventions. And the great effort of the great poets of ancient Greece was to reveal and express, from the interior to the exterior, the reality, movement, and compulsion of this god-haunted, god-tormented universe in which they lived. There was an immediate, urgent and vital connection between literature and life. The poet's function was not simply to amuse or decorate: it was to speak of what it was of the utmost importance that man should know; and to speak of it in a way, in a language that man could understand—in a language which was itself living and real, the actual language of the people among whom the poet lived.

This intimate connection between literature and life was gradually lost. Literature ceased to be an expression of life, of an experienced reality, and became something else. When, following the conquests of Alexander the Great, that world known as the Hellenistic world emerged, its chief centres were those commercial agglomerations like Alexandria, Antioch, Ephesus, which studded the whole Middle-Eastern area. These cities were rather like new towns of today. They were laid out on the lines of the cities of ancient Greece, but laid out as it were *in vacuo*. They were culturally rootless, with no local traditions of their own. But they were the outcome of the Greek diaspora, and their main language was Greek. So that when it became a question of trying to fill the vacuum, or trying to find something to make up for their lack of native cultural roots, it was only natural that they should look back to ancient Greece. In the literature of ancient Greece the citizens of these Hellenistic cities sought the cultural basis for their own civilization. They sought to imitate the models provided by ancient Greece, and to mould their world according to the patterns of fifth century Athens. They adopted the language of the past, they tried to think in categories of the past, to fit their lives into the framework of a bygone outmoded age. They wanted their epics and hymns to be like those of Homer, their prose like that of their Attic models. They produced glossaries of difficult poetic words, glossaries of Homer, systematic grammars, vast tomes on Attic metaphors and on comic and tragic diction. What in fact they were trying to do was to fashion a perfect instrument for the imitation of those classical models which they regarded as the ideal forms of culture, of civilization itself. The more perfect they could make this instrument, the more completely would they be able to conform life and thought to those Attic prototypes which they so venerated.

This imitative habit, cult of the classical past, continued with the Romans. Rome took over the classical heritage in its Hellenistic form. More and more did literature cease to be a direct expression of life, and more and more did it aspire to be but a copy of past literary models. Its language became ever more remote from ordinary speech, and ever more a matter of artistic convention and scholarship, derivative and pedantic. In this way the last centuries of the Roman Empire saw those imitative tendencies which had characterized all literature since the death of Alexander the Great developed to an unprecedented degree. Life and literature had fallen apart. Literature had degenerated into being little more than the instrument of classical education, the means whereby that Procrustean operation of forcing life into the classical mould could be most effectively performed. At the same time, as a counterpart to this process, the image of the ancient Greek world itself became more and more abstract, atrophied and artificial. Cut off from its living roots; divorced from all historical reality; set apart from the present; its gods turned into vacuous man-made effigies, effete literary fictions or devices of a dreamlike etiolated prettiness, ancient Greece became a kind of lost paradise, a great golden past in which souls too timid or trivial for anything else could find relief from the horrors and afflictions of contemporary megalopolitan life.

The next landmark in this story is the Renaissance. At the time of the Renaissance, this 'classicism' was 'reborn'. Why was this? Renaissance man, it is commonly said, is an individualist. The individualism of the Renaissance—not, incidentally, a sudden growth, but one going back through the Middle Ages to the Hellenistic world—this individualism represented a revolt against Christian thought and the type of society that goes with it: a more corporate, impersonal, and hierarchic type of society than that demanded by the Renaissance man. But this revolt had to find a cultural and ideological basis somewhere, just as the Hellenistic world had to find such a basis somewhere. And as the Hellenistic world looked back to ancient Greece for this basis, so the Renaissance humanists in their turn looked back, not to ancient Greece (as they might have thought they were looking back), but to the form which the literature and thought of ancient Greece had been given in Hellenistic and Roman times. Hence their cry of 'back to the classics'. In the classics were thought to be embodied the values according to which Renaissance man desired to live. They were to be the models for the new civilization which was just emerging, the new humanist world. Imitate the classics and all would be well. So far did this attitude develop that Petrarch, for instance, typical of the new mentality, laid it down that only Greek and Latin were suitable languages for literature. Only Greek and Latin authors should be read for guidance on how to live, how to enjoy nature, how to cultivate friendship, and so on. Thus, imitation and ideological interests went together, and the great work of providing modern European civilization with its cultural basis had begun.

There was another aspect to this undertaking. The classics were to serve as models for the new humanist way of life. Well and good. But to gather the classics together, to prepare and edit them for printing, to produce them in such a way that their language and structure could be adopted for current literary use—this was an enormous task. It needed a considerable degree of learning, an elaborate technical knowledge. These were things that not everyone possessed or could acquire. Only a few could master them—a small select company of scholars, of finely trained classical experts. Hence from the very foundation of our modern western civilization the enormous prestige attaching to classical scholarship, for it was the classical scholars who had to perform the task of providing this civilization with its intellectual and cultural models in a form that could be assimilated.[1]

By the end of the sixteenth century the classical scholars had in fact fulfilled their creative role—that of giving a cultural basis to the middle class revolution of the Renaissance. Classicism had by then become the possession of popular writers and was no longer the privileged reserve of scholars. It had become embedded, even fossilized, in those most stubborn and recalcitrant of all institutions, the schools and universities of Europe. From now on classical scholars could bask in reflected glory, enjoy a status and an esteem not for the work they were now doing but for the work which their pioneering predecessors had done a century or two before. The work they were now doing and were to do for the next few centuries had none of this pioneering or creative quality. More and more it was devoted to the mere gathering of information about the ancient world and its goings-on, and to filing this information in fat handbooks (or more recently in diminutive articles) where those who wished could get at it with the least possible bother. It was a task of preservation and diffusion: of trying to maintain the classical discipline and of propagating its ideals among the new mercantile classes; of remoulding the taste of the educated European so that it conformed to these ideals—was, that is, non-religious, rational, materialist, and looked back to the ancient world and in particular to fifth-century Athens as both the cradle and the great period of the arts, the sciences, civilization itself.

How well they performed their task may be gathered from the emergence, under their direct influence, of a new type of humanism.

[1] For a full account of this development see: R. R. Bolgar, *The Classical Heritage* (Cambridge, 1953).

7

This was the humanism of those who had made good in the new bourgeois world of modern Europe, had grown rich and possibly picked up a title in the process, had imbibed through education the classical taste, and who were now consequently in a financial and cultural condition to indulge this taste in a way which flattered their own vanity and was in harmony with the finest ideals of civilization. This new humanism was not that of scholars and schoolmasters, of universities and schools. It was that of learned societies and dilettante gentlemen. Its adepts preferred the gathering of objects to the gathering of information, preferred coins, statues, vases, inscriptions to the annotation of texts and the compiling of dictionaries. Addison the essayist discussed the relevance of coins to literary criticism; and Gibbon, escaping from Oxford, spent £20 on 20 volumes of the *Memoirs of the Academy of Inscriptions*.

Above all these new humanist gentlemen liked travel. Italy was still of course the main centre of the European tour, since it was relatively accessible, and was in addition the scene of the extraordinary discoveries at Herculaneum and Pompei. But the fortunate few ventured further afield. The fortunate few got as far as Greece. And here the wheel came full circle. Here, in a way, Greek met Greek—the humanist, nourished on the classics, considering himself the latest, and finest, flower of the classical tradition, came back to the place where, as he thought, it had all started, to the native land of the Greeks. And here precisely was the rub.

It was towards the end of the eighteenth and beginning of the nineteenth centuries that these gentlemen travellers began to reach Greece in any number, at a time when the Greek people were preparing for their war of independence from the Turks. It was the age of Romanticism, of new ideas about liberty and nationality. The Greek cause caught the imagination. It seemed to combine everything: all the classical associations, the struggle for freedom, the rights of nations. The country which had given birth to European civilization—which was taken to be the only civilization there was—was at last itself going to be reborn. The wheel, as was said, had come full circle; and many were the romantic philhellenes who took up the Greek cause. Shelley was one of them. In his preface to his drama, *Hellas*, published in 1822, he expresses perfectly the romantic phil-hellenes' state of mind: 'The apathy of the rulers of the civilized world to the astonishing circumstances of the descendants of that nation to which they owe their civilization—rising as it were from the ashes of their ruin, is something perfectly inexplicable to a mere spectator of the shews of this mortal scene. We are all Greeks. Our laws, our literature, our religion, our arts, have their root in Greece. . . . The human form and the human mind attained to a perfection in Greece. . . . The modern Greek is the descendant of those glorious beings whom the imagination almost refuses to figure to itself as belonging to our kind. . . .' And in the final chorus of the drama he sings of this reborn Greece:

> The world's great age begins anew,
> The golden years return,
> The earth doth like a snake renew
> Her winter weeds outworn. . . .
>
> A brighter Hellas rears its mountains
> From waves serener far;
> A new Peneus rolls his fountains
> Against the morning-star. . . .
>
> Another Athens shall arise. . . .

This might go unchallenged as long as one didn't visit Greece or know too much about the modern Greeks. But if one did go, as our humanist gentlemen, Byron among them, went, then things were more difficult. For the image of Greece these gentlemen carried with them was that artificial image enshrined in the classical tradition which they had received from their preceptors at various establish-ments of higher learning. Greece was the land of sylvan nymphs and piping shepherds, of the great god Pan down by the river, of old Triton blowing his horn, of islands where burning Sapphos sang, of Arcadia and straight noses. This image, in spite (or perhaps because) of its lack of connection with any historical reality, was for those travellers at the end of the eighteenth and beginning of the nineteenth centuries extremely real. And the rub came because the historical reality of Greece at this same period was anything but classical. Thus, on the one hand there was the legend-wrapped Greek, descendant of his half-divine ancestors, now once again in the forefront of the battle for freedom and justice—'hereditary bondsman' still, but son of the heroes of Thermopylae and Salamis; and on the other hand there was the Greek of flesh and blood, probably entirely ignorant of the heroes of Thermopylae and Salamis, member perhaps of some wild Peloponnesian tribe, and to all intents and purposes conspicuously lacking in those virtues and features with which centuries of classical legend had encrusted the ancient Greek. He wasn't rational. He wasn't enlightened. He knew little of his ancestors and cared less for their monuments. And worst of all his life and its activities were vilified by his subscription to a religion which he had inherited directly from that Christian Byzantium which to the humanists (suckled on the inane maledictions of their Gibbon) stood for practically everything that was non-classical, obscurantist, barbarous, of the Dark Ages. The world of the Greek revival received the news of this discrepancy between the ancient and modern Greeks with an ill-concealed sense of pain and bewilderment. If the members of this world were themselves Greeks—as, with Shelley, they were quite sure they were—how could the modern Greeks be Greek, or even have anything to do with glorious Hellas?

It was not long before an answer was found. It was a remarkably simple answer: the modern Greeks were not Greeks. Or at most very few of them were Greeks. The great majority was Slav or, more precisely, Albanian. 'The Albanian race occupies no inconsiderable portion of ancient Greece', wrote the historian Finlay; and he goes on to specify where these Albanian colonists have settled: all Attica and Megara, the greater part of Boeotia, parts of Locris, Andros, and Euboea; Marathon, Plataea, Salamis, Mantinea, Olympia; Poros, Hydra, Spetsai; and so on: practically the whole of Greece. Many of the famous so-called 'Greek' heroes of the War of Independence were, we are told, really Albanians. Even the 'national' Greek dress—the fustanella—is in fact the dress of one of the great Albanian tribes, the Tosks, and was only adopted after the War of Independence in recognition of the warlike virtues of the Albanians, though, Finlay adds, 'the calico fustanella hangs round the legs of the Greeks like a paper petticoat, while the white kilt of the Tosk, formed from a strong product of native looms, fell in the graceful folds of *antique* drapery'—the implication being that at least the Albanians had some connection with ancient Greece, even if the modern Greeks had none. All this, ably supported by the researches of the German scholar, Fallmerayer, was a great relief. The descendants of Pericles and Phidias were dead, and those living beneath the broken stumps of the Parthenon were 'the unmoral refuse of mediaeval Slav migrations, sullying the land of their birth with the fury of their politics, and the malformation of their small brown bodies.'

Thus the good classicist could breathe again; could, oblivious of Adam's fall, go on measuring his walls and gathering his sherds without having to worry himself about whether the mirage in whose name ultimately he performed these jejune activities was really more than the product of a stunted imagination. But in fact the release was only temporary. By the end of the nineteenth century other winds were abroad, threatening and disruptive, signs of the beginning of that shift spoken of at the start of this introduction. First, the classical idea of ancient Greece itself began to be doubted. It was felt that the ancients may have been far less rational and enlightened than imagined. Behind the classical poise, dark and uncontrollable forces were discerned—Dionysiac forces, mysteries and orgies, strange rites, sexual and savage, a vast irrational cthonic world. Irrational but vital. Religious but creative. Nietzsche went as far as to say that Greek decadence set in with the classical period, when the reason began to cripple and deny the expression of the dark forces. And as if to confirm this, archaic sculpture began to be unearthed—sculpture beside which the classical mode seemed flaccid and vacuous. In addition, there were the excavations of Schliemann at Mycenae and Troy, and a bit later, after the turn of the century, those of Evans at Knossos. The image of ancient Greece suddenly became more complex, harder to fit into the classical framework.

Then, the appalling ugliness of the huge industrial world being built up in the West, and particularly in England, in the nineteenth century—a world from which art seemed to be more and more excluded, in which it seemed increasingly separated from life and society—made several people wonder when this sundering of art and life first began to take place; and as they saw it, it first began to take place with the revival of the classical tradition at the time of the Renaissance. Already Blake had written: 'The Classics! it is the Classics, and not Goths nor monks, that desolate Europe with Wars.' And the counterpart to the enquiry into when art and life in modern England had fallen apart was a returning for inspiration to an epoch in which they still seemed to interpenetrate and coalesce. This epoch was identified with the pre-Raphaelite period, the mediaeval period. Those leading this enquiry began to find their models in this period, in the Christian art and life of the Middle Ages so abused by Gibbon and his like. But searching in and behind these models they began to discern the outlines and influences of Byzantium and Byzantine art. Mostly it was what outlines and influences they could discern in Italy—at Venice, Ravenna, or in Sicily. Burne Jones visited Ravenna in 1873 to see its 'heavenly churches'—churches which, it may be remembered, had made no impression on Shelley or Byron some six decades earlier. Burne Jones himself designed mosaics: the revival of mosaics was part of that general 'revival' of the arts centring round William Morris and his followers. Both Oscar Wilde and Arthur Symons visited Ravenna and wrote about Byzantine art. In 1894, Lethaby and Swainson published the first serious study of St Sophia, 'the most interesting building on the world's surface', as they called it; and in 1912 Dalton published his work on Byzantine art. A breach had at last been made in that asphyxiating world of classical preconceptions to which since the time of the Renaissance the theory and practice of the arts had for the most part been confined.

Thirdly, the persistent presence of a contemporary people, Slav migrants or not, living in the land of Greece, speaking the Greek language, and possessing a wealth of custom and belief in which

classical scholars themselves perceived overtones and undertones of
ancient myth and religious practice, was something that couldn't be
written off for ever as essentially unrelated to the Greek scene. To
start with, if an unmixed genealogy was to be the criterion of what
constitutes a people, then no one would come off very well, least of
all the English. In fact, the identity of a people depends on more
subtle factors than this: depends on common ways of thought and
feeling, on common assumptions and attitudes, on common religious
beliefs and practices. And here, for what it was worth, the modern
Greeks could claim a far greater continuity of inheritance from the
ancient Greek world than could their western detractors. In a sense,
this has been partially at least their misfortune, for many of them,
putting themselves too readily and uncritically to learn at western
schools, have themselves become victims of the classical image of
antiquity (which they now regard as *their* antiquity), a lapse which
has led, and still leads, to many abuses and confusions, often at the
expense of what is of value and beauty in their own proper tradition.
But this apart, the fact that on closer acquaintance the modern Greeks
were discovered to possess certain qualities and characteristics to
which parallels could be found in the writings of ancient authors
meant that it was impossible to dismiss them altogether as having
nothing to do with their so-called ancestors; but on the other hand
the fact that they so desperately failed to conform in so many other
ways to the classical ideal of humanity meant that, if they couldn't
be dismissed, some adjustment might have to be made to this
ideal itself. In other words, it began to become evident that instead of
the classical yardstick being used to measure the degree of the
'Greekness' of anything, including the modern Greeks, some other
standard of what constitutes the essence of Hellenism would have to
be found, one to which the classical artifice whose history we have
been tracing would itself have to give way.

All this soon began to have its effects. We have already noted
Virginia Woolf doubting whether the classical image of Greece was
anything but a dream; and the new perspectives of ancient Greek
history and art being opened up, those of the archaic period and,

further back, of Knossos were influencing the minds of creative
writers like D. H. Lawrence:

> Little islands out at sea, on the horizon
> keep suddenly showing a whiteness, a flash and a furl, a hail
> of something coming, ships a-sail from over the rim of the sea.
>
> And every time it is ships, it is ships—
> it is ships of Cnossos coming, out of the morning and the sea,
> it is Aegean ships, and men with archaic pointed beards
>   coming out of the Eastern end. . . .

At the same time, the measure of the impact of Byzantine Greece can
be gauged by the fact that while Byzantium has no place—as far as
I am aware—in the imaginative world of English romantic poets like
Keats and Shelley, it is at the very centre of the imaginative world of
such a poet as W. B. Yeats, who in two of his greatest poems chose
Byzantium as the only fit symbol for the profound compound meaning he wished to convey, and who regarded early Byzantium as the
most complete example known to recorded history of that supreme
type of society in which religious, aesthetic, and practical life were one.
And more recently writers such as Lawrence Durrell have sought to
penetrate into the living landscape of Greece itself and to grasp its
mystery and power: 'Greece: the vertical, masculine adventurous
consciousness of the archipelago, with its mental anarchy and in-
discipline touched everywhere with the taste of agnosticism and spare
living: Greece born into the sexual intoxication of the light, which
seems to shine upwards from inside the very earth, to illuminate those
bare acres of squill and asphodel.'

The result is that the image of Greece has now assumed new
dimensions, a new complexity. The Greece of the classical heritage
and of the romantic philhellene has gone, and anyhow has always
been irrelevant to the Greek situation. Greece is not and never has
been a lost paradise or a haven for tourists or an object of study, and
those who approach her as if she were any of these will always fail to
make any real contact with her. For to achieve this it is not enough to

act in the manner of those who singly or in droves are to be seen pouring exhaustively and exhaustingly over the Greek landscape, guide-book or notebook in one hand, camera or tape-measure in the other, hurrying from site to site, from island to island, pausing here to observe the niceness of the view, there the shortcomings of the food or drainage, elsewhere how graced with or delightfully free from western virtues the natives are; for this is merely an avoidance of experience or understanding. He who would wish for these must have a more receptive and unhurried kind of temperament, one that is able to let things be what they are and to express their own natures rather than serve as the raw material for some purpose or other, be it only one's own pleasure. He must have sought out not the past but the living fate of Greece, which is not a doom but a destiny, a process rather in which past and present blend and fuse, in which nature and man and something more than man participate: a process, difficult, baffling, enigmatic, with its element of magic, its element of tragedy, working itself out in a landscape of bare hills and insatiable sea, in the miraculous cruelty of the summer sun, in the long generations of the lives of the Greek people. The following anthology has been compiled, not indeed to define this process (for that is impossible), but to indicate something of the vitality and richness of certain of its manifestations as well as of reactions to them.

P.S.

Katounia, Limni
Spring, 1963

THE APPROACH

SOMEWHERE between Calabria and Corfu the blue really begins. All the way across Italy you find yourself moving through a landscape severely domesticated—each valley laid out after the architect's pattern, brilliantly lighted, human. But once you strike out from the flat and desolate Calabrian mainland towards the sea, you are aware of a change in the heart of things: aware of the horizon beginning to stain at the rim of the world: aware of *islands* coming out of the darkness to meet you.

In the morning you wake to the taste of snow on the air, and climbing the companion-ladder, suddenly enter the penumbra of shadow cast by the Albanian mountains—each wearing its cracked crown of snow—desolate and repudiating stone.

A peninsula nipped off while red hot and allowed to cool into an antarctica of lava. You are aware not so much of a landscape coming to meet you invisibly over those blue miles of water as of a climate. You enter Greece as one might enter a dark crystal; the form of things becomes irregular, refracted. Mirages suddenly swallow islands, and wherever you look the trembling curtain of the atmosphere deceives.

Other countries may offer you discoveries in manners or lore or landscape; Greece offers you something harder—the discovery of yourself.

2

A POT of basil may symbolize the soul of a people better than a drama of Aeschylus.

3   *The Dark Crystal*

THE journey to Greece is the most intellectual of all journeys. Thither least of all are we driven by that half-sensual curiosity which is and always has been the unconscious motive of so many journeys; and we are almost shocked when, as soon as we set foot on her soil, she receives us with what we least expected: a fragrance that is enchanting and wholly oriental, a mixture of orange-blossom, acacias, laurel, and thyme.

We have entered upon a pilgrimage of the mind, and we have quite forgotten that this land could clothe itself in an atmosphere which is not that of our memories. We strain towards sights we wish to see with too much impatience of spirit; we carry within us too many souls whose desire to reach these hills and these ruined temples is mingled with our own. We arrive lost among a crowd of ghostly companions, but as soon as we step on this soil, and feel the stone of Greece under our feet, and breathe the clear and sun-laden air, they leave us all in the lurch. We are standing in the antechamber of our longings, and we feel that we no longer have our guides. . . .

The first impression this country gives—no matter from where one enters it—is one of severity. She precludes all reverie, even historical. She is dry, bare, full of expression, and almost frightening, like a face that is terribly reduced by famine; but over all hangs a light the like of which the eye has never previously beheld and which entrances it, as if it had only at that moment awoken to the discovery of what sight means. This light is at once both unspeakably glaring and unspeakably soft. It gives to the tiniest detail a clarity, a soft clarity, which makes one's heart beat faster, and it mantles what is nearest to one—I can only put this as a paradox—in a transforming mist. . . . This light is bold and it is young. It is the mental image of youth, forcing its way right through to the very kernel of the soul. Until now I held water to be the most wonderful epitome of changelessness. Yet this light is ageless in a more penetrating way. . . .

Whoever lives in this light, lives truly; with no aspiration, nostalgia, or grandezza, he lives. To live in the light—that is it. To leave this light, for existence among the shadows—that was the terrible, inconsolable thing. 'Better to be a slave than Achilles here'—whoever has never seen this light cannot understand such a saying. . . . I see from the top of a hill a few goats somewhere on a slope. The tinkling of their bells, the lifting of their heads, all this is real and yet at the same time as if drawn by the most inventive draughtsman. These creatures have in them something divine, something derived from the air, as well as something animal; this light is the ceaseless marriage of spirit and world. A steep cliff, a few pines, a small field of wheat, a tree whose aged roots cling to the rock full of crevices, a cistern, an evergreen shrub, a flower: the individual thing has no ambition to be merged into the whole, it is independent, but in this light independence is not the same thing as loneliness. Here if anywhere was the individual born, but to a divine and communal destiny. In this air one is wonderfully distinct—but one is not lonely, any more than any of the gods were ever lonely, whether they might appear from the waters or glide through the air. And here all creatures are gods. This pine, beautiful as a column of Phidias, is like a goddess. These spring flowers which scatter fragrance and sparkle down a sloping meadow— it has been said before, and rightly said: they stand there like little gods. . . .

4   *Philhellenism*

WHAT then is real Philhellenism? What has inspired and still inspires strangers from northern lands and other continents, to fight, or die, or give the remainder of their lives to Greece? Is it hexameters and lifeless stone? Is it the abstract of freedom, or the hatred of infidel misgovernment? Is there, in fact, explanation?

When a man is drawn to a woman, he may want her body; there is explanation in that. But when he falls in love, motive defies analysis. The Greek sea-board is also of two elements. In the brown mountains, the rosy air and the sapphire sea; in the golden temples and classic sites; in the broken churches and luminous mosaics, sad residue of the Empire; in the temperament of the people itself; in these lies the body. And the other? It is the essence which defines the Romiosyni, the Greek world, and eludes the comprehension of man. Byron knew it. When he set sail the second time for Greece, invested with all the paraphernalia of mock-romance, he alone, of all his contemporaries, harboured no illusions of 'a race of heroes'. He said once, to a friend, who had suggested visiting Homeric sites in Thrace: 'Do I look like one of those emasculated fogies? Let's have a swim. I detest anti-quarian twaddle.' For Greeks, the epitaph of the greatest Philhellene is written in those words: 'Let's have a swim.'

5   *Byron on the Greeks*

AT present, like the Catholics of Ireland and the Jews throughout the world, and such other cudgelled and heterodox people, they suffer all the moral and physical ills that can afflict humanity. Their life is a struggle against truth; they are vicious in their own defence. They are so unused to kindness, that when they occasionally meet with it they look upon it with suspicion, as a dog often beaten snaps at your fingers if you attempt to caress him. 'They are ungrate-ful, notoriously, abominably ungrateful!'—this is the general cry. Now, in the name of Nemesis! for what are they to be grateful? Where is the human being that ever conferred a benefit on Greek or Greeks? They are to be grateful to the Turks for their fetters, and to the Franks for their broken promises and lying counsels. They are to be grateful to the artist who engraves their ruins, and to the antiquary who carries them away; to the traveller whose janissary flogs them, and to the scribbler whose journal abuses them. This is the amount of their obligations to foreigners.

Socrates and Others

NOT feeling any enthusiasm myself about Athens, my bounden duty of course is clear, to sneer and laugh heartily at all who have. In fact, what business has a lawyer, who was in Pump-court this day three weeks, and whose common reading is law reports or the newspaper, to pretend to fall in love for the long vacation with mere poetry, of which I swear a great deal is very doubtful, and to get up an enthusiasm quite foreign to his nature and usual calling in life? What call have ladies to consider Greece 'romantic', they who get their notions of mythology from the well-known pages of 'Tooke's Pantheon'? What is the reason that blundering Yorkshire squires, young dandies from Corfu regiments, jolly sailors from ships in the harbour, and yellow old Indians returning from Bundelcund, should think proper to be enthusiastic about a country of which they know nothing; the mere physical beauty of which they cannot, for the most part, comprehend; and because certain characters lived in it two thousand four hundred years ago? What have these people in common with Pericles, what have these ladies in common with Aspasia (O fie)? Of the race of Englishmen who come wondering about the tomb of Socrates, do you think the majority would not have voted to hemlock him?

The Trojan Horse

THE Greeks are remarkable for their finesse and intriguing spirit. This last quality has long been considered as the distinction of the Fanariotes, but I conceive it to belong to all the Greeks without exception. Talented, versatile, indefatigably active, subtile, and insinuating, they prefer obtaining their object by intrigue and strategem to gaining it honestly by industry and perseverance, in neither of which qualities, however, are they at all deficient. A Greek merchant is always endeavouring to undermine, outgeneral, and counterplot his competitors or customers, and will prefer gaining fifty pounds by ingenuity and finesse to double the sum obtained in the regular course of trade. This is the national propensity, and we cannot quarrel with it. It proceeds rather from a peculiar talent than from any inordinate desire of gain: and, though certainly unfavourable to perfect honesty in their dealings, is not incompatible with it. It is, however, to this peculiar feature in their character that the Greek merchants, settled in European and Asiatic ports, owe the reputation for unfairness which they have obtained from the indignation of those they have outwitted. A Greek merchant is, if we may so speak, a species of *amateur deceiver*; it is less a love of filthy lucre which urges him to cheat, than his desire to exercise his wit and cleverness: and we may generally conclude, that the complaints we constantly hear of the dishonest practices of the Greeks are the result of their subtlety of spirit, exercised on unusual and perhaps illegitimate objects.

8

IN no land as in this does one feel what divinity there is in the aspect of distant mountains.

9   *The Greek Experience*

FROM that height of joy in which man feels himself completely and utterly a deified form and self-justification of nature down to the joy of healthy peasants and healthy semi-human beasts, the whole of this long and enormous gradation of the light and colour of *happiness* was called by the Greek—not without that grateful quivering of one who is initiated into a secret, not without much caution and pious silence—by the godlike name: Dionysos. What then *do* all modern men—the children of a crumbling, multifarious, sick and strange age—*know* of the *compass* of Greek happiness, how *could* they know anything about it! Whence would the slaves of 'modern ideas' derive their right to Dionysian feasts!

When the Greek body and soul were in full 'bloom', and not, as it were, in states of morbid exaltation and madness, there arose the secret symbol of the loftiest affirmation and transfiguration of life and the world that has ever existed. There we have a *standard* beside which everything that has grown since must seem too short, too poor, too narrow: if we but pronounce the word 'Dionysos' in the presence of the best of more recent names and things, in the presence of Goethe, for instance, or Beethoven, or Shakespeare, or Raphael, in a trice we realize that our best things and moments are *condemned*. Dionysos is a *judge*! Am I understood? There can be no doubt that the Greeks sought to interpret, by means of their Dionysian experiences, the final mysteries of 'the destiny of the soul' and everything they knew concerning the education and the purification of man, and above all concerning the absolute hierarchy and inequality of value between man and man. There is the deepest experience of all Greeks, which they conceal beneath great silence—*we do not know the Greeks* so long as this hidden and subterranean access to them remains obstructed. The indiscreet eyes of scholars will never perceive anything in these things, however much learned energy may still have to be expended in the service of this excavation;—even the noble zeal of such friends of antiquity as Goethe and Winckelmann, seems to savour somewhat of bad form and of arrogance, precisely in this respect. To wait and to prepare oneself; to await the appearance of new sources of knowledge; to prepare oneself in solitude for the sight of new faces and the sound of new voices; to cleanse one's soul ever more and more of the dust and noise, as of a country fair, which is peculiar to this age; ... to rediscover the South in oneself, and to stretch a clear, glittering, and mysterious southern sky above one; to reconquer the southern healthiness and concealed power of the soul, once more for oneself; to increase the compass of one's soul step by step, and to become more supernational, more European, more super-European, more Oriental, and finally more *Hellenic*—for Hellenism was, as a matter of fact, the first great union and synthesis

25

of everything Oriental, and precisely on that account, the *beginning* of the European soul, the discovery of *our 'new world'*;—he who lives under such imperatives, who knows what he may not encounter some day? Possibly—a *new dawn!*

10   *The Landscape*

THE beauty of Greek nature seems to be due above all to two particular characteristics. The first is variety combined with extreme simplicity: the simplicity in the formal elements, the lines of the horizon; the variety being due to the light which, especially at sunrise and sunset, changes the scene magically every moment, as though clothing it in a different dress. Our attention is thus always held by this gradual transformation, the image before us being renewed through the play of light and shadows. The façade in itself is of extreme simplicity: clear sky, attractive and gentle horizon, streams and the sea's inlets. But the colours of the mountains, the surface of the sea, the tones of the sky, are always changing according to the state of the atmosphere. This happens also elsewhere, but as it is above all the light that gives this perpetual variety to the scene, and as the light is exceptional in Greece, these compelling alternations are more perceptible and manifold.

The other characteristic is the feeling of calm and repose. Rarely does the atmosphere grow forbidding, and when it does it soon clears up again: its disturbance is as a passing cloud of anger. The vibrant light of the stars, the waves of scent-laden breezes are so gentle, so calm, that it seems that the elements become rarified and are diffused into the harmony of that image of His own beauty in which God created them. . . .

11   *The Light*

THIS light has many odd foibles and conjuring tricks. One of these is the lens-like function of the air. All the vapours that roam the Italian atmosphere and muffle the outlines of things are absent here. A huge magnifying glass burns up the veils of distance, making objects leagues away leap forward clearly as though they were within arm's length. The eye shoots forth a telescopic braille-reading finger to discern the exact detail and texture of a church, a wood or a chasm ten miles off. Things in the distance co-exist on equal terms with those hard by; they have a proprietary and complementary share in the patterns that immediately surround one. A distant cordillera completes a curve begun by the vein along the back of a plane-tree leaf, a far off belfry has the same intensity as a goat's horn a few yards away, a peninsula leans forward to strike the stem of a dried-up thistle at right angles. Mountain ranges that should melt with the heat-haze and recession, lean forward and impend till one is at a loss to say whether a hill is a small nearby spur or a far-away Sinai. Perpendiculars only exist in walls and towers and tree trunks—unless the trees are olives, in which case they unite and revolve like dancers or contortionists—and the only horizontal is the horizon. The sea stands bolt upright and the sun's track across it is not a highway that retreats with the curve of the globe's surface, but, till sunset flattens it and lays it on its back again, a blazing pagoda. At this late afternoon hour, the hard-hearted mountains turn golden and lavender, the valleys become ground porphyry and powdered serpentine. Where the weathered limestone has fallen away in a landslide, the virgin rock glows bright orange as though infernal forges were at work within. The light also performs several simultaneous and contradictory acts; it chisels and sharpens everything so that the most fluid curve can be broken up at once, by a shift of focus, into an infinity of angles; it acts like an X-ray, giving mineral and tree and masonry an air of transparence; and it sprinkles the smoothest and most vitreous surface with a thin layer of pollen like the damask on a moth's wing. The stones and walls, as well as staying warm to the touch long after the light has left, are absorbent to the light; they glow as if lit from inside with a wick that burns down very slowly as darkness deepens. The strangest phenomenon of all occurs with the shadows. What little there is at noon is grey and dead, and when the colours revive in the afternoon, they are a cool clear blue and archways are curving waterfalls. But in the late evening they outglare the solids that fling them, falling across white walls or grey stone court-yards or the dust of a pathway with an intensity like a magnesium flare, standing from the surfaces that register them in electric-blue and orange and sulphur-green shapes as separately as though they were in high relief or deep intaglio. The motionless trench dug by a tree-shadow or the shifting and instantaneous bird-shaped cavity that crosses a terrace looks far more real than the tree trunk or the swooping bird which they echo; both of these the light, by comparison, has immaterialized. It is probably because of all this that a strong mystical and sentimental significance pervades the actual surface of the earth, the rocks and the stones, of Greek mountains. The adjective *theo-badiston*, 'trodden by the feet of gods (or God)' in ancient Greek and in the Byzantine liturgy, comes to mind. In an old ballad which describes a quarrel between two great mountains, free Olympus is held to be good because it is *Klephtopatiméno*, 'trodden by klephts', as opposed to the '*Tourkopatiméno*, the Turk-trampled, the shameful flank of wretched Ossa.

These characteristics have a strange effect on the Greek land-scape. Nature becomes supernatural; the frontier between physical and metaphysical is confounded.

12   *The Everliving Fire*

HERACLEITUS the Ephesian is most clearly of this opinion [that there will some time be a change into the essence of fire]; he considered that the world in one sense is eternal, but in another sense is in the course of destruction, knowing that the world of this world-order is none other than a modification of the eternal world. But that he knew that the world exclusively as such, composed of all reality, is eternal, he makes clear by these words: 'This (world)-order (the same for all) did none of the gods or men make, but it always was and is and shall be: an everliving fire, kindling in measures and going out in measures.'

13   *The Spell of Beauty*

UNTIL now all I have said has been about the fourth type of madness, that which makes a man mad who, seeing here some object of beauty which reminds him of true beauty, grows wings and longs to fly upwards, but cannot, and like a bird gazes at what is above him, scorning things below. This is the best of all inspirations and is of the highest value to him who has it and shares in it; and it is he who, loving what is beautiful and partaking of this madness, is called a lover. For as has been said, every soul of man has by nature seen the true realities, since otherwise it could not have entered into a living human being; but it is not easy for every soul to recollect those realities from what it sees here on earth, either because it had but a brief glimpse of them in its former state or because after falling hither it had the misfortune to be so turned by certain persuasions towards injustice that it has forgotten the holy things it once saw. Few there are then whose strength of recollection is sufficient; but these when they see here some likeness to the realities of the other world, are struck dumb and are no longer in control of themselves, though because of the inadequacy of their vision they don't understand what they suffer from. Now of justice and sobriety and of other things precious to the soul there is no light in their earthly likenesses, though a few, moving towards these images with their dull organs of sense, may just discern the archetypes they imitate. . . . But beauty, as I said, was radiant among those archetypes; and since coming here we have found it shining most distinctly through the most distinct of our bodily senses. For sight is the sharpest of these senses, though wisdom it cannot perceive—for wisdom (as each of the other beloved realities) would arouse a terrible love should such a clear image of it be given as could come through sight; but now beauty alone has this fate, and hence is most distinctly seen and most beloved.

The Isles of Greece

THE sun is not in love with us,
    Nor the corrosive sea;
Yet both will burn our dried-up flesh
In deep intimacy

With stubborn tongues of briny death
And heavy snakes of fire,
Which writhe and hiss and crack the Greek
Myth of the singing lyre.

The dusty fig-tree cries for help,
Two peasants kill one snake,
While in our rocky heart the gods
Of marble hush and break.

After long ages all our love
Became a barren fever,
Which makes us glow in martyrdom
More beautiful than ever.

Yet when the burning horses force
Apollo to dismount
And rest with us at last, he says
That beauty does not count.

LUCKY mountains, lucky fields,
    They have no fear of Death;
They don't expect the Murderer,
They only wait for lovely spring,
For summer to make the mountains green,
To strew the fields with flowers.

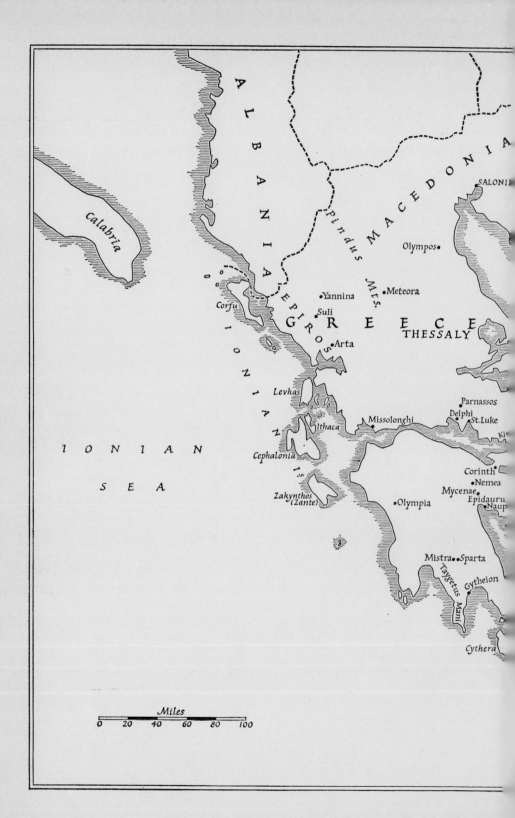

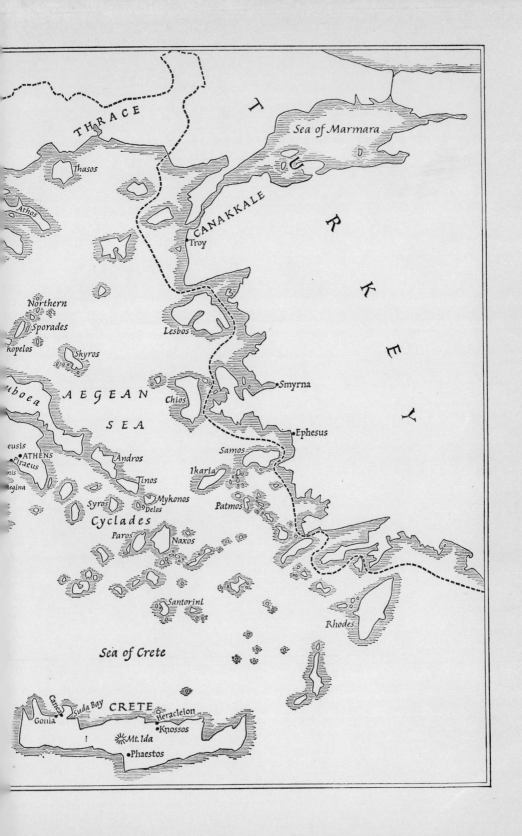

ATHENS AND ATTICA

A FRENCH man-of-war, lying in the silvery little harbour, sternly eyeing out of its stern port-holes a saucy little English corvette beside, began playing sounding marches as a crowd of boats came paddling up to the steamer's side to convey us travellers to shore. There were Russian schooners and Greek brigs lying in this little bay; dumpy little windmills whirling round on the sunburnt heights round about it; an impoverished town of quays and marine taverns has sprung up on the shore; a host of jingling barouches, more miserable than any to be seen even in Germany, were collected at the landing-place; and the Greek drivers (how queer they looked in skull-caps, shabby jackets with profuse embroidery of worsted, and endless petticoats of dirty calico!) began, in a generous ardour for securing passengers, to abuse each other's horses and carriages in the regular London fashion. Satire could certainly hardly caricature the vehicle in which we were made to journey to Athens; and it was only by thinking that, bad as they were, these coaches were much more comfortable contrivances than any Alcibiades or Cymon ever had, that we consoled ourselves along the road. It was flat for six miles along the plain to the city; and you see for the greater part of the way the purple mount on which the Acropolis rises, and the gleaming houses of the town spread beneath. Round this wide, yellow, barren plain,—a stunt district of olive-trees is almost the only vegetation visible—there rises, as it were, a sort of chorus of the most beautiful mountains; the most elegant, gracious, and noble the eye ever looked on. These hills do not appear at all lofty or terrible, but superbly rich and aristocratic. The clouds were dancing round about them; you could see their rosy, purple shadows sweeping round the clear, serene summits of the hills. . . .

33

The Face of Attica

STAND in an open place of Athens. At the Zappeion, at Patissia, where you like. Climb a small slope, a hill, Ardettos, Lycabettos, Philopappus, the Acropolis, wherever you like. Go if you prefer up to the small church of St Demetrios, beneath the Acropolis, and turning to the right where a road has been cut out for you continue on a few paces until all opens out before you. There is best, for then your head is one with the line of all the hills and mountains and you are neither too high nor too low.

Go there either one dry cloudless red-dawn of a day, or at a bright noontime, or, better, three hours before sunset, when all is more clear and simple to the uninitiated eye. Stay there, two, three, four, five hours. Nothing will happen to you at once. It is so good, so pleasant, to sit down on the ground and to stroke the grass and the stones, with which so soon you will be one. Sit without thought, without purpose; allow yourself to be bewitched by what is visible and in your mind's dark-room photograph hills, mountains, shores, waters, smoke, colours, whatever there is.

What do you see?

A whole world.

And each thing of this world delicate, dry, coloured. Follow with your eyes your fingers stroking the earth. Dry earth, fine, crumbled, hollow, fragments of many-coloured stone, often fragments of vases from a crumbled world. Look more carefully: a plant, just discernible, just protruding above the surface, minute, very delicate, many-coloured—you can just tell whether it is dead or living. Observe what is more visible, the stones beside you, the grass. Each pebble, each stone, each blade of grass, perfectly set, shaped most distinctly, imposing its features like an individual, like a person. Each blade of grass, from its root to its crest, to its final ray, all most beautiful to see. Each stone, grass-blade, little flower, plant, bush is outlined so clearly, is so distinct, so different, with such intensity

34

proclaims its existence, its individuality, that each pebble, blade of grass is like a Mr A., a Mr B. Observe the nearby flowers of the asphodel: one by one like human faces they gaze at you; observe the least stripe of its petals: in a large one you can make out all its globular seeds. Expand your gaze to the flowering asphodels which dress the slopes of the hills opposite, their pink shimmering lights breathing a gentle delight. Wherever you look you see, one by one, asphodels, you have the sense of the air and light between them. Observe, observe carefully each solid stone, each bulk, each protrusion of earth, each blue-grey rocky outcrop; observe all the details, the veins, the waters, the shades, the cuts in each hill, the diggings, the arabesques which nature playing with matter has made on each hill: it is as if you held in your hand a case of carved sandal-wood. A goat is on the distant hills, above the slaughter-houses, or on Philopappus: it is like a goat of finest workmanship held in your hand. In the far away mountains you can see all their construction, their precipices, all the lines of their body; you perceive, you feel their character, their expression completely. Observe the olive grove, which seems from where you sit like a thick clump: where there is a slight gap you make out one by one the olive trees. Even the sparse trees of Attica are distinct personalities. . . .

All the rocks, the hills, the mountains sit one by one like beautiful women of the people, dreaming modestly, like mothers holding in their arms fine children, like Byzantine Madonnas bending their head slightly with deep love; the small hills sit at the feet of the big hills like girls leaning their heads on the knees of their lovers, caressed and meditative. . . .

It is a single waving line. Everywhere a most simple, a most delicate curve moist and elusive as the huge quiet breathings of the sea, like the huge quiet waves, giving deep sensual delight. The straight line, the upright line of the one-boned Englishman, of the lance-like Englishwoman, is a line which produces strength, has resistance, it is a line that repels. A hill's curving line, the softly curving throat of a woman, is a line creating sympathy, desire to caress, it attracts the kiss; the line of a woman or of a hill is what attracts, what asks for

35

the caress. And it is strange that the curves of the Parthenon are thought to be so marvellous, for it is obvious that the true artist having to raise lines on a hill of Attica will but seek to harmonize his lines with those curves that surround him. . . .

It is this same line whose likeness we find in all ancient statues and works of art, in Byzantine Madonnas and the saints, in the demotic songs, in the young men and in the village lad, the village girl of today: of all these the body is a delicate line, all the movements and gestures are delicate, and the face has that intoxicated look of melancholy, expresses that strange mixture which we are of light festivity and of a certain modest and melancholy thoughtfulness.

A single waving line, circular and most musical. Beside all the other impressions the most powerful is that of music. It is like that of our circling dance of beautifully dressed, lightly joined bodies of young men and women, waving rhythmically and singing of the desires and sorrows of mortal life. Watching it one thinks that one hears always, from the circle of earthly lines, the friendliness and love of the song's joy and sadness which comes from the dance; and that music, changed from sight into sound, is like the long cry of passionate Aphrodite for the wounded Adonis, the highest poetical expression of the Greek earth.

18   *On the Acropolis*

WE passed the whole morning in the examination of the citadel. The Turks had formerly stuck the minaret of the mosque to the portico of the Parthenon. We ascended by the half-destroyed staircase of this minaret; we seated ourselves on a broken part of the frieze of the temple, and looked around us. We had Mount Hymettus on the east; the Pentelicus on the north; the Parnes on the north-west; the Mounts Icarus, Corydallus, or Aegaleos on the west, and beyond the former was perceived the summit of the Cithaeron and to the south-west and south appeared the sea, the Piraeus, the coasts of Salamis, Aegina, Epidaurus, and the citadel of Corinth.

Below us, in the hollow whose circumference I have just described, were seen the hills and most of the monuments of Athens; to the south-west the hills of the Museum with the tomb of Philopappus; to the west the rocks of the Areopagus, the Pnyx, and the Lycabettus; to the north the little Mount Anchesmus, and to the east the hills which overlook the Stadium. At the very foot of the citadel lay the ruins of the theatre of Bacchus and of Herodes Atticus. To the left of these ruins stood the huge detached columns of the temple of Jupiter Olympius; and still further off, looking toward the northwest, we perceived the site of the Lyceum, the course of the Ilissus, the Stadium and a temple of Diana or Ceres. In the west and north-west quarter, towards the large wood of olive trees, M. Fauvel pointed out the site of the outer Ceramicus, the Academy, and its road bordered with tombs. Lastly, in the valley formed by the Anchesmus and the citadel was seen the modern town.

You must now figure to yourself all this space, partly waste and covered with a yellow heath; partly interspersed with olive groves, fields of barley, and vineyards. Your imagination must represent shafts of columns and heaps of ancient and modern ruins scattered among these cultivated lands; and whitened walls, and the inclosures of gardens intersecting them. You must scatter over this space Albanian women fetching water, or washing the garments of the Turks at the wells; peasants going and coming, driving asses, or carrying provisions on their backs to the city. You must conceive all these mountains which have such fine names, all these celebrated ruins, all these islands, all these seas not less famous, illumined by a brilliant light. From the summit of the Acropolis, I beheld the sun rise between the two peaks of Mount Hymettus: the crows which build their nests around the citadel, but never soar to its summit, hovered below us; their black and polished wings were tinged with roseate hues by the first radiant beams of Aurora; columns of light, blue smoke ascended in the shade, along the sides of the Hymettus, and marked the gardens where the bees are kept; Athens, the Acropolis, and the ruins of the Parthenon, were coloured with the most beautiful tints of peach-blossom: the sculptures of Phidias, struck

37

horizontally by a ray of gold, started into life, and seemed to move upon the marble from the mobility of the shadows of the relief: in the distance, the sea, and the Piraeus, were perfectly white with the light; and the citadel of Corinth, reflecting the brilliancy of the rising day, glowed on the southern horizon like an encrimsoned rock of fire.

From the spot where we were placed, we might, in the prosperous times of Athens, have seen her fleets standing out of the Piraeus to engage the enemy, or to repair to the feasts of Delos; we might have heard the griefs of Oedipus, Philoctetus, and Hecuba burst from the theatre of Bacchus; we might have listened to the applauses of the citizens and the orations of Demosthenes. But, alas! no sound met our ears, save a few shouts from an enslaved populace, issuing at intervals from those walls which so long re-echoed the voice of a free people. To console myself I said what we are obliged to be continually repeating: Every thing passes away, every thing must have an end in this world. Whither are fled those divine geniuses, who reared the temple on whose ruins I was seated? This sun which, perhaps, beamed on the last moments of the poor girl of Megara, had witnessed the death of the brilliant Aspasia. This picture of Attica, this spectacle which I contemplated, had been surveyed by eyes that have been closed above two thousand years. I too shall soon be no more, and other mortals, transitory as myself, will make the same reflections on the same ruins. Our lives and our hearts are in the hands of God; let him then do with both what he pleases.

19   *Socrates Prophesying*

IT will not be long, men of Athens, before you are accused, by those who want to insult the city, of putting Socrates, a wise man, to death—for they'll call me a wise man, even if I'm not. If you'd waited but a little, I would have died in any case: you see how old I am, how far on in life, how close to death. I'm not saying this to all of you, only to those who've condemned me. . . . And to them too I wish now to prophesy; for I'm now there, on the threshold of death, where it is most common for man to prophesy. And I say to you, my killers, that you will yourselves be punished directly after my death with a punishment far worse than the death you have given me. For what you have done to me you have done with the idea that it will free you from having to give an account of your lives; but I tell you the result will be quite the opposite to this. Many more will there be now to examine you—men whom I held in check, though you weren't aware of it; and they will be more cruel, for they are younger, and you will be more harassed. For if you think that by killing people you prevent anyone from saying that you've acted wrongly, you are mistaken: that escape is neither possible nor noble. The best and most simple release is not to suppress others but to make oneself as good as one can. With this prophecy to you who have condemned me I take my leave.

20   *St Paul at Athens*

AND they that conducted Paul brought him unto Athens: and receiving a commandment unto Silas and Timotheus for to come to him with all speed, they departed.

Now while Paul waited for them at Athens, his spirit was stirred in him, when he saw the city wholly given to idolatry. Therefore disputed he in the synagogue with the Jews, and with the devout persons, and in the market daily with them that met with him. Then certain philosophers of the Epicureans, and of the Stoics, encountered him. And some said, 'What will this babbler say?' and some, 'He seemeth to be a setter forth of strange gods': because he preached unto them Jesus, and the resurrection. And they took him, and brought him unto Areopagus, saying, 'May we know what this new doctrine, whereof thou speakest, is? For thou bringest certain strange things to our ears: we would know therefore what these things mean.' (For all the Athenians and strangers which were there spent their time in nothing else, but either to tell, or to hear some new thing.)

Then Paul stood in the midst of Mars' Hill, and said, 'Ye men of Athens, I perceive that in all things ye are too superstitious. For as I passed by, and beheld your devotions, I found an altar with this inscription: TO THE UNKNOWN GOD. Whom therefore ye ignorantly worship, him declare I unto you. God that made the world and all things therein, seeing that he is Lord of heaven and earth, dwelleth not in temples made with hands; neither is worshipped with men's hands, as though he needed any thing, seeing he giveth to all life, and breath, and all things; and hath made of one blood all nations of men for to dwell on all the face of the earth, and hath determined the times before appointed, and the bounds of their habitation; that they should seek the Lord, if haply they might feel after him, and find him, though he be not far from every one of us: for in him we live, and move, and have our being; as certain also of your own poets have said, 'For we are also his offspring.' Forasmuch then as the offspring of God, we ought not to think that the Godhead is like unto gold, or silver, or stone, graven by art and man's device. And the times of this ignorance God winked at; but now commandeth all men everywhere to repent: because he hath appointed a day, in which he will judge the world in righteousness by that man whom he hath ordained; whereof he hath given assurance unto all men, in that he hath raised him from the dead.'

And when they heard of the resurrection of the dead, some mocked: and others said, 'We will hear thee again of this matter.'

So Paul departed from among them. Howbeit certain men cleaved unto him, and believed: among the which was Dionysius the Areopagite, and a woman named Damaris, and others with them.

21   *The Acropolis, 1826*

A Christian came and told us secretly that the Turks would move with great strength against my post and would capture the rooms beneath the Serpetze . . . and would enter the fort. For in that place were the mouths of the subterranean tunnels of the Turks and our own as well. We had also one tunnel prepared against them but we hadn't put any gunpowder in. Then, when we learnt of the move-ment of the Turks, we hurried Lagoumitzi to go and secure it, to put in the gunpowder. Lagoumitzi said to me: 'The tunnel is beneath the Turks and will resound when I secure it, and the Turks will hear me; and I shall be in danger. If you protect me,' he said to me, 'I enter; otherwise I shan't go in, for I'm in danger.' 'Go and do your job and I'll protect you. And if I die, then you die.' Lagoumitzi went in. I had been without sleep so many nights; night and day we had worked to make trenches; and I had made my rampart also. I went to sleep. The Turks, hearing the hammering of Lagoumitzi, gathered a number of themselves together and made an assault, and came to outside my rampart. . . . Then my men engaged with the Turks. I rose suddenly from where I was lying. I stood on the rampart. The Turks shot at me, I shot at them in the mass. They gave me a burst and wounded me in the throat. Then I made a step to come down from the rampart. I fell. The place was narrow; my men were fighting from the outer rampart. They trod on me and went on and, the place was narrow, they crushed me. They saw also the blood, they thought that I was killed. When all had passed and few were left and these were going into the fort, then the Turks would have gone in with them. Katzikostathis was inside; he left his post and fled and went through the door into the fort, into the church; and no one was fighting the Turks. Then I rose half-unconscious and I kept some ten men outside with the knife; I didn't let them go in. And I shut the door which they had open and we started to fight and we fought with pistols. Neither the Turks could fire a rifle, nor could we; and we fought for about three hours there. The Turks made a charge, they wounded me again in the head, on the crown. My body was covered with blood. My men sought to take me to go in; then I say to them: 'Brothers, whether we go in or whether we remain outside we are lost, if we don't hold the Turks and free Lagoumitzi.' (For the Turks had the mouths of the tunnels and Lagoumitzi at their mercy.) I tell them, if we don't hold out and they capture Lagoumitzi, the fort is lost and ourselves with it. But we will hold out. Then the brave

Greeks stood like lions. . . . The afternoon passing, I shared out the cartridges between the men; other friends joined us. A fresh lot of Turks came also; they fired at us furiously, entered the rooms, took possession of them all and opened the loopholes and fired into the fort. They came at us furiously to take our rampart also. . . . I was wounded again very badly in the back of the head; the cloth of the fez went into the bone, to the covering of the brain. I fell as dead. The men dragged me in; then I came to myself. I said to them: 'Leave me to die here, so that living I don't see the Turks over-run my post.' Then the poor Greeks grieved for me; they fought bravely, they drove the Turks from our rampart, and they closed them all in the rooms. . . . Then Lagoumitzi escaped and came out to us; he found me in that state. He told me he would stay there, I to stay in the fort for the doctor to bind me up. I said to him: 'Go in. If I die, the fort isn't lost; if you die, it is lost.' Our men held on above the Serpetze and threw burning rags and grass into the rooms. The smoke choked the Turks. Our whole company held their rifles ready. Near evening, the Turks made to come out, our men fired at them in the mass and Turks enough were killed.

22   *Kifissia: November*

ALL day sunshine, though now there's a chill at evening. Trees still green, and full with fruit. Outside the door is a big lotus tree, hung all over with ripe red loti, which we eat. Now too they begin to bring in the oranges and the grapefruit—marvellous creatures each the size of a child's head, and glowing still from the sun, generally with a bright green leaf clinging, which gives an even greater new-born feeling, the feeling that they are come straight from some dark unimaginable womb. The whole atmosphere is alive, sensual. It may be the light that does it, a very fine, *translucent* light, almost at times harsh with brightness. Nothing superfluous or false can exist in this light. It cleans and washes everything, and somehow in it everything possesses a great freshness, a great clarity and definiteness.

All is like a breathing plasm: the mountains are huge animals, you can reach out your hand and touch them. Leaves of trees flow in the blood-stream. All has this vital plastic quality. The result is that one is much more in contact with natural things, much more personal and friendly towards them than in the more hostile northern climes: they do not seem to be objects, but subjects. The moon for instance breaking suddenly over the crest of the mountain is really some old, yet very young, goddess, bathing the world in her cool, trembling light; and one feels a great reverence.

THE WAY, THE MYSTERIES,
AND SALAMIS

YOU yourselves saw how he went from here, no friend leading him but he the guide of all. When he had reached the spot where the paths cross and the abrupt threshold descends with brazen steps into the earth, close to the rocky hollow recording Theseus' pact with Peirithous, he stopped and there, between that rift and the Thorician rock, the hollow pear-tree and the marble tomb, he sat down and took off his wretched garments. Then calling to his daughters he bade them bring running water for washing and libation and they climbed the steep green hill and quickly did as their father asked, washing and dressing him as for death with proper ceremony. When all was done according to his will and nothing was left to do, a peal of thunder came from beneath the earth. The girls shuddered as they heard it, and fell at their father's knees, weeping and beating their breasts and crying out aloud. Hearing their sudden bitter cry he threw his arms about them and said: 'Children, henceforth you will have no father, for all that is mine ends today and no longer do you have to keep this long attendance on me. Harsh it has been, I know, for you, though one word makes all such burden light. That word is love; and more than from any other man have you had love from me, whom now you will be without through the whole of your life to come.' Then all three clinging to each other wept and sobbed. When at last they stopped their tears and cried aloud no more, and there was silence, suddenly a voice summoned Oedipus, making their hair stand up on end in fear; for God was calling him, again and yet again: 'Oedipus, Oedipus, what holds you back? Too long do you delay.' He, knowing it was God who summoned him, called King Theseus to him and said: 'O dearest friend, give your right hand in faithful pledge to my daughters—and you, children, give him yours; and promise you will never forsake them, but will always do what is best for them.' King Theseus, a valiant man, with no further word of grief swore to do as he was bid. This promise given, Oedipus at once groped with blind hands for his children, saying: 'Children, show your courage and go from this place, so you do not see or hear things unlawful for you. Go quickly, and let only King Theseus stay to witness what is done.' Thus we all heard him speak and with streaming eyes we and the children left him. After a little though we turned our heads and looked behind us: Oedipus was no more to be seen, and only the king stood there, his hand raised to shade his eyes as if from some terrifying unendurable sight. Then a moment later we saw him pray with a single prayer to earth and heaven at once. But by what death Oedipus died no man but Theseus can tell. For in that hour no fiery bolt fell nor did the sea raise any storm, but some messenger of God took him or earth's foundations were cleft, gently and painlessly, to let him in. For without a cry or any pang of sickness has this man gone, in a way that is most wonderful.

24   *The Pantokrator at Daphni*

INSIDE the church, in the cooler light, the high walls and piers rise to support the dome from which looks down the tremendous mosaic picture of the Almighty. The height seems greater than one knows it to be in reality; but there the effect of height is not, as in some Gothic buildings, to draw the eyes upwards towards something shadowy and indistinct. Here, as in the Parthenon, something of spiritual value is expressed by solidity, clarity and proportion. There is no mystification, no fumbling, nothing quaint, nothing that reaches in the direction of the impossible. Instead, what is miraculous is what is possible and real and open to inspection.

First, perhaps, it will be this perfection of the architecture that will hold and fascinate the eye. But soon the vision will become concentrated and fixed on limited expanses of wall or vault or dome where the famous mosaics shine or glimmer in gold and blue or paler colours.

In the dome itself is the huge figure of the head and shoulders of Christ the Pantokrator. It is a figure of stupendous power and authority. The piercing eyes, the long index finger clasping the jewelled book will seem to follow one as one moves below, and here in particular the curvature of the stone gives a depth and concentration to the picture that can scarcely be reproduced on a flat surface. Tremendously imposing as is this artist's vision of Christ, what will again, perhaps, seem most impressive is its reality. Here, certainly, are eyes 'acquainted with sorrow', but they are also severe and capable of penetrating anything in the nature of an illusion. Here indeed is a God who is not mocked, a God who, in this respect, may remind one of the Christ in Piero della Francesca's Resurrection and in other respects of the work of El Greco; but a God who is as far as can be from those common artistic conceptions of the West to which such adjectives as 'gentle', 'meek', 'benevolent', 'long-suffering', or 'charming' may often be applied. Here the severity of brow and mouth is not due to any contraction of the muscles; the searching eyes are capable both of sympathy and of accurate judgment; the delicate lean fingers are strong. Every line, even the two straggling hairs on the forehead, has powerful significance. And the bright book, whether Bible or Book of Judgment, held in that long hand, seems to embody a doctrine that is irrefutable and vital. Here is Man raised above the stature of Man, the Christian God represented as possessing fully the power and the wisdom necessary to supplant Apollo and Zeus. Something new, certainly, has entered the world of artistic imagination with those long curved fingers and that hierophantic book. Something new too in the look of the eyes. But one would like to know whether any of that combination of dignity and reality was descended or re-created from the great lost statues of the past that were hidden away from the light, though shining in gold and ivory, in the inner temples of Zeus at Olympia and of Athene of the Acropolis. Reality (not realism) and power are words that constantly come to the mind in any consideration of Greek art at any period. So far as this period of the 11th century is concerned, it would be hard to imagine anyone, however committed to one side of a false opposition, who, after looking at the picture of Christ in Daphni, could use the word 'decadence' of Byzantine art.

25   *The Sacred Way*

THROUGH the new wound which fate had opened in me
    the setting sun seemed to enter my heart
with the impetus of water flooding suddenly
the breach in a sinking ship. . . . For again at dusk
like one long sick when first he ventures forth
to milk life from the outside world, I walked
solitary along the road which starts
from Athens, and has Eleusis as its sacred
terminus. For that road always seemed to me
as the Soul's road. . . . It bore, like an enormous
river, slow ox-drawn carriages upon it, full
of sheaves or piled high with wood, and other
carriages, which quickly passed before me,
the people who were in them shadow-like.

But out beyond, as if the world were lost
and nature alone remained, hour after hour
a quietness held sway . . . And the rock I found
rooted at one side was like a throne
long predestined to me. And as I sat
I held my hands upon my knees, forgetting
whether I had set out today, or whether
ages ago I'd walked this very road. . . .

But then, round the near corner into this
quietness three shadows entered. A Gypsy
came from opposite and, dragged along by chains,
two heavy-footed bears trod after him.
And then, as they came near to where I sat
the Gypsy saw me and, before I was aware,
drew the tambourine from off his shoulder,

beat upon it, and with his other hand
tugged fiercely at the chains. And the two bears
rose on their hind-legs wearily. The one
(her greater size proclaimed she was the mother),
her head adorned with tassels of blue beads,
a white amulet on top, towered up
suddenly enormous, as if she were
the Great Goddess's primordial image,
the Eternal Mother's, she who in sacred sorrow,
as with time she assumed a human form,
was in her longing for her daughter called
here Demeter, in her longing for her son
elsewhere Alcmene or the Madonna.
And the small bear beside her, like a big
doll, an innocent child, rose up as well
not knowing yet how long he had to suffer
or the bitterness of slavery mirrored in
the burning eyes the mother turned upon him.

But since, being weary, she was slow to dance,
the Gypsy, with a single dexterous jerk
on the chain fastened to the young bear's nostril,
bloody still from the ring put in, it seemed,
but a few days before, suddenly made her,
as she groaned with pain, straighten up and then,
turning her head towards her child, dance
livelily. . . .
        And I, as I watched, was drawn
outside and far from time, free from forms
closed in time, from statues and from images.
I was outside and removed from time. . . .
And nothing did I see before me but
the huge bear with the blue beads on her head
raised by the ring's wrench and her own tenderness,
sad enormous testifying symbol of

all the world, of the present and the past,
sad enormous testifying symbol of
all primaeval suffering, for which still
the mortal centuries have not yet paid
the tax of the soul.

For the soul as yet
has been and is in Hell.

And the whole time
I—slave of the world that I too am—kept
my head bowed as into the tambourine
I threw a single penny.

But as the Gypsy
went away at last, again dragging
the lumbering bears behind him, and vanished
in the dusk, my heart prompted me to take
once more the road which terminates among
the ruins of the Soul's temple, at Eleusis.
And as I walked my heart within me groaned:
'Will the time come, will the moment ever come
when the souls of the bear and of the Gypsy,
and my own soul as well, which I call initiated,
shall feast together?'

And as I continued on,
night fell, and again through the same wound
which fate had opened in me, I felt darkness
enter my heart as water floods the breach
of a sinking ship. . . . But as if my heart had
thirsted for this flood, when it had sunk down
as though to drown into the pitch-black dark,
when it had sunk down to the pitch-black dark,
a murmur spread through all the air above me,

a murmur,

and it seemed to say:

'It will come. . . .'

26   *The Great Mother*

THIS holiness of Nature is a fragile thing: it wilts in proportion as her own virginal purity is tampered with, her modesty pried into, her austere exuberance 'tamed', as the brutal saying goes. 'Avoid tampering' is a spiritual maxim the Taoist sages made into the keynote of their teaching; the world's busybodies have gone on neglecting it to their own and our great peril. Under the continual measuring and delving and lumping together which now has reached its climax, the face of the Great Mother is becoming so disfigured that soon it may be unrecognizable, with all its eminences 'conquered', its furrowing dales 'brought under the discipline of a map' (as another blasphemy hath it), its underwater—sky even—contaminated, the whole so blotched and flayed and carved up and reshuffled that only the all-seeing Intellectual Eye will still be able, across the wreckage of a dishallowed world, to perceive the Motherly Presence there where she subsists. . . .

27   *Portent of Battle*

MOREOVER Dicaios the son of Theokydes, an Athenian, who was an exile and had become of great repute among the Medes at this time, declared that when the Attic land was being ravaged by the land-army of Xerxes, having been deserted by the Athenians, he happened then to be in company with Demaratos the Lacedemonian in the Thriasian plain; and he saw a cloud of dust going up from Eleusis, as if made by a company of about thirty thousand men, and they wondered at the cloud of dust, by what men it was caused. Then forthwith they heard the sound of voices, and Dicaios perceived that the sound was the mystic cry *Iacchos*; but Demaratos, having no knowledge of the sacred rites which are done at Eleusis, asked him what this was that uttered the sound, and he said: 'Demaratos, it cannot be but that some great destruction is about to come to the army of the king: for as to this, it is very manifest, seeing that Attica is deserted, that which utters the sound is of the gods, and that it is going from Eleusis to help the Athenians and their allies: if then it shall come down in the Peloponnese, there is danger for the king himself and for the army which is upon the mainland, but if it shall direct its course towards the ships which are at Salamis, the king will be in danger of losing his fleet. This feast the Athenians celebrate every year to the Mother and the Daughter; and he that desires it both of them and of the other Hellenes, is initiated in the mysteries; and the sound of voices which thou hearest is the cry *Iacchos* which they utter at this feast.' To this Demaratos said: 'Keep silence and tell not this tale to any other man; for if these words of thine be reported to the king, thou wilt lose thy head, and neither I nor any other man upon earth will be able to save thee: but keep thou quiet, and about this expedition the gods will provide.' He then thus advised, and after the cloud of dust and the sound of voices there came a mist which was borne aloft and carried towards Salamis to the camp of the Hellenes: and thus they learnt (said he) that the fleet of Xerxes was destined to be destroyed. Such was the report made by Dicaios the son of Theokydes, appealing to Demaratos and others also as witnesses.

28 *The Eleusinian Mysteries*

LET us therefore more attentively consider the fable, in that part of it which is symbolical of the descent of souls; in order to which, it will be requisite to premise an abridgement of the arcane discourse, respecting the wanderings of Demeter, as preserved by Minutius Felix. 'Persephone,' says he, 'the daughter of Demeter by Zeus, as she was gathering tender flowers, in the new spring, was ravished from her delightful abodes by Pluto; and being carried from

thence through thick woods, and over a length of sea, was brought by Pluto into a cavern, the residence of departed spirits, over whom she afterwards ruled with absolute sway. But Demeter, upon discovering the loss of her daughter, with lighted torches, and begirt with a serpent, wandered over the whole earth for the purpose of finding her till she came to Eleusina; there she found her daughter, and discovered to the Eleusinians the plantation of corn.' Now in this fable Demeter represents the evolution of that self-inspective part of our nature which we properly denominate *intellect* (or its being unfolded from its quiet and collected subsistence in the intelligible world); and Persephone that vital, self-moving, and animating part which we call *soul*. But lest this analogy of unfolded intellect to Demeter should seem ridiculous to the reader, unacquainted with the Orphic theology, it is necessary to inform him that this goddess, from her intimate union with Rhea, in conjunction with whom she produced Zeus, is evidently of a Saturnian and zoogonic, or intellectual and vivific rank; and hence, as we are informed by the philosopher Sallust, among the mundane divinities she is the divinity of the planet Saturn. So that in consequence of this, our intellect in a descending state must aptly symbolize with the divinity of Demeter; but Pluto signifies the whole of material nature; since the empire of this god, according to Pythagoras, commences downwards from the Galaxy or milky way. And the cavern signifies the entrance, as it were, into the profundities of such a nature, which is accomplished by the soul's union with this terrestrial body. . . .

Pluto, then, having hurried Persephone into the infernal regions, i.e. the soul having sunk into the profundities of a material nature . . . , the wanderings of Demeter for the discovery of Persephone commence. . . . What emblem can more beautifully represent the evolutions and processions of an intellectual nature into the regions of sense than the wanderings of Demeter by the light of torches through the darkness of night, and her continuing the pursuit till she proceeds into the depths of Hades itself? For the intellectual part of the soul, when it verges towards body, enkindles, indeed, a light in its dark receptacle, but becomes itself situated in obscurity: and, as Proclus somewhere divinely observes, the mortal nature by this means participates of intellect, but the intellectual part becomes obnoxious to death. The tears and lamentations too, of Demeter, in her course, are symbolical both of the providential energies of intellect about a mortal nature, and the miseries with which such energies are (with respect to partial souls like ours) attended. Nor is it without reason that Jacchus, or Bacchus, is celebrated by Orpheus as the companion of her search: for Bacchus is the evident symbol of the partial energies of the intellect, and its distribution into the obscure and lamentable dominions of life. . . .

It only now remains that we consider the last part of this fabulous narration, or arcane discourse, in which it is said, that after the goddess Demeter, on arriving at Eleusina, had discovered her daughter, she instructed the Eleusinians in the plantation of corn. . . . Now the secret meaning of this will be obvious, by considering that the descent of intellect into the realms of generation, becomes, indeed, the greatest benefit and ornament which a material nature is capable of receiving: for without the participation of intellect in the lowest regions of matter, nothing but irrational soul and a brutal life would subsist in its dark and fluctuating abode. As the art of tillage, therefore, and particularly the plantation of corn, becomes the greatest possible benefit to our sensible life, no symbol can more aptly represent the unparalleled advantages arising from the evolution and procession of intellect into a corporeal life, than the good resulting from agriculture and corn. . . .

29   *An Easter Visit to a Poet at Salamis*

WE landed on the island among a group of fishermen who had come to the monastery in order to have their boats blessed. Then we began to walk the little distance uphill to the white building of the monastery itself and the shade of the trees that stood outside it. Here we were welcomed by Sikelianos and by his beautiful wife. The poet looked older than I have seen him look before or since, yet his face lit up as he greeted us and as we exchanged the salutations 'Christ is risen,' 'Yes indeed he is risen.'

Under the trees, in the dappled shade, was a long table with plates of red Easter eggs and many other varieties of hors-d'oeuvre. A little distance away, over a trench filled with charcoal, the whole body of a lamb was turning on a spit. We went to examine it, to sniff the savour and to exchange greetings with the servant who was cooking it and who proudly expatiated on its excellence. The process of cooking was almost completed and we sat down in the open air to this memorable feast, memorable not only for the quantity and quality of what was eaten but for an atmosphere of dignified gaiety, of a kind of joyous calm, sympathy and affection. The sun streamed through the branches of the trees and the mild air was silent except for the tinkling of sheep bells or the occasional shouts of shepherds in the hills above us. We had come, indeed, to pay our respects to a friend and to one of the greatest poets of Europe, but there was no formality, unless the most exquisite manners can be described as formality, about our reception. Tired and ill as the poet evidently was, he was just as evidently delighted to be entertaining us. Of the conversation I can, unfortunately, remember little, since what struck me most was the kindness and distinction of the man together with the anxious attention paid to him by his wife and by those of his friends who knew him best and were, in all their gaiety, seeking to spare him any exertion that might be overtiring. I remember on this occasion, as on others, his warm smile, his grave attention to any remark that was addressed to him, the deep seriousness of his voice, particularly when he was quoting poetry, his sudden flashes of amusement. For long we sat over our meal, eating, drinking and talking. I learnt afterwards that Sikelianos was much more ill than he seemed to be. His pleasure in seeing friends and his natural delight in hospitality had constrained him to make an effort which any doctor would have discouraged. Yet his friends knew that he would behave as seemed to him fitting whether or not he was upon the point of death.

In the afternoon he was indeed persuaded to rest; but when we left in the evening he was much weaker and his weakness could

scarcely be disguised even by the warmth and perfection of his man.
ners. As we crossed over the water we talked of him again, but this
time with an added affection and with an acute anxiety. There were
some of his friends who believed that this might be the last occasion
on which they would see him, and it was clear that for them, in this
event, it would be as though for some time the sun were taken from
the sky.

Fortunately our apprehensions were unjustified. In a short time
Sikelianos resumed his usual vigour and I have many memories of
the firm clasp of his hand and of his ringing voice. Yet still the
memory of this Easter feast in Salamis is among the most endearing,
since it recalls most vividly to me the affection in which he is held
together with his own affectionate and noble nature.

KITHAERON, CORINTH, AND THE ARGOLID

WHEN at dawn the herded cattle were moving peak-wards I saw three bands of women dancers, one led by Autonoë, one by your mother Agave, the third by Io. Asleep they were, resting their bodies, leaning back on pine-boughs, or on the ground, careless heads on oak-leaves—sober, not, as you said, drunk with wine and the flute's sound and love-hunting in the woods. Then your mother, hearing the horned beasts low, leapt up among her crowd and cried: 'Awake!' Chasing sleep, they rose, a strange company, young women, old women, girls. First down their shoulders they let their hair fall, then, where the clasps had come undone, they tied their fawn-skins, binding them with snakes which licked their cheeks. Some, cuddling young fawns or wild wolf-cubs, gave them their own white milk— young mothers with full breasts and children left behind. Then they wove crowns of ivy, oak, and flowering briony. One, taking her thyrsus-rod, struck the rock, whence cool water leapt. Another poked her rod in earth, and the God sent up a wine-fount; and those who sought a white drink, scraped the ground with their finger-tips, and milk streamed forth; and from their ivy-rods sweet honey dripped. . . .

We fled to escape their tearing, and unarmed they swept down on the pasturing cattle. Then might you have seen your mother rend the full-uddered lowing heifer with her hands, others rip a calf to bits; ribs or cloven hoofs you might have seen flung here and there, and flesh hung on pine-trees dripping blood. Proud, fierce-horned bulls were thrown to earth, dragged down by the women's countless hands. More quickly than you could close your royal eyes was the flesh stripped from them. Like winged birds they swept down to the plains where by the streams of Asopus the rich Theban harvest grows; on Hysiae, on Erythrae, nestling beneath Kithaeron, like soldiers they swooped, looting as they went, seizing babes from houses; and all they laid unbound on their shoulders, and nothing, neither bronze nor iron, fell to the dark earth; and they put fire on their hair and it did not burn. The villagers, livid, took arms against them. Then, sir, was the marvel—barbed points did not touch them; but they, women, flinging their thyrsus-rods, dealt wounds all round, and, not without some God, put men to flight. Then they went back to whence they came, to the springs the God had sent them; and they washed the blood, and the snakes licked the stains from their cheeks. Therefore, sir, receive this God, whoever he be, into the city, for, besides all else, they say, I hear, that he gave the grief-suspending vine to men. Where there is no wine, there is no love, and man has no further joy.

31   *In the Yerania Mountains*

IT was a long climb up the open mountainside, where stunted shrubs clung like coils of wire to the rocks and sun glared off the naked stone, to the goat-pens of Aéra. Eight months before, I had found the truck of the Greek Alpine Club parked here, and the driver eating his lunch with a family of shepherds, an old man with curly, silver hair and an old woman with spectacles and a long apron—and several sturdy young men and their wives and barefooted children. I had eaten my picnic beside their pine-branch hut, listening to the few words they addressed to one another, contemplating an existence measured by the needs of animals, by patriarchal laws and the simplicities of weather and the seasons; they had not talked to me. Now ahead of me I recognized the huts, and suddenly three huge dogs charged towards me and circled round and round my legs, snarling like wild beasts, their jaws vibrating and slavering, until the same old woman emerged from her hut and with a well-aimed stone sent all three stampeding into the woods. Then she withdrew. For the next two hours I walked along a path that kept its altitude along the mountain's northern flank a few hundred feet below the ridge, breathing again the crystalline air that poured out of the fir forests over the high fields of limestone. These rolled away from the ridge like the backs of whales, rising to smaller peaks that pointed up out of the forests clinging to their flanks, as if hanging in mid-air over the soft blue of the Corinthian Gulf. Far below, the brown fields of the Isthmus—a giant tendon holding the Peloponnese to the continent— and across the water the hazy, warm recesses of Kithairon and Helikon faded into dusk. Even with night falling fast, I felt the marvellous intimacy of the Greek landscape with the sea running in and out of land and the mountain-tops so close to one another. Soon I could no longer see the water of the Gulf; then before me rose the silhouette of a rocky spur above the spring of Koura. Below the path on one of the broad, open saddles were the fires of a shepherds' settlement, and the voices of women carried across the still air. This was not the hour to make my appearance, though they were Andoni's relatives, and I walked quietly so as not to arouse the dogs I could see circling round the firelight. Then at my feet I heard the deep gurgle of water flowing out of the rock into a wooden trough. I drank so much at once it ran down my neck, and it was so cold my teeth hurt. Above the spur, on a little plateau covered with the remains of ancient goat-pens, I was laying out my sleeping-bag when from the forest above came a rushing sound of bells and the dry clatter of innumerable hoofs grating over the stony slope. Suddenly the night echoed to a piercing whistle, yells and imprecations as the shepherd swept the goats before him, flinging stones to right and left.

'Ho ho ho hoo-oo, hey-ey, your father and mother and all their horns and whoooo, your Antichrist, hey-ey!'

A stone rebounded off the rock beside me; I crept off to the top of the spur, while the herd flowed like a dark patch towards the goat-pens on the saddle. For some time I could hear the herdsmen milking and the barking of the dogs and the voices of the women. Then I played the reed flute with which I had beguiled solitary hours on many mountain-sides, sometimes pausing to listen to the stillness after a soft or shrill echo had died away. Down the hill someone put out the fire, then all was quiet. I lay back on the ground and received the imprint of stars on my eyes as I fell asleep.

When I opened them again, a sickle moon hung in the sapphire sky of four o'clock in the morning. Gradually it went white. Birds began to sing in the depth of the forest and the goats came up the mountainside again in the shadowless light. Across the Gulf the summits of Helikon and Parnassos showed red through the morning haze, then stood out yellow against the bright blue day. The sun rose like a blazing eye, bringing immediate warmth; long, dewy shadows of stunted firs stretched over the open slopes where a woman was laying out coloured blankets in the sun. Five bay ponies grazed on the col, their long tails waving. Everywhere the mountain glistened as if the night had washed it.

32 *Drinking the Sun of Corinth*

DRINKING the sun of Corinth,
reading the marble ruins,
striding vineyards and seas,
sighting along the harpoon
a votive fish that slips away,
I found the leaves which the sun's psalm memorizes,
the living land that passion joys
in opening.

I drink water, cut fruit,
thrust my hand into the wind's foliage;
lemon-trees water the summer pollen,
green birds break my dreams,
I leave with a glance,
a wide glance, where the world becomes again
beautiful from the beginning to the heart's measure.

33 *The Winged Horse on Acro-Corinth*

I travel by train along the coast, in sight of Salamis, from Eleusis to Megara and on to Corinth.

Fields of poor barley, a few scattered horses, an olive-grove or, as we would say, an orchard by the sea. Only the bare mountains, in open formation, austere, gracious, set the Greek stamp on the horizons. But even their elegance and dignity could become tedious, the weather overcast. It is a familiar landscape, a coastal road in Provence.

The Provençal Corniche must indeed have been very similar before ostentatious foreigners from the world over forced us to consider it as vulgar. Here at least is no pretentious architecture, no exotic vegetation. Wild herbs among the stones and, on the reddish earth, small olive trees, motionless and ancient. This constancy of sea and mountain has a beauty like that of plain surfaces in architecture which allow the main motif to proclaim itself more clearly.

The main motif in Greece is always the light. He who has never seen the Saronic gulf on such a morning as this is unaware of what a field of poppies can look like. Joyous purple, like a hero's wide wounds. Beyond are the sheets of gold. It is thus, in great masses, that flowers are best enjoyed. The light glitters from the mountains, turns the sea opaline. Fresh cordons of silver in the blue of the sea!

Is it delight we feel? We recover our balance. Anguish, torment, delirium are of night's kingdom; the light scatters them, calms us. A mediaeval Greek chronicler, to express his scorn of one of our crusading knights, says that he was 'a man passionate in all things.' We might regard this as a compliment; here, there is nothing superior to a man in control of himself.

But this does not mean, where the Greek is concerned, the suppression of the unconscious or of that fine spontaneity which springs from our deepest imagination. Since I've been in Greece I've realized what has stilted our Parnassian Hellenism. Leconte de Lisle exaggerated the outstanding importance of the part played by the will in art. He has led us to neglect the splendid treasures an artist holds in his heart. No poet is without wings (even though he fears that Pegasus may be lost among the high solitudes where he alone is his own spectator). It is a question of measure. And Greece has discovered the precise point of perfection. In the Greek skies the spirit always returns undizzied and untired, like a strong faithful bird, to rest on the promontory.

We reach Corinth at noon. Ewes are gathered under a tree. The sleeping goatherd holds a kid in his arms. Nothing stirs on the stony ground. A donkey lays his great unbridled bulk down in the grass, and from a distance I see his tail flicker with pleasure.

At Corinth, on the 6th of May, the highest mountains are still snow-covered, while heat oppresses the plain. The landscape has lost that compact harsh perfection that reduced us to silence on the Athenian Acropolis. With its crown of ruins, Acro-Corinth is like a very ancient Semiramis.

I climb the high, vast, burning Acropolis to visit the legendary fountain, still active, the Pirene fountain, source of all poetry. For hours I scramble over a wilderness of Turkish ruins, of high Frankish feudal walls, of Byzantine towers and ancient Greek foundations; all that I have to regret is the time when the winged horse, Pegasus, came to drink from the Pirene and was seized by a hero.

Around me Greece displays her capes, her gulfs, her islands, her two seas, the snows of Parnassus burnished red and the confusion of the mountains of Achaea. I feel I stand on the poop of the centuries, immersed in, overcome by an indefinable drunkenness. But near the Pirene fountain no fine frenzy goes uncontrolled. This I proved for myself that evening. All my thought, which this immense spectacle had sought to distract, was brought back to the narrow mirror of the spring, and the rich fable unfolded in images beneath my eyes, while a music spoke to me. . . .

34   *Nemea*

A SONG in the valley of Nemea:
Sing quiet, quite quiet here.

Song for the brides of Argos
Combing the swarms of golden hair:
Quite quiet, quiet there.

Under the rolling comb of grass,
The sword outrusts the golden helm.

Agamemnon under tumulus serene
Outsmiles the jury of skeletons:
Cool under cumulus the lion queen:

Only the drum can celebrate,
Only the adjective outlive them.

A song in the valley of Nemea:
Sing quiet, quiet, quiet here.

Tone of the frog in the empty well,
Drone of the bald bee on the cold skull,

Quiet, Quiet, Quiet.

35   *Mycenae*

HERE, as so often in Greece, the turning of a corner reveals
something new and unexpected. A few steps from the place
where the road stops will bring one suddenly to the entrance of the
Acropolis, a porch built of massive blocks of stone above which stand
the famous lions which gave the gate its name. The impression is immediate and overpowering. Here is a place of colossal strength, the
remains of the most ancient civilization in Europe, something to which
we are irrevocably connected, yet something different from the paths
of what progress we have made and, in its difference, somehow
sinister, cruel, violent and overwhelming. The walls are built for magnificence as well as for defence, and the sheer size of the blocks of stone
is an aspect of this magnificence. The fortresses of Eleutherae and of
Aegosthena, in spite of their strength, have a kind of grace, even a
humanity, about them. But Mycenean architecture strikes one as

being, in its size and overloading of weight, somehow devilish. It is not that it is stiff and massive and geometrical like the monuments of Egypt. This people, with all their display of overwhelming power, were also capable of an almost sensual delicacy in their art. Rather, perhaps, one is inclined to feel that the splendour actually achieved was something accidental, that these architects were not in the least interested in what among us are the accepted standards of taste. So the most perfect examples of their work, the great bee-hive tombs, were designed, if for any eyes at all, then for the eyes of the dead and of a funeral cortege.

To the right of the entrance, below the Acropolis itself, is what is assumed to be the royal cemetery, excavated by Schliemann in 1876, where, according to popular tradition, were buried the bodies of Atreus, Agamemnon and Cassandra. Past this circular pit in the ground one ascends to the summit of the hill and on the way can amuse oneself with the conjectures or certainties of archaeological guides as to the precise positions of the various parts of the great palace of the Atridae. Here one may imagine Cassandra standing in terror at her second sight, the visions of slaughtered children and of further slaughter still to come. Here perhaps was the bath where Agamemnon was murdered; here the chamber where Clytemnestra and Aegisthus enjoyed their guilty loves; here Orestes revealed himself as an avenger and here first became aware of the pursuing presence of the Erinyes. Far more than this may be imagined on this grey rock which, in the spring, is scarlet with anemones and which, even then, has a grim aspect as though the very scarlet of the flowers was the stain of blood.

I have seen it at all seasons and even in the sunniest weather when the air is full of the murmurs of insects, a sound interrupted continually by the distant noise of goat bells, when light drenches the two great hills between which the citadel of Mycenae stands above its steep gorges, when the grey of these mountains seems white and blazing against the blue sky and when, if one looks out to the plain of Argos below and the sea beyond, one will be surveying a view whose calm, flat and various extent must soothe and fascinate the eye—even then this small but immensely powerful rock seems to crouch, alert and instinct with a different kind of life, between mountains that are savage, dominating from its small stature the whole rich plain with a kind of domination that is certain, uncanny and ferocious, like that exercised by a weasel over a rabbit.

I have stood here too in grey and rainy weather when skeins of mist have hung in the gorges and blanketed the two peaks behind. In such conditions, perhaps, this ancient fastness might be expected to wear a desolate and a Gothic air. But it is not precisely so. Nothing here can be imagined of the romantic or the picturesque. Desolate, certainly, and haunted the place may seem, but with a quality that recalls nothing medieval, nothing in the novels of Sir Walter Scott.

As one walks round the summit of the citadel or descends on the further side, admiring the great bastions built above the sheer descent into the gorge, the Cyclopean architecture of the passage that leads down to the hidden well, everything will confirm one's first impressions. And it is difficult indeed to understand why this place should have an impact on the mind which is as powerful as that made by Delphi, though so extremely different. In Delphi one feels the presence of God or of some sublimity which appears divine; but mysterious and unaccountable as is the full force of this feeling, there are certain geographical features—the tremendous rocks, the high mountain air, the richness and profusion of that stream of olives—which can easily be associated with ideas of sublimity and holiness. At Mycenae one's impressions can be, as I have said, opposite of what might be expected. There is no vast extent even of the ruined walls; there is nothing remarkable in the foundations of the courts of palaces; the hill itself, though immensely strong, is not high; nor is it in the least conspicuous, being folded away between two much higher mountains. Yet, of all places, this one pre-eminently, savagely and masterfully exists, so that the whole smiling landscape down to the sea seems to be within its clutches. No doubt one's memories of the bloody legend of the house of Atreus will affect one's sensations when one is standing on the ground where one may imagine Orestes to have stood; yet people who are ignorant of these legends will be affected in the same way as oneself. Here as elsewhere, it seems to me, we are confronted by a reality, in this case something almost monstrous, which is inexpressible by the ordinary resources of our language. There is something here which remains, making itself felt and feared. Its presence has been felt and described by many witnesses. I do not think that many are impervious to it, though all will grope, as I am groping, vainly for the definite words to describe their feelings.

36   *Mycenae*

THE cities of the hero age thine eyes may seek in vain,
   Save where some wrecks of ruin still break the level plain,
So once I saw Mycenae, the ill-starred, a barren height
Too bleak for goats to pasture,—the goat-herds point the site.
And as I passed a grey-beard said, 'Here used to stand of old
A city built by giants, and passing rich in gold.'

37   *Arrival at Mycenae*

IT is now two years since I first climbed up to Mycenae with my brother, one torrid August afternoon. Behind us the plain of Argos was a lake of flame. The mountains were tawny and savage as a lioness. We climbed on foot, in silence, suffocated, almost breathless, the eyes dazzled. Now and then a silent eddy rose suddenly at the edge of the path like a column of dust and dry herbs; and it pursued us soundlessly, with a phantom's tread. On seeing it approach I couldn't prevent an instinctive fear, as if these mysterious forms had renewed in me the terror of ancient crimes. At the top of a large trench, Leonard, picking up a snake's cast off skin, said to me jokingly: 'It was in Clytemnestra's heart.' And he wound it like a ribbon round my hat. The wind fluttered the small shiny tail before my eyes, making it rustle like a dry leaf. A terrible thirst burnt my throat. We looked for the Perseia fountain in the hollow beneath the citadel. I was so exhausted that as soon as I put my arms and lips into the

icy water I fainted. When I recovered my senses it seemed that I was in a place of dream, outside the world, as if after death. The wind blew furiously, and the eddies of dust followed each other over the height and were lost in the sun, which seemed to devour them. I was filled with an immense sadness, a sadness such as I had never felt, unforgettable. I thought I had come into some place of exile from which there was no return; and everything before my eyes took on a funeral look, giving me I know not what presentiment of anguish. . . .

38   *Cassandra at Mycenae*

CASSANDRA: Apollo! Apollo!
             God of the Ways! My destroyer!
             Where? To what house? Where, where have you
                 brought me?
CHORUS: To the house of the sons of Atreus. If you do not know
                 it,
             I will tell you so. You will not find it false.
CASSANDRA: No, no, but to a god-hated, but to an accomplice
             In much kin-killing, murdering nooses,
             Man-shambles, a floor asperged with blood.
CHORUS: The stranger seems like a hound with a keen scent,
             Is picking up a trail that leads to murder.
CASSANDRA: Clues! I have clues! Look! They are these.
             These wailing, these children, butchery of children;
             Roasted flesh, a father sitting to dinner.
CHORUS: Of your prophetic fame we have heard before
             But in this matter prophets are not required.
CASSANDRA: What is she doing? What is she planning?
             What is this new great sorrow?
             Great crime . . . within here . . . planning
             Unendurable to his folk, impossible
             Ever to be cured. For help
             Stands far distant.

CHORUS: This reference I cannot catch. But the children
I recognized; that refrain is hackneyed.

CASSANDRA: Damned, damned, bringing this work to completion—
Your husband who shared your bed
To bathe him, to cleanse him, and then—
How shall I tell of the end?
Soon, very soon, it will fall.
The end comes hand over hand
Grasping in greed.

CHORUS: Not yet do I understand. After her former riddles
Now I am baffled by these dim pronouncements.

CASSANDRA: Ah God, the vision! God, God, the vision!
A net, is it? Net of Hell!
But herself is the net; shared bed, shares murder.
O let the pack ever-hungering after the family
Howl for the unholy ritual, howl for the victim.

CHORUS: What black Spirit is this you call upon the house—
To raise aloft her cries? Your speech does not lighten me.
Into my heart runs back the blood
Yellow as when for men by the spear fallen
The blood ebbs out with the rays of the setting life
And death strides quickly.

CASSANDRA: Quick! Be on your guard! The bull—
Keep him clear of the cow.
Caught with a trick, the black horn's point,
She strikes. He falls; lies in the water.
Murder; a trick in a bath. I tell what I see.

CHORUS: I would not claim to be expert in oracles
But these, as I deduce, portend disaster.
Do men ever get a good answer from oracles?
No. It is only through disaster
That their garrulous craft brings home
The meaning of the prophet's panic.

CASSANDRA: And for me also, for me, chance ill-destined!
My own now I lament, pour into the cup my own.

72

	Where is this you have brought me in my misery?
	Unless to die as well. What else is meant?
CHORUS:	You are mad, mad, carried away by the god,
	Raising the dirge, the tuneless
	Tune, for yourself. Like the tawny
	Unsatisfied singer from her luckless heart
	Lamenting 'Itys, Itys', the nightingale
	Lamenting a life luxuriant with grief.
CASSANDRA:	Oh the lot of the songful nightingale!
	The gods enclosed her in a winged body,
	Gave her a sweet and tearless passing.
	But for me remains the two-edged cutting blade.
CHORUS:	From whence these rushing and God-inflicted
	Profitless pains?
	Why shape with your sinister crying
	The piercing hymn—fear-piercing?
	How can you know the evil-worded landmarks
	On the prophetic path?
CASSANDRA:	Oh the wedding, the wedding of Paris—death to his people!
	O river Scamander, water drunk by my fathers!
	When I was young, alas, upon your beaches
	I was brought up and cared for.
	But now it is the River of Wailing and the banks of Hell
	That shall hear my prophecy soon.
CHORUS:	What is this clear speech, too clear?
	A child could understand it.
	I am bitten with fangs that draw blood
	By the misery of your cries,
	Cries harrowing the heart.
CASSANDRA:	Oh trouble on trouble of a city lost, lost utterly!
	My father's sacrifices before the towers,
	Much killing of cattle and sheep,
	No cure—availed not at all

73

> To prevent the coming of what came to Troy,
> And I, my brain on fire, shall soon enter the trap.

Note: Atreus, in revenge for Thyestes seducing his wife, killed Thyestes' young children and served them to him as meat.

39 *Nauplia*

HAIL to you, renowned Nauplia! I see your forts and I tremble, because I am a rayah. You are like great Alexander armed, you stand ready for battle. Trumpets sound on the air. Forts to the right, forts to the left, before, behind! The air I breathe smells of blood. Dark is the sea round Vourtzi, that abortion of an island, with walls instead of rocks, cannon-balls and bullets instead of pebbles.

One glance at the mountains is enough to reveal that this place is a place for murder. Elsewhere, plants of gladness grow. Here death stalks, and the devil, ascetic, has built a monastery on the rocks. Look up and tell me: do you not see that scroll unfurled in the gloomy sky? It has words upon it, and they say: 'This is the renowned Nauplia. Here armies are doomed to wrestle, kingdoms to fight, heads to be cut by the guillotine. This place is fearful and terrible. Blood and fire and smoke!'

I look round and ask where I am. In the time of the Greek captain, the valiant Leon the Curly-Headed, in the time of General Morosini, in the time of the Mavromichaels? But have not men from all corners of the earth mingled at this cross-roads . . . ?

The history of Nauplia is like a fable. No blood or race have its walls not seen. Every so often it has changed hands. He who today besieged it has tomorrow defended it, and then the other way round once more.

A glance at her history gives an idea of what Nauplia has known. I pass over early times and begin with the Franks.

1200. Leon the Curly-Headed, of Nauplia, 'captain of the Greeks and a terrible profane soldier', fought with the Franks. The Frank

Boniface closed him in on Acro-Corinth. But when he saw Boniface move off towards the Isthmus he fell upon him and routed him. . . . Villehardouin besieged Nauplia. Leon is killed by a knight, close to the ancient Tiryns.

1210. Besieged for a year by Villehardouin, aided by four Venetian galleons. The town surrendered, on the understanding that the Greeks keep the western fort, the Franks taking the other.

1340. The Dukes of Athens capture Nauplia. The Catalans besiege it but do not capture it.

1389. The Frankish princess Maria sells it, as her own property, to Venice. . . .

1463. Mahomet orders the Pasha of Athens to enter the Morea and fight the Venetians. Bertoldo d'Este is sent to protect Nauplia. . . . Bertoldo is shortly killed and the Turks succeed in driving the Christians back as far as Nauplia, where they are cut to pieces, but the city remains with the Venetians, and five thousand Turks are killed.

1473. The Venetians secure Nauplia, above all on the side of the Frankish fort. They build a powerful fortress on the isle of St Theodorus, now called Vourtzi. . . .

1537. New war between Turks and Venetians.

1538. The Venetians lay the foundations of the fort of Palamidi.

1540. The Venetians surrender Nauplia to the Turks by treaty, with Monemvasia and the islands of the Archipelago.

1686. Morosini lands at the port of Tolos, close to Nauplia. Captures Palamidi easily and besieges the city. . . . Nauplia is surrendered to the Venetians.

1687. Morosini repairs the old forts of Acro-Nauplia and orders the building of powerful garrisons on Palamidi. Nauplia becomes capital of the province of Romania and of all the Morea (Napoli di Romania).

1694. Morosini dies at Nauplia.

1714. Sultan Ahmet III opens war with the Venetians, breaking the treaty of Carlowitz. Nauplia besieged by land and sea.

1715. Turks capture Nauplia.

1781. Staikos Staïkopoulos besieges Nauplia with Demetrios

Tsokris, and Bouboulina blockades it from the sea. The Turks make a sortie from the gates and throw down from the fort pieces of the Greeks they have captured. Hunger and sickness in Nauplia. To lighten the burden, three hundred Christian captives, women and children, are released. Meanwhile, the English ship 'Josephus' lands supplies. The Greeks make an assault but fail.

1822. The French admiral Jourdain captures Vourtzi, sets a large cannon up on it and with flaming shot bombards the houses of Nauplia. Captain Mehmet Pasha tries to supply the besieged, but is frustrated by the fire-ships of the Greeks. The Turks finish by eating dead animals. They send word to the Greeks that they wish to surrender. But Colocotronis does not accept since the Turks ask to be allowed passage to Corinth. Demetrios Moskonisotis enters Nauplia by night and opens the gates to the Greeks. Staïkopoulos sends word to Colocotronis. Colocotronis reaches Palamidi and orders fire on Nauplia. Then sends letter to garrison-commander Ali-Pasha, asking for his surrender, which is given. . . .

1828. Nauplia becomes capital of Greece. On the 8th of January, President Capodistria lands, greeted by cannons from the forts and from ships.

1831. The Mavromichaels Constantine and George kill Capodistria. The first is lynched by the crowd; George seeks refuge in the French consulate and a few days later is shot before his father, his last words being: 'Brothers, concord, love!'

1833. 18th of January the Russian ship "Anna" and the French "Cornelia" anchor, with between them the English frigate "Madagascar", with King Otho on board. On January 25th, at sunrise, 21 cannons are fired, and at midday Otho lands, with acclamations and splendour.

Disturbance and disorder. Bad administration of the Bavarians. Colocotronis imprisoned as traitor. . . .

1834. Colocotronis condemned to death and shut up on Palamidi. Otho leaves Nauplia and goes to his new capital, Athens. . . .

All these things go round and round in my head like a swarm of bees, as I gaze at the dumb stones. Opposite me stands the circular fort of Morosini, two short squat towers, barbaric, as if built by Tartars or by Kalmouks. Grassy steps lead up to a dark hole, a tiny door, and within one sees only piles of stone and pitch blackness.

Higher up, the walls are destroyed—they are older and were built more hastily. The ancient towers lean: gout has attacked their damp feet. Up on Acro-Nauplia, everywhere heaps of stones, above all on the side of the sea. But on the other side in a single undamaged line stretch the battlements, built with two ears, in the Frankish style, and above them stands majestically the old clock-tower.

Everywhere ancient walls, well-built turrets, iron doors, some standing, some fallen two or three hundred years since, dark cells, every kind of tower, unliftable bars, locks, cannons, hinges, mortars, shot, ramrods, marble balls. A number of stone lions carved here and there on the fort, beasts with human heads, grind their teeth holding clutched in their strong claws a book with the words: 'Pax tibi, Marce Evangelista meus.' Some are lean, others broad-faced, others with hair standing on end as if angry that you gaze at them and ready to spring out and maul you. Of some the face is shot away, of others the feet are crippled, but they stand fearless in their broken marble niches, upright, crowned with their thick manes, chests swollen with courage and tails raised in the air. Might! The tameless might of the Venice of Morosini. . . .

I climb up and sit in a watch-tower and then I shift, until I find somewhere comfortable. In full daylight, I am frightened. These heavy forts seem to weigh on my breast. The Middle Ages, as they are called, oppress one, reduce one to melancholy. Ancient sites are quiet. Among marble one is not frightened. They have submitted to their fate without resistance, they lived as long as they lived, they grew old and died in due season. They rest in God, as they say of the saints. But this wild fighter, his veins swollen with boiling blood, has had his manhood struck once, twice, three times by the archangel's lance, but he has not submitted. He crouches on bent knee, armed to the teeth, covered by his shield, sword in hand, as if unwilling to recognize that his hour has come, because his energies are still unspent.

Numberless armies pass before me, of all nations, each with its standard and its armour. Rock and fort echo the trumpets, bowels shake at the drum's sound. Foot-soldiers like ants. Cavalry loaded with iron, belly and breast bound with chains and mail. Their sweating heads are closed in iron helmets, giving them a daimonic look. In one hand they carry their heavy swords, six feet in length, crossed before the breast, others with lances with red tassels that wave in the air. In their left hand they carry their shields, each with its decoration. . . . This endless procession continues hour after hour, until I raise my tired eyes and look down on the city. I see palaces, churches, houses with towers, shops and arsenals, closed within walls. . . . The roads are full of all kinds of people in all kinds of costume, noblemen, mercenaries, traders, dealers, Jews, slaves, Hungarians, Arabs, Maltese, walnuts of every walnut-tree. The harbour is called Porto Catena, because there used to be a chain slung from the isle of St Theodorus to the mainland, to secure it against enemies. Inside and outside the chain ships of all styles are anchored, galleons, galleys, brigantines, captured corsairs, feluccas coming and going like bees. . . .

I shake my head, and all is scattered and disappears. So everything that is written, with the i's dotted and the t's crossed, is fable! All I see living is that donkey which grazes down there below me. How can one believe that within this silence is suffocated all that commotion of which the memory alone is enough to break the head! How is it that this nothing is all that is left of that furious crowd, of that violence and of that passion! How is it that this dry thorn is the richest fruit produced by this cursed wilderness on which I tread, after it has been manured by so many bodies! Not days, not months, not years, but for centuries have fought here the most blood-thirsty men of earth, beasts and men, endlessly, generation after generation. Where are the wing-swift horses which blew smoke from their nostrils into the sky? All, men, horses, arms, have vanished. Why then this vain fury, the pain, the uncontrollable struggle? Why the unjust waste of life, without any gain either to the one side or to the other? I talk with the dust, and I receive no answer. . . .

40

ARCADIA is bounded on the East with Eliso, on the West with Misenia, on the North with Achaia inferiour, and on the South with a part of Laconia and the sea: It was formerly termed Pelasgia, and lastly it tooke the name from Arcas the sonne of Jupiter and Calisto, the people whereof, did long imagine they were more auncient then the Moone;

> This soyle of Whom Arcas great patrone was,
> In age the Moone excell'd, in wit the Asse.

But because it is a tradition of more antiquity then credit, I doe rather note it, then affirme it: And as men dread the thunderbolt, when they see the lightning, so ignorance and idolatry placed amongst us, and round about us, may be a warning to the professours of the trueth, to take heed of the venome, least by their Arcadian antiquitie surpassing the Moone, they become novices to some new intended massacre, for as powder faild them, but alas, not poison! so now with policy they prevaile in all things: how long the holy one of Israell knoweth, but certainely, our sinnes are the causes of their domineering and of our carelesse drouping.

In this Desart way, I beheld many singular Monuments, and ruinous Castles, whose names I knew not, because I had an ignorant guide: But this I remember, amongst these rockes my belly was pinched, and wearied was my body, with the climbing of fastidious mountaines, which bred no small griefe to my breast. Yet notwithstanding of my distresse, the rememberance of these sweet seasoned Songs of Arcadian Sheepheards which pregnant Poets have so well penned, did recreate my fatigated corps with many sugred suppositions. These sterile bounds being past, we entered in the Easterne plaine of Morea, called aunciently Sparta, where that sometimes famous Citty of Lacedemon flourished, but now sacked, and the lumpes of ruines and memory onely remaines. Marching thus, we left Modena and Napoli on our right hand, towards the sea side, and on the sixt day and night, we pitched our tents in the disinhabited villages of Argo and Micene, from the which unhappy Helen was ravished.

This cursed custome of base prostitution, is become so frequent, that the greater sort of her mercenary sexe, following her footsteps, have out-gone her in their loathsom journeies of Libidinous wayes: she being of such an infinite and voluptuous crew, the arch mistresse and ring-leader to destruction, did invite my Muse to inveigh against her lascivious immodesty, as the inordinate patterne of all willing and licentious rapts:

> I would thy beauty (fairest of all Dames)
> Had never caus'd the jealous Greekes to move
> Thy eyes from Greece, to Ilion cast flames,
> And burnt that Trojan, with adulterate love:
> He captive like, thy mercy came to prove
> And thou divorc'd, was ravish'd with a toy:
> He swore faire Helen was his dearest dove
> And thou a Paris swore for to enjoy:
> Mourne may the ghosts, of sometimes stately Troy.
> And curse that day, thou saw the Phirigian coast:
> Thy lecherous lust, did Priams pride destroy,
> And many thousands, for thy sake were lost.
> Was't nature, fortune, fancy, beauty, birth,
> That cros'd thee so, to be a crosse on earth.
> Some of thy sexe, baptiz'd with thy curst name,
> Crown'd with thy fate, are partners in thy shame.
> Helens are snakes, which breeds their lovers paine,
> The maps of malice, murther and disdaine:
> Helens are gulfes, whence streams of blood do flow
> Rapine, deceit, treason, and overthrow:
> Helens are whoores, whiles in a Virgin Maske,
> They sucke from Pluto sterne Proserpines taske:
>> Curst be thou Hell, for hellish Helens sakes,
>> Still crost and curst, be they, that trust such snakes.

Here in Argos I had the ground to be a pillow, and the world-wide-fields to be a chamber, the whirling windy-skies, to be a roofe to my Winter-blasted lodging, and the humide vapours of cold Nocturna, to accompany the unwished-for-bed of my repose. What shall I say then, the solid and sad man, is not troubled with the floods and ebbes of fortune, the ill imployed power of greatnesse, nor the fluctuary motions of the humerous multitude; or at least, if he be sensible of his owne, or their irregularities, or confusions, yet his thoughts are not written in his face, his countenance is not significant, nor his miseries further seene than in his owne private suffering; whereas the face and disposition of the feeble one, ever resembleth his last thoughts, and upon every touch, or taste of that which is displeasant and followes not the streames of his appetite, his countenance deformeth it selfe, and like the Moone, is in as many changes as his fortune, but the noble resolution must follow Aeneas advice in all his adventures;

> Per varios casus, per tot discrimina rerum,
> Tendimus in latium, &c.

> By diverse wayes, and dangers great we mind,
> To visit Latium, and Latinus kind.

In all this country of Greece I could finde nothing, to answer the famous relations, given by auncient Authors, of the excellency of that land, but the name onely; the barbarousnesse of Turks and Time, having defaced all the Monuments of Antiquity: No shew of honour, no habitation of men in an honest fashion, nor possessours of the Country in a Principality. But rather shut up in prisons, or addicted slaves to be cruell and tyrannicall Maisters: So deformed is the state of that once worthy Realme, and so miserable is the burthen of that afflicted people: which, and the appearance of that permanancy, grieved my heart to behold the sinister working of blind Fortune, which always plungeth the most renowned Champions, and their memory, in the profoundest pit of all extremities and oblivion.

41   *The Grove of Asclepius at Epidaurus*

THE sacred grove of Asclepius is surrounded on all sides by mountains. No death or birth takes place within the enclosure; the same custom prevails also in the island of Delos. All the offerings, whether the offerer be one of the Epidaurians themselves or a stranger, are entirely consumed within the bounds. . . . The image of Asclepius is, in size, half as big as the Olympian Zeus at Athens, and is made of ivory and gold. An inscription tells us that the artist was Thrasymedes, a Parian, son of Arignotus. The god is sitting on a seat grasping a staff; the other hand he is holding above the head of the serpent; there is also a figure of a dog lying by his side. On the seat are wrought in relief the exploits of Argive heroes, that of Bellerophontes against the Chimaera, and Perseus, who has cut off the head of Medusa. Over against the temple is the place where the suppliants of the god sleep. Near has been built a circular building of white marble, called Tholos (Round House), which is worth seeing. In it is a picture by Pausias representing Love, who has cast aside his bow and arrows, and is carrying instead of them a lyre that he has taken up. Here there is also another work of Pausias, Drunkenness drinking out of a crystal cup. You can see even in the painting a crystal cup and a woman's face through it. Within the enclosure stood slabs; in my time six remained, but of old there were more. On them are inscribed the names of both the men and the women who have been healed by Asclepius, the disease also from which each suffered, and the means of cure. . . . The Epidaurians have a theatre within the sanctuary, in my opinion very well worth seeing. For while the Roman theatres are far superior to those anywhere else in their splendour, and the Arcadian theatre at Megalopolis is unequalled for size, what architect could seriously rival Polycleitus in symmetry and beauty?

IT is the morning of the first day of the great peace, the peace of the heart, which comes with surrender. I never knew the meaning of peace until I arrived at Epidaurus. Like everyone else I had used the word all my life, without once realizing that I was using a counterfeit. Peace is not the opposite of war any more than death is the opposite of life. The poverty of language, which is to say the poverty of man's imagination or the poverty of his inner life, has created an ambivalence which is absolutely false. I am talking of course of the peace which passeth all understanding. There is no other kind. The peace which most of us know is merely a cessation of hostilities, a truce, an interregnum, a lull, a respite, which is negative. The peace of the heart is positive and invincible, demanding no conditions, requiring no protection. It just is. If it is a victory it is a peculiar one because it is based entirely on surrender, a voluntary surrender, to be sure. There is no mystery in my mind as to the nature of the cures which were wrought at this great therapeutic center of the ancient world. Here the healer himself was healed, first and most important step in the development of the art, which is not medical but religious. Second, the patient was healed before he ever received the cure. The great physicians have always spoken of Nature as being the great healer. That is only partially true. Nature alone can do nothing. Nature can cure only when man recognizes his place in the world, which is not in Nature, as with the animal, but in the human kingdom, the link between the natural and the divine. . . .

I think that the great hordes who made the long trek to Epidaurus from every corner of the ancient world were already cured before they arrived there. Sitting in the strangely silent amphitheatre I thought of the long and devious route by which I had at last come to this healing center of peace. . . . As I entered the still bowl, bathed now in a marble light, I came to that spot in the dead center where the faintest whisper rises like a glad bird and vanishes over the shoulder of the low hill, as the light of a clear day recedes before the velvet black of night. Balboa standing upon the peak of Darien could not have known a greater wonder than I at this moment. There was nothing more to conquer: an ocean of peace lay before me. To be free, as I then knew myself to be, is to realize that all conquest is vain, even the conquest of self, which is the last act of egotism. To be joyous is to carry the ego to its last summit and to deliver it triumphantly. To know peace is total: it is the moment after, when the surrender is complete, when there is no longer even the consciousness of surrender. Peace is at the center and when it is attained the voice issues forth in praise and benediction. Then the voice carries far and wide, to the outermost limits of the universe. Then it heals, because it brings light and the warmth of compassion.

Epidaurus is merely a place symbol: the real place is in the heart, in every man's heart, if he will but stop and search it. Every discovery is mysterious in that it reveals what is so unexpectedly immediate, so close, so long and intimately known. The wise man has no need to journey forth; it is the fool who seeks the pot of gold at the rainbow's end. But the two are always fated to meet and unite. They meet at the heart of the world, which is the beginning and the end of the path. They meet in realization and unite in transcendence of their roles. . . .

In Greece one has the conviction that *genius* is the norm, not mediocrity. No country has produced, in proportion to its numbers, as many geniuses as Greece. In one century alone this tiny nation gave to the world almost five hundred men of genius. Her art, which goes back fifty centuries, is eternal and incomparable. The landscape remains the most satisfactory, the most wondrous, that our earth has to offer. The inhabitants of this little world lived in harmony with their natural surroundings, peopling them with gods who were real and with whom they lived in intimate communion. The Greek cosmos is the most eloquent illustration of the unity of thought and deed. It persists even today, though its elements have long since been dispersed. The image of Greece, faded though it be, endures as an archetype of the miracle wrought by the human spirit. A whole people, as the relics of their achievements testify, lifted themselves to a point never before and never since attained. It was miraculous. It still is. The task of genius, and man is nothing if not genius, is to keep the miracle alive, to live always in the miracle, to make the miracle more and more miraculous, to swear allegiance to nothing, but to live only miraculously, think only miraculously, die miraculously. It matters little how much is destroyed, if only the germ of the miraculous be preserved and nurtured. At Epidaurus you are confronted with and permeated by the intangible residue of the miraculous surge of the human spirit. It inundates you like the spray of a mighty wave which broke at last upon the farther shore. Today our attention is centred upon the physical inexhaustibility of the universe; we *must* concentrate all our thought upon that solid fact because never before has man plundered and devastated to such a degree as today. We are therefore prone to forget that in the realm of the spirit there is also an inexhaustibility, that in this realm no gain is ever lost. When one stands at Epidaurus one *knows* this to be a fact. With malice and spite the world may buckle and crack but here, no matter into what vast hurricane we may whip our evil passions, lies an area of peace and calm, the pure distilled heritage of a past which is not altogether lost.

43   *Ouzo Unclouded*

HERE is ouzo (she said) to try you:
        Better not drowned in water,
Better not chilled with ice,
Not sipped at thoughtfully,
Nor toped in secret.
Drink it down (she said) unclouded
At a blow, this tall glass full,
But keep your eyes on mine
Like a true Arcadian acorn-eater.

EUROTAS, TAYGETUS, HELEN, AND MISTRA

AT eight in the morning, I set out for Amyclae, now Scla-bochorion, accompanied by my new guide, and a Greek cicerone, very good tempered, but extremely ignorant. We took the road to the plain at the foot of Taygetus, following shady and very agreeable by-paths, leading between gardens, irrigated by streamlets which descended from the mountain, and planted with mulberry, fig, and sycamore trees. We also saw in them abundance of water-melons, grapes, cucumbers, and herbs of different kinds. From the beauty of the sky, and the similarity of the produce, a traveller might imagine himself to be in the vicinity of Chambery. We passed the Tiasa, and arrived at Amyclae, where I found nothing but the ruins of a dozen Greek chapels, demolished by the Albanians, situated at some distance from one another, in the midst of cultivated fields. The temple of Apollo, that of Eurotas at Onga, the tomb of Hyacinthus, have all disappeared. I could not discover a single inscription; though I sought with care the celebrated necrology of the priestesses of Amyclae, which the Abbé Fourmont copied in 1731 or 1732, and which records a series for nearly a thousand years before Christ. Destructions succeed each other with such rapidity in Greece, that frequently one traveller perceives not the slightest vestige of the monuments which another has admired only a few months before him. Whilst I was searching for fragments of antique ruins among heaps of modern ones, I saw a number of peasants approach with a papa at their head. They removed a board set up against the wall of one of the chapels, and entered a sanctuary which I had not yet discovered. I had the curiosity to follow them, and found that the poor creatures resorted with their priests to these ruins to pray: they sung litanies before an image of the Panagia, daubed in red upon a wall that had been painted blue. How widely different was this ceremony from the festival of Hyacinthus! The triple pomp, however, of the ruins, of adversity, and of prayers to the true God, surpassed, in my opinion, all the splendours of the earth....

89

Night drew on apace, when I reluctantly quitted these renowned ruins, the shade of Lycurgus, the recollection of Thermopylae, and all the fictions of fable and history. The sun sank behind the Taygetus, so that I had beheld him commence and finish his course on the ruins of Lacedaemon. It was three thousand five hundred and forty-three years since he first rose and set over this infant city. I departed with a mind absorbed by the objects which I had just seen, and indulging in endless reflections. Such days enable a man to endure many misfortunes with patience, and above all, render him indifferent to many spectacles.

We pursued the course of the Eurotas for an hour and a half, through the open country, and then fell into the road to Tripolizza. Joseph and the guide had encamped on the other side of the river near the bridge, and had made a fire of reeds, in spite of Apollo, who was consoled by the sighing of these reeds for the loss of Daphne. Joseph was abundantly provided with necessaries: he had salt, oil, water-melons, bread, and meat. He dressed a leg of mutton like the companion of Achilles, and served it up on the corner of a large stone, with wine from the vineyard of Ulysses, and the water of Eurotas. I made an excellent supper, having just that requisite which Dionysius wanted to relish the black broth of Lacedaemon.

After supper, Joseph brought me my saddle, which usually served me for a pillow: I wrapped myself in my cloak, and lay down under a laurel on the bank of the Eurotas. The night was so pure and so serene, and the Milky Way shed such a light, reflected by the current of the river, that you might see to read by it. I fell asleep, with my eyes fixed on the heavens, having the beautiful constellation of Leda's swan exactly over my head. I still recollect the pleasure which I formerly received from thus reposing in the woods of America, and especially from awaking in the middle of the night. I listened to the whistling of the wind through the wilderness, the braying of the does and stags, the roar of a distant cataract; while the embers of my half extinguished fire glowed beneath the foliage of the trees. I loved even to hear the voice of the Iroquois, when he shouted in the recesses of his forests, and when, in the brilliant star-light, amid the silence of nature, he seemed to be proclaiming his unbounded liberty. All this may afford delight at twenty, because then life suffices, in a manner, for itself, and there are in early youth a certain restlessness and inquietude, which incessantly encourage the creation of chimaeras—*ipsi sibi somnia fingunt*; but in maturer age, the mind contracts a relish for more solid pursuits, and loves, in particular, to dwell on the illustrious examples recorded in history. Gladly would I again make my couch on the banks of the Eurotas, or the Jordan, if the heroic shades of the three hundred Spartans, or the twelve sons of Jacob, were to visit my slumbers; but I would not go again to explore a virgin soil, which the plough-share has never lacerated. Give me now ancient deserts, where I can conjure up at pleasure the walls of Babylon, or the legions of Pharsalia—*grandia ossa*; plains whose furrows convey instruction, and where, mortal as I am, I trace the blood, the tears, the sweat of human kind.

45	*Taygetus*

TAYGETUS rests on powerful foundations, full of sombre folds; its base is tormented by deep gorges, dark blue and wood-lined, all fortified with ridges and huge buttresses. These strong outposts invade, assault the plain, and one sees them die there like heroes of ancient warrior villages. On this first construction rise formidable escarpments. Above them, as though on a third level, towers the wild region of glaciers and avalanches. And still higher point the summits, admirable in their variety.

Among this massive ascension of brows, dark woods, gulfs, ridges iridescent and frozen, Taygetus splits into sudden fissures, into unexpected and magnificent accents.

How much force and grandeur there is in the movements of Taygetus, as it bases itself firmly in the plain, bed of sensuality, and hurls itself with five snow-covered peaks into the sky! No literary daring could paint this glittering, powerful intensity, these colours, solid, whole, never equivocal, these great rough diversities rising effortlessly from the level of the orange groves to the sparkling glaciers above. By what lyrical flight may the spirit which this savage mass exhales be conveyed?

Taygetus, where through the rocks' density breathes an immense Spartan soul, raises us from the sad lascivious sensuality of the Eurotas. . . .

Ah, the flight of the Eurotas as it flows with Helen through its gentle valley towards Gytheion—flight that troubles but does not embroil us! Its course as it winds towards the gulf of Cythera, at the hour when the sun, slipping behind the mountain, still makes the spring tremble, is the eternal heart-rending image of the departure of voluptuousness. At the age of forty it is at Sparta that I would choose to settle. Sparta is not like Venice: a note of tenderness sounding in the midst of pleasure; it does not like Toledo throw an order, a cry into the battle; it leaves Jerusalem to its lamenting. Taygetus intones a paean.

A heart immersed in poetry, once it has known this vitality beneath which the guilty plain lies quivering, would die for an ideal. Its desire to be heroic springs forth clear and joyful. From now on nothing will content it but a proud repose at the city's breast, a well-founded and resplendent memory.

No hesitation, no groping. Sparta is ever the tamer of men. Three decisive and emphatic colours are all it needs to direct the soul. Sparta did not come into being as the caprice of a systematic spirit. It was the necessary product of the earth. It is the landscape where Taygetus rises with scornful pride over an intoxicating plain which imposed the famous institutions of Lycurgus.

Ever-tragic hills of russet Menelaeon; Eurotas, escaping through a desert of pebbles and laurels; glittering peaks of five-fingered Taygetus: now when the people you formed to be your living soul have long disappeared, you still spread your influence over the stones. The natural powers that supported the land of Helen and Lycurgus remain. These indifferent sublimities ignore the history they enshrine, and whether the city lives or dies they continue to speak.

An atmosphere of divine youthfulness always envelops the

masses of Taygetus. Over its snows I see primitive Centaurs wandering. Castor and Pollux wrestle in the forests of its flanks. The mysterious cortege of Bacchants rush past with terrible cries. What do these furies signify? Why these young daughters of Sparta, cheeks enflamed, thyrses and torches in their hands, dresses tucked up to the knees? Let us celebrate with the poets those whose inmost heart Dionysos has penetrated. He is the inspirer of the most generous decisions; he creates a people of *evelpides*, of men confident of their destiny . . . Cassandra is ever violated on the altar. The swan assaults Leda. The daughters of Platanistas sing an eternal epithalamium to the young bride closetted with her groom. This night, at Gytheion, Paris will possess Helen.

46 *Helen*

M Y eyes and heart are renewed this morning. For I have breathed the air that caressed the beauty of Helen.

In the poor museum at Sparta there are a large number of bas-reliefs showing the Dioscuri. Generally they are holding their horses by the bridle. Sometimes they stand naked with their magician's caps on, leaning on their lances. Between them is their sister Helen, with a wide-brimmed hat, rigid, in the attitude of an archaic idol. Are those jewels in her hands? Is it a broken chain? Sad between these two men, unintelligible and perhaps limited, she sends me from the depths of the ages a thousand feelings of sadness, fear and desire.

Here she is then, a small craft, before she embarked on the deep seas. . . .

This Helen bound in her girdle of Asia is the still shut flower of the magnolia which when it unfurls the next morn will transfigure its tree. But this crude Helen of the museum contains in herself more than the colours and scents of a marvellous tree of roses. From the walls of Troy she gazed on combats of which she was the prize. What silence! What distant look! The ridges of Taygetus and its warlike promontories cast their shadow over this primitive Helen.

Although her influence spreads everywhere, don't imagine she belongs to all landscapes, this daughter of Tyndareus. She was born in this valley, of the Eurotas and Taygetus. In vain has she played her great adventure through the ages: her legend keeps the form of these unforgettable models, and her sensuality enjoys its full empire only in a heroic setting.

After Helen had journeyed over the whole world, Goethe seized her in his arms, and the old prophet sought to reinstate her on the horizon of Sparta. He did not say explicitly that he set his magnificent scene in the castle of Villehardouin, but no one can be in doubt of it: this golden burg, to the West of the plain, on the buttresses of Taygetus, is Goethe's poem, dominating the ruins of Mistra like a crown.

47   *The Broken Walls*

AS soon as the great mountain which the ancients called Taygetus and the simple people Five-Fingers comes into sight above the plain, one sees scattered at its feet on the eastern side some smaller mountains, and on these, as if supports of the great backbone, rest its snowy peaks, rising up one behind the other. On one of these lesser mountains, looking towards the sun, Mistra is built. The peak of the mountain is sharp, but the whole of it is unnaturally precipitous and stands up proudly. At its feet a river runs out into the plain, where the village is today. Old Mistra is higher up, on the mountain-side. The way is paved and passes between ruins. To the right and left, water-eaten walls one behind the other, walls of palaces, towers, churches, cottages, mosques, springs, baths, of a whole city. Every so often you come across ruined rooms, and other hanging buildings, which stand like bears, like whatever shapes you can imagine, waiting for a cloud-burst or a storm to disperse them altogether.

At first as you go up you meet on your left hand a fine Frankish tower in good condition; it seems that this tower stood at a corner of the walls which used to surround the city. By it is a church called Perivleptos, built by a certain Leon Mavromata in about 1390.

Then the houses begin, old and new mixed together. High up, in the upper part of the city, is a monastery with a fine church and a wonderful belltower, surrounded by a wall and adorned with trees and flowers. It is called Pantanassa, built by Manuel Cantacuzene in about 1360 and renovated by John Frankopoulos in 1445.

Following along the way which leads to the lower city you come to the Metropolis.... All round is a confusion of palaces, old houses, rooms, walls, towers, all destroyed; the churches of Aphentiko, the Saints Theodorus, St John, St Sophia, and others scattered here and there....

On the north of the mountain is a small crest and there stands the royal palace of the Cantacuzenes, and, slightly behind, that of the Palaeologoi. Huge walls full of big windows, rusted, rotten, crumbling day by day. Every so often a piece dislodges itself and falls to earth. The stones return to their mother, unknown, like every other stone of the mountain. The poor hill-dweller gathers them and builds his cottage to keep out the cold and the rain, and they, submissive to their fate, see and hear the sufferings of poverty, just as they used to see and hear once the secrets of the king and what was said in councils that affected the world.

Where there was wood in the buildings is now an empty hole, because the wood has rotted away. First the man who was once the master disappeared, then his clothes, then the wood, then the stones were scattered and thus all came to rest. Roofs and floors were soon sunk and the four walls only remained, and these also crumbled and dissolved, especially to the south. The northern corner lasted longer, until there remained standing a single column of wall, beaten by wind and becoming more slender, more decayed, until it reached the point at which even nature was ashamed to order one of her valiant envoys, the air, the earth-quake, the thunder-bolt, to finish off such an adversary. Then a crow flew over and settled lightly on the top of this column, and there as it began to preen its wings for lice, suddenly the stones fell apart and rumbled down with a hollow noise, as if dissolved back into the earth.

Why do I speak and write of such things? You can go yourself and lament, as you see still the chimneys, and the fire-places where they used to cook, and the baths where the noble women bathed, and the stone from which the king mounted his horse, and the place where his throne stood, and the treeless garden where he walked, oppressed with worry.

All round the palaces are upright walls, fallen walls, of every shape and size, stone as if from a thousand quarries, domes, half-eaten altars overturned, orphaned columns, pulpits painted with rain-washed saints. Here a hole, a hole there, wherever you stand, and in the holes nothing but grassy shells, piles of bone, such as not even a starving jackal would glance at. The marjoram and other herbs smell like incense, and as I wander round I sing psalms as if in remembrance, as if saying a mass for the dead. Every now and then I stop, and then I go on again, and I sing with tear-filled eyes, I sing for the harsh lot of man, for my mother and for my father buried in Turkey, some thousands of miles away. I weep for the poor, for the noble, for Palaeologus, even if he was a king, for he was a man who suffered, a shipwrecked man, a victim bled for the crimes of others.

By the time I had reached the ravine which cuts the mountain on the west, verse by verse I had sung all the funeral prayers: 'The dance of the saints found the source of life and the door of Paradise; I also have found the way of repentance; I am the lost sheep: summon me, Saviour, and save me.' 'Image am I of your ineffable glory, even if I bear the marks of error; have pity on your creature, Lord, cleanse him with mercy, prepare for me the longed-for country, make me again citizen of Paradise. . . .'

Thus little by little I reached the palace said to be that of Lascaris. Just then the bell from Pantanassa sounded for even-song, and shortly after the small bell of Mitropolis began to speak mournfully, with a sweet accent, as if an innocent girl was singing. No one was in sight. I stood alone, perched among ruined houses, before the house of Lascaris, a poor refugee, without home, unkempt, sleepless, weather-beaten, driven out by the Turk as these men were, and I sang and chanted above the bones and the colours: 'Remember of the prophet crying, I am earth and ashes; and again I beheld your works, and I saw in the tombs the image of God fashioned most beautifully for us, formless, without glory, having no shame; O miracle, what mystery is this that has befallen us. . . !' And again: 'I saw the naked bones and I said: What is a king, or soldier, or rich man, or hungry man, or just man, or sinner. . . !'

48   *The Ascent of Mistra*

IT was on a morning of joy that I crossed the little river of Parori and began to climb the ruin-charged slopes. The sun warmed the violet flowers that carpeted the ruins and drew their scents from them. Soon the orange-trees thinned out and, as the sound of the torrent grew less, the zones of pleasant vegetation gave place to those of aridity. We trod over broken flagstones, through tortuous alleys, beneath posterns and machicolations. From the escutcheoned roofless palace no face looked down on our progress.

I entered a small church with a green dome, beautiful in its peace; there was not an inch of the wall that was not covered with frescoes, like faded silks: I recall a Christ on a white ass entering into a mediaeval city, with the supper already prepared beneath the Byzantine dome. A little further on I visited two chapels adjoined to one another as one bower precedes another more secret bower; I had to bend, so low they were, and my two hands touched both walls at once. Elsewhere my guide showed me the tomb of a Byzantine Empress; he called her the beautiful Theodora Tocco. Near newly opened tombs were baskets filled with skulls and tibia. Those neglected baskets seemed to me like those at which voluptuaries might glance between bouts of pleasure in order to quicken the savour of life.

Mistra crumbles away with no sadness. Its convents, its mosques, its Latin and Byzantine churches have about them an atmosphere deliciously young and friendly. Amid this luminous devastation I saw cypresses of an extraordinary darkness; in the court of the metropolitan church, one of them was worth a column of Phidias, while a lilac gave off its scent at its foot.

What a curious inhumanity I feel on this mountain of fire! It spiritualizes me. I sense no breath from the centuries in these palaces, unless it be that of Chateaubriand, who sheltered beneath one of these roofs. Of what significance to me are these indefinite beings? But above the portico of the church called Pantanassa there is a small loggia where a fig-tree leans. There I rested, breathless not so much because of the ascent beneath the sun but because of my burning desire to embrace everything; and there, finding the plain beneath me, I rejoiced that I was alive and that the world was so beautiful.

We know other dead cities from the Middle Ages: Baux, for example, in Provence, or San Gemignano near Siena. Their picturesque quality charms our taste; but Mistra fills my soul with poetry. An orange-tree which casts its fruit on the machicolation brings suddenly before my eyes the seraglio of Helen's grand-daughters, where the rough Champenois, my brothers, lost their strength and tasted something of an ancient culture. Here was one of the harems where our knights grew effete. Better still, here was the castle raised by magic near the palace of Menelaus to shelter the love of Helen and Faust. . . .

It was here, and no where else, that Faust could possess Helen. It was through these tortuous alleys that Tyndareus' daughter, fleeing the uncertain palace of ancient Sparta, found refuge with the gothic warrior.

The child born of their love, Euphorion, leapt and danced on the ruins before me: 'Ever higher! I must rise! Always further! I must see. . . . Let me leap now! To spring into the air is what I want! I don't want to walk on earth any longer.' From church to chapel, to mosque, to palace, to convent, across gaping cisterns and beneath collapsing stones, I am drawn invincibly towards the summit, towards the kastro. The higher I climb, the more deserted, though the more escutcheoned, do the ruins become. What stays the same is the desolation: below, a desolation atrocious and scented, above, an embroidered desolation. Among the debris of history and art I see some pigs running, snouts to the earth, and chickens made as beautiful as pheasants by the sun. I halt in a large square where the high walls with their embattled towers are the remains of the palace of the Byzantine despots. Then, from gap to gap, through breach or beneath a tottering archway, I clear the tower-flanked walls which form the various lines of the fortifications.

This mountain is built like an intelligence. Fragments from all periods and from the most diverse races are here woven into a single whole: a patchwork held together by a vigorous ivy humming with bees.

At last I reach the crest of the citadel. Between the ruins and the cisterns barley is growing. What spaces, what light! To my left rises a deserted peak bearing only tufts of pine; behind unfold the escarpments of Taygetus, sown with sparkling villages and crowned with glaciers. From this side comes a chill wind, for Mistra protects, conceals a deep dark gorge into which a huge cascade pours. But powerful though these confined views to the East may be, I have to turn from them to enjoy and expand into the immense light-filled plain.

Sheer beneath my feet the silvery ruins flash down lead-coloured slopes. From my Champenois battlements, beneath the Byzantine churches, I see the voluptuous gardens which cover the ruins of Sparta. The Eurotas flows seaward between the hills that form its valley, beneath a dust of the sun burning with all the reds, ocres and greens. From Taygetus to Menelaeon, from the island of Cythera to the mountains of Arcadia, I gaze on, I respire the valley of Lacedaemonia.

From up here all thought assumes an amplitude, an ease, a youthfulness, as if one had drunk of happiness and immortality. Only on the slopes of Vesuvius have I known this intoxication. And even Vesuvius, when its ashes have burnt my eyes, my lips, and the soles of my feet, has not stirred my soul so much as this volcano of history and poetry. Here Islam, the Crusades, Byzantium, and then my schoolday Sparta, powerful and morose, mingle, vaporize beneath the action of the sun, the sea and the sky. The plain is beneath my intoxication like the lyre of a poet.

Here then is the land of Helen! Although history has rudely crowded the lovely bed of Tyndareus' daughter, the acrid smell of love remains. All my senses marry with the sleep of Helen. She rests her head on the hills of the Shepherds; the ships that die against her guilty feet come from the kingdom of Venus.

Ignorant, I cannot grasp, in the cold corridors of our museums, the lessons of the tree of Greece. But that it should appear to me, this tree, as a bush of flames in the centre of the gardens of Sparta, is what I desire and what I find to be in just accord with the spirit of antiquity.

Helen once again turns her face towards us and stirs in our breast an ardour no human child can assuage. Two lovely frozen rays pursue us from her eyes, double counsel persuading us either to a noble death or to strike the lyre.

49   *Gemistos Plethon*

PLETHON passed the greater part of his life at Mistra. The choice of Mistra as his place of residence is of particular significance for the understanding of his life and work. In his memorandum to the Emperor Manuel he wrote: 'We are Hellenes', and he added that the Peloponnesus was the original source of the most noble Greek tribes which, springing from there, gave birth to the great history of the Greek nation. In the setting of the sad decline of the Byzantine Empire, this reaffirmation of a Hellenic consciousness represents a resistance and a reaction; it announces and determines the future of the Greek nation. Plethon had wished to play a major part in shaping this future and it was to this end that he dedicated his intellectual powers. His tenacious will, his clear intelligence armed with an encyclopedic knowledge, made it possible for him in fact to act in many spheres. In one of his numerous historical works, the *Hellenika,* he described Plato at the court of Syracuse, trying to persuade the tyrants to adopt his political ideas. His two memoirs leave no doubt that Plethon wished to play in relation to the Byzantine princes a role similar to that of the philosopher. His whole thought was directed to an integral reorganization of life. The interminable discussions for the union of the churches had shown him how little Christianity could serve as a principle of union. He ended by seeing in these disputatious Christians sophists who discuss not for the sake of truth but in order to triumph over their adversaries with a view to obtaining certain political benefits. This mercantile spirit in supernatural matters was something that Plethon could not tolerate; according to him, such mercantilism amounted to a denial of God's Providence, on which everything depends. It is for this reason that he did not subscribe to the union of the churches proposed at Florence and composed in 1448 a treatise on the procession of the Holy Spirit in which he attacked on the level of dogma the ideas of Bessarion (who supported the union) and condemned the Latins. He concluded that it was not union with the Latins that would save the Hellenes; the Hellenes would not be saved unless they trusted to divine Providence, unless they corrected the errors and faults they had committed against God, whether these were in the form of opinions they held or of deeds they had done. It is clear that it is not a question here of a theologian debating in the interests of Christendom, but of a Hellene and philosopher. He refused to subscribe to the union of the churches and at the same time he sought a new principle of universal union. He knew the Plato of the tradition of Psellos, by way of neo-Platonism; he was more and more drawn towards the syncretic mysticism of the Alexandrians and he ended by dreaming, in the mid-fifteenth century, of renewing the efforts of Porphyry, Iamblichus and Proclus; on the ruins of the Christian cult he wished to establish a new universal religion. 'I heard him say,' wrote George Trebizond with reference to Plethon, 'when he was in Florence, that in the not distant future all men in the whole world would by common consent and in the same spirit embrace one and the same religion. And when I asked him whether this would be the religion of Jesus Christ or that of Mahomet, he replied: neither the one nor the

other, but a third, which would not be different from that
of antiquity.'

WHATEVER the nuns' isolation the natural beauty of their
situation must fortify the weakest soul. For those epicures in
landscape who demand not only form but colour, for whom central
Europe is but a chromatic photograph and an Alp in a sunset comparable only to the asbestos in a gas-stove, the Levant is without peer.
And in all the Levant, in Europe or Asia, pagan or Christian, there is
no place where the divine soul of the earth can so fill the heart, so
suffocate the eyes with tears, so make man proud, as the Eurotas'
valley. Last year, as this, we had come every morning from Sparta.
And at the end of each day we had plodded home along the dusty
road through the olive groves, bidding the peasants good evening and
good night. Never in life will the memory of those May nights escape;
of the air enveloping, dark and real, the breathing human kiss of earth;
of the bells of the birds dropping round and full from the trees, with
a red vein to their silver curves; of space lit with the scattered mer-
cury of the stars; of one star balanced on the black brow of Taygetus
and suddenly, as by a hand, snatched off; and last, of the meticulous
scholastics from under the bridge: *Brekekekex Coax Coax.*

Now it is on rainy October days that we sit up in the Pantanassa,
drinking coffee in the Byzantine white-pillared cloister beneath the
egg-topped tower. Below us, the stone of the ruined houses, brown
and grey, merges into the hill. Then the walls stop. And the last roots
of the great mountain behind slide out into the valley, where the
rich red earth is dotted grey with olives or striped with the spring-
green of vines. Over all hangs the odour of fresh rain. With distance
the trees lose their detail in patches of colour, Sparta hiding a white
toy town in their thickets. Each way the valley stretches, till on the
east, as we look north, a soft glint of the sea parts the rival ranges
for ever. All along the twining silver river floats a veridian haze. Far

away rise the parallel hills, deepest sapphire, sweeping high and regular as far as the eye can see, with the black and white clouds rolling up, and their shadows like foreign armies traversing the plain. In all lurks the colour of light, of the fire of the earth, burning in watered leaf and sodden plough, catching even the sounds as they run hazard through the air: this colour which Greece knows and other lands do not; and which Greeks have brought to rest, not in stone, but paint.

51   *Triplets for Beautiful Mistra*

ON the clay of the Greeks lowly gleaming
Mistra like an innocent passion
reposes its dead in the sun.

Pantánassa, the evening light
pours through your coloured windows
the scent of stars.

How joy moistens the early leaves
and dew glints on a stone ascent—
the eagle of glory alone on the floor of Byzantine beauty.

There I recall John's city
and weightless pavements blue
in the reflection of the Attic twilight.

Bitter road leading to what is past,
flowering apple-trees moving up to God,
susurrating poplars, the sky's pyx.

And in outdoor forgetfulness, O humble mud-brick cottage,
the skull of a bus
in the wall's shadow.

Caught are we all in the sky's trap—
the numberless apple-trees, phial-like churches, the spring
as a woman's womb outside in the fatherland.

I inhale the smoke of burning laurel:
aloft in the inhabited sky alone
knowing the divine joy of the elements.

I appease the wind with laments
as the vetch stirs desolate
and pinks wound with the scent of festivals.

I left my love in her body, I became a journey.
Gazing deeply into her hair beyond time
I do not exist, stabs upon her hair.

Ruined palaces like women unknown and blind:
vanity
gains the terror of beauty.

Take the oil-lamp, you who will guide our thirst—
the hour is as a funeral pyre—
in the night of Mistra drink with us of this hyacinth.

Behold Taygetus at night over the kastro
while the sky proclaims the sea's blueness
and cries are heard from invisible dogs.

What do you wait for, Greek, facing the stars?
Pain was made for you and beauty
was given you like water great and endless.

THE MANI, CHAROS, RIVERS, OLYMPIA

AT sunrise we were riding at anchor and across the water the harbour front of Yitheion slumbered in the early light. Everything was so quiet; many windows were still closed, and the little tables were empty along the embankment. After standing on deck for a good ten minutes I noticed above the rooftops a white tinge showing through the dusty sky—the high snows of Taygetus, floating there with nothing underneath but the warm haze of the early spring morning. Then the ship started south down the coast of Mani. I have never seen anything like it in all Greece, where the wildest scenery is always a background to the lives of people and the highest mountain only casts a longer shadow under the plane tree in the village square, and in the deepest gorges and along the edge of cliffs the tiny paths are travelled over by the feet of donkeys in endless journeyings from one village to another, and there are always goat-pens in the rocks. There was no sign of anything human on these yellow slopes rising out of the water, radiant and bare as pyramids. The barbarians must have been a terror for the Spartans, even the Spartans of the *basse époque*, to have fled here for refuge. Kakovóuni, the Evil Mountain, the terror of all ships that sailed round Tainaron, where the Turks never dared to penetrate. . . . I looked in vain for some of the villages shown on my map, with the angry-sounding, harshly aspirated names—Skóutari, Kotrónas, Koúrnous, Káyio, Xangiá—and then I read what it says about Mani in the guide-book: 'One of the most original parts of Greece, both for its scenery and the customs of its inhabitants. It is wise, however, to have a recommenda-tion; they still practise the blood-feud, and are fierce and inhospitable, though loyal to the guest once accepted. . . .'

As we drew close to Tainaron, where the last cliff of Taygetus drops into the sea, I saw the first tall stone towers and then the cum-brous, truncated mass of Cape Grosso fissured and streaked with blue-black shadows striking down into the water. A brown bay

107

closed round the ship as it headed in towards a cluster of houses on
the shore. I had known all along it would put in at Yeroliména, that
this was the last stop but one. Decisions are never sudden; they are
only the final stage in the slow maturing of desires; often in the moment one is hardly conscious. Squinting through the glare, I watched
the row-boat coming out to meet us, then grabbed hold of my pack
and hurried aft in time to drop down with two or three other passengers, and a few minutes later I felt the keel grating on the rocks
while the steamer vanished round Cape Grosso. Someone helped me
out on to the pebbly beach of a port just big enough for a few fishing-
boats. People thronged around me in total silence, with swarthy faces
close to mine, faces the colour of earth with eye-sockets like black
holes under the vertical sun. Here there was no gabble of tongues,
none of the glistening, mercurial web of glances avid of perception:
all eyes looked straight ahead. Everybody was armed; round the port
and up and down the street shot-guns and rifles pointed behind each
man's back, with cartridge-belts slung one upon the other across
chests and shoulders, holsters slapping and revolver handles sticking
out of trouser pockets, while the swarm of intent and speechless men
moved like troops in a village just behind the lines. . . . One man
standing beside a donkey had several weapons strapped about him
and on his head the rough-textured cap of the *Agrophylakes*, the
gendarmes of the countryside who watch over the villagers' fields
and recall stray herds off neighbours' property. Because he was
standing still I pressed towards him through the crowd and asked the
way to Tsímova. . . .

'My name is Vasíli', he said. 'I shall show you the way from my
village. Let us go.'

He climbed on to the donkey, and out of the crowd an old man
with a beard, also mounted, joined us as we proceeded into the
country. The path was a narrow trough full of stones like a torrent-
bed with high walls on either side thrown up out of what I was slow
to realize were tilled fields—fields of stones, completely bare of soil,
where the thick spears of wheat grew as by a miracle under the
scrawny olive-trees.

Gazing to right and left, I lost my balance on a loose boulder in the path and stumbled from stone to stone until Vasíli leaned out from his saddle and caught me by the arm, saying, 'Be careful how you walk in Mani. . . .'

The old man turned off and disappeared under the branches of the olive trees. At another crossing several soldiers joined us on the path, and at the next two women who talked with the others in bold, loud, careless voices. When they left us, I confided to Vasíli that I had grown used to hearing women talk quietly in Greece, if they talked at all.

'This is Mani,' he replied; 'women fight together with the men. The Turks were more frightened of our women than of us. A woman can be fearless here because no one is going to touch her. Sometimes when a stranger comes into a house, the father will put his daughter into the same bed with him to sleep, to show his trust. A stranger here is regarded highly. If anyone does him an injury, his host will set about shooting the offender, and then both families fight until no one is left on either side. A war between families only stops when a stranger comes, for it is only he who can pass freely from house to house. But if anything should happen to him, woe betide! The fighting after that will be worse than anything that went before. What can you do? People have to die; there is no room here. . . . Every once in a while at weddings or christenings when many are gathered together, people will let their guns off without looking where they fire, let Charon take whom he will. . . .'

I said, 'Doesn't the race die out?'

Vasíli laughed. 'That's why we make children.'

'To be killed?'

He exclaimed, 'Look around you. How can one expect to live in such a place!'

A TIGHT-meshed network of walls covers this sloping country till the loose ends trail a little distance up the flank of the Taygetus and die away among the boulders. They are there for no purpose of delimitation. It is merely a tidy way of disposing of the stones that otherwise cumber the fields in order that, here and there, an inch or two of dusty earth may afford enough purchase for wheat grains to germinate. A little crescent-shaped bastion of flat stones shores up the precious soil round the roots of each olive tree. Winding labyrinths of walled lanes meander among the walls and trees as arbitrarily, it would seem, as the walls themselves. The solid rock of the Mani breaks through the sparse stubble fields in bleached shoulders and whales' backs and tall leaning blades of mineral and all is as white as bone. Sometimes groups of these blades cluster so thick that they give the illusion of whole villages; but when you reach them after clambering a score of walls, there they are in all their bare sense-lessness: fortuitous dolmens and cromlechs and menhirs. Once in a while, however, the wreck of an almost pre-historic ghost village does appear: a sudden gathering of walls, the shells of half troglo-dytic houses with broken slab-roofs and thresholds only to be entered on all fours, the rough-hewn blocks pitched headlong by wild olive and cactus with only a rough cross incised on a lintel or a carved unidentifiable animal to indicate that they date from later than the stone age. The only other buildings are innumerable microscopic chapels, their shallow slab-roofed vaults jutting like the backs of armadilloes; an occasional farmstead, and the abandoned peel-towers of the Nyklians. The pale marble world of rock and gold stubble and thistle and silver-grey olive-leaves shudders in the mid-day glare, and one feels prone to test the rocks (like spitting on a flat-iron) before daring to lay a hand on them or to lie down in an olive's fragmentary disc of shade. The world holds its breath, and the noonday devil is at hand. . . .

On the other side of a hot valley rose a long saddle of rock on either end of which a village was gathered and each village was a long solid sheaf of towers. There were scores of them climbing into the sky in a rustic metropolis, each tower seeming to vie with the others in attaining a more preposterous height: a vision as bewildering as the distant skyline of Manhattan or that first apparition of gaunt medieval skyscrapers that meets the eye of the traveller approaching San Giminiano across the Tuscan plain. But there were no bridges or ships here, no bastioned town wall or procession of cypresses to detract from the bare upward thrust of all those perpendiculars of sun-refracting facet and dark shadow. The tops were sawn off flat, the gun slits invisible. These two mad villages of Kitta and Nomia shot straight out of the rock in a grove of rectangular organ pipes, their sides facing in every direction so that some of the towers were flanked with a stripe of shade, some turned bare and two-dimensional towards the sun, others twisted in their sockets and seeming to present two visible and equal sides, one in light and one in shade, of symmetrical prisms. Nothing moved and in the trembling and fiery light they had the hallucinating improbability of a mirage.

We crossed the intervening ossuary of hillside and stepped inside the nearest town. The canyons of lane that twisted through the towers were empty and silent as though the inhabitants had fled an aeon ago or a plague had reaped them all in an afternoon. And yet there were signs of recent life: a dozen sacks of dried carob-pods in a courtyard, a child's cart made out of a box and fitted with castors of cotton-reels, a scythe leaning against an iron-studded door. A cat stretched sound asleep along the coping of a wall. Cobbles or slabs of stone alternated with the muffling dust underfoot and tower after tower soared on either hand. The town was empty or locked in catalepsy, paralysed in a spell of sleep which seemed unbreakable. The main square was scarcely larger than a room, and the steep ascending planes of masonry that elbowed it in on all sides lent it the aspect of the bottom of a dried-up well from whose floor sprang a few motionless mulberry trees. The heat and stagnation, the heavy breathlessness of the air and the warm smell of the dust cast a mantle of utter strangeness over this town. It seemed not Greece at all but a dead city of Algeria or Mauretania that a marauding desert tribe had depopulated and abandoned, vanishing into the Sahara or the Atlas mountains three lusters ago. An admonishing silence hung in the air enjoining the newcomer to walk on tiptoe and laying a finger across his lips.

54   *The Women of Mani*

Kitris, Maina,
April 18, 1795.

TO SEE patriarchal and primitive manners, a traveller should visit Maina. . . . We entered it yesterday, and soon came to one of the towers of its chiefs, to whom we had letters. We found a spirited, hearty fellow, who received us with open arms, welcomed us to the country, and entered into a very interesting and animated conversation on the present state of it. . . . He then took leave of us, and one of his men, armed, walked before us to the fair lady's castle, where we now are—another battlemented tower, with portholes on all sides in case of defence, surrounded by a small village on the shore. At our approach, an armed man came out to know our business, and walked with our other guard before us to the house. We were received by her uncle, the late governor of the country, to whom, as well as to her, we had strong letters. The lady is about twenty-eight; her husband, who governed here, is dead, and she is mistress of the territory. . . . Her castle was really enchantment; her uncle, a hearty, fine old man, dined and supped with us, and we were waited on by beautiful girls, in the true mode of patriarchal times. He lived in one tower with four daughters and his wife. Two of his daughters were children, and visited us—they were beautiful beyond measure; and of his older daughters one was, I think, the handsomest woman I ever saw. To give you some idea of their style of dress: On their heads is a plain small circle, either of shawl worked with gold or, sometimes, a red or green velvet cap embroidered round with gold, forming a coronet. Over this floats a long veil of white embroidered muslin.

One end hangs over their right shoulder behind, and the other, hanging loose across their breast, is thrown also over the right shoulder. They wear a tight, high camisole of red silk and gold, buttoned with coloured stones across the breast. A short waistcoat, which is cut quite low, and clasps tight round their waist, is made of muslin and gold, with small globe buttons. A red sash and long flowing robes of white muslin and gold are below. Over these they wear a red, green, or light-blue silk gown, cut straight, and entirely open before, embroidered in the richest manner, the long sleeves sometimes of different colours. On their necks are rows of gold chains in the English mode exactly. They do not wear trousers so low as the women in other parts of Turkey. This is chiefly the description of the lady of the house; you will suppose the colours are varied for different tastes and different ranks. The contour of the dress is much the same, and as the women are naturally lovely, with complexions you would suppose born in the coldest of climates, you may imagine the enchantment of the place, and will conceive how we regretted leaving our lodging. . . . I must allow that the ladies, beautiful as they are, are rather *farouches* in their ideas of honour, as at one captain's where we had a ball they apologized for not having better music, as a favourite fiddler having made too free either with the person or reputation of a fair lady here aroused the vengeance of the *softer sex*, and she shot him through the head upon the spot. The gentlemen, too, would have rather alarmed you as partners, for each of them danced with a large brace of loaded pistols in his belt, and by way of entertaining the ladies a shot was fired out of the window about every ten minutes to enliven the dance. At Cardamyle we saw the ladies exercise at throwing stones. . . .

55   *Mavromichaelis of the Mani*

WHEN the Greek revolution broke out, Pietro Bey Mavromichaelis, the head of one of the most numerous and esteemed families of Maina, was governor of that territory. The revolution was very fatal to Pietro Bey's numerous family. Nine of his near relatives, sons, brothers, and cousins, perished in the struggle. But they had all done good service, and their country remembered their exertions and deplored their loss; and on the arrival of Capodistrias, Pietro Bey was elected to fill the office of senator. Unfortunately, however, various misunderstandings between him and the president gave rise to mutual distrust and disagreement.... It was one of the regulations of the constitution, that no senator should absent himself from the seat of government without the permission of the president. Pietro Bey had occasion to visit his property in Maina, and demanded leave of absence for this purpose. It was refused: and the haughty old chief, little accustomed to have his motions controlled by the caprice of another, left Nauplia in high indignation, and took the road to Maina. Capodistrias had him arrested, brought back to Nauplia, and lodged in a dungeon in the lofty fortress of Palamede, which commands the town. Here the old man was confined for many months, notwithstanding the repeated entreaties and remonstrances of his friends, some of which were couched in language which should have opened the eyes of the president....

George Mavromichaelis was the second son of Pietro Bey, and though not a military man, had served his country with equal devotion to her cause and credit to himself. His personal appearance was singularly prepossessing; his features were peculiarly national; his long black hair curled in glossy ringlets down his shoulders—his countenance was mild and sweet, and bore an expression of gentle and dignified composure—but his broad forehead, and full dark eye, were indicative of great energy and determination. His dress was studiously elegant, and seemed as though a little too much attention might have been bestowed upon it. On the whole, George Mavromichaelis was one of the handsomest men to be met with, even in a land unrivalled in specimens of manly beauty.

One Sunday morning, in October 1831, the president left his house to attend public worship in the principal church of Nauplia. As he approached the door, followed by a few guards, the people respectfully made way for him to pass, when a pistol-shot was heard, and Count John Capodistrias fell into the arms of his nearest attendants, and expired almost immediately. The bystanders all started back at the report, and George Mavromichaelis and his uncle stood forth the obvious perpetrators of the deed. The latter was instantly cut down by a one-armed man, who had been long attached to the president's person; but George escaped by the assistance of some of the crowd, and took refuge in the house of the French consul, by whom, however, he was a few days after given up to the proper authorities. Augustin Capodistrias, brother of the deceased president, procured a decree of the senate that the murderer should be tried by a court martial. Mavromichaelis was brought to trial, and sentenced to be shot.

Early on the morning appointed for his execution, he was led out on the ramparts which face the north-east, by a small detachment of the regular troops, or *tactici*, as they are called. He seemed little changed either by his confinement or his situation; his tread was as firm and manly, and his countenance was dignified and peaceful, as when he was honoured, happy, and free. He stepped a few paces from his executioners, who were drawn out to receive him, and looked at them for a moment or two with unmoved composure. He shewed no weakness—made no confession—asked no delay—refused the bandage with which they wished to hide from him the stroke of death—then, extending his arms towards the assembled multitude, he exclaimed, 'Fellow-countrymen, farewell! I die unjustly,—but I die for my country!' 'Soldiers, fire!' The men fired—the unfortunate victim sunk without a struggle or a groan, and his gallant spirit passed away to its last account.

What must have been the sensations of the agonized father, as from his dungeon, in the overhanging rock, he listened to the volley of musketry which terminated the earthly career of his only remaining son, I will not attempt to paint. It seemed to be acknowledged even by his enemies that he had suffered enough. He was shortly after released, and a Russian brig appointed to convey him to Maina. I obtained permission to accompany him.

As might be expected, the voyage was a melancholy one. The

bereaved old man was generally sunk in what Campbell calls 'the silent soliloquies of sorrow'; and though every now and then he could be roused when the conversation turned upon some of the scenes in which he had been an actor, yet at such times he would suddenly stop in the middle of a sentence, and relapse into his former sullen taciturnity; and it was truly heartbreaking to see the deep shade of anguish which passed across his furrowed brow, and the tears of agony which rolled down his weather-beaten cheeks, as the image of his dying son was forced back upon his recollection by some trifling occurrence, or some careless word.

We landed at Maina; and Pietro Bey asked us, in a manner which shewed that a refusal would have been painful, to go and share the hospitality of his castle for at least one night. We accordingly accompanied him to his residence. It was situated among a sea of mountains, which rose on every side like waves in a storm. The house itself, like most of the Greek habitations, was poor, old, and ruinous; there were but few trees near it: altogether it was a wild scene, and but for the rich, soft, southern climate, would have seemed bleak and desolate. Our host was received with great respect and evident attachment by all his dependants; and a rude banquet was soon prepared for us. . . .

When the banquet was over, the venerable chieftain rose from his seat, and, after struggling for a few moments with his feelings, said to us, in a voice tremulous with emotion, 'Strangers, I thank you for having brought me from a place which I must hate for ever, to my own sequestered dwelling. I shall quit it no more, but will die in the habitation of my forefathers. Greece and I are henceforth strangers— I will mingle no more in her affairs. I have sacrificed to her everything I had; my enemies have made me childless, and nothing now is left to me but lonely, hopeless, tearless desolation.' He spoke these few words with a passionate burst of grief, then sunk down on his seat, and covered his face with his hands. We respected his sorrows, and were silent.

Death and Lamentation

MOURNING and funeral rites have an importance in Greece that exceeds anything prevailing in western Europe, and the poorer and wilder the region—the fewer the tangible possessions there are to lose, and the less the possibilities of material consolations and anodynes—the more irreparable and sad seems loss by death. The expression of this distress is correspondingly more articulate. In these regions the thread of life is brittle. Survival seems something of a day-to-day miracle and life itself, in spite of the impetuousness with which it can be cut off, is doubly precious.

There is, in practice, little belief in a conventional after-life and the rewards and sanctions of Christian dogma. In spite of the orthodox formulae of the priest at the graveside it is not for a Christian eternity, for a paradise above the sky, that the dead are setting out, but the Underworld, the shadowy house of Hades and the dread regions of Charon; and Charon has been promoted from the rank of ferryman of the dead to that of Death himself, a dire equestrian sword-wielder. 'Charon took him', a widow will sigh, contradictorily enmeshing her torso with a dozen signs of the cross. 'He has left me for the Underworld. . . . It was his destiny, it was written. He had eaten his bread and he had no days left. May God forgive all his sins and may the All Holy Virgin give me strength. . . .'

The thread of life, then, is very brittle. In the remote mountains of Greece, on the bare rocks by day and by the glimmer of rush-lights at night, the skull seems close to the surface and struggling to emerge. One sees it plainly beneath the hollow eye-sockets and cheeks and the jawbone's edge, and in old people, wasted by toil and poverty and fever and worry, it looms—the moment the bright glint of conversation fades to the dark and fatalistic lustre of thought—pathetically close. Death is a near neighbour, slight ailments cause exaggerated anxiety among the most robust and more serious illnesses often induce the despair of a wild animal, an inability to fight against death which meets Charon half-way. Invalids often waste away without reason and their eyes reflect neither the impending joys of paradise nor the terrors of hell fire—the temporary rigours of Purgatory and the mists of Limbo have been omitted from Orthodox theology—but extinction, the loss of friends, the end of everything. The bright day is done and they are for the dark, and when the soul flutters away at last no one knows whither it is flying and a shrill and heartrending wail of bereavement goes up.

57   *The Passing of Charos*

WHY are the mountains dark, and why so woe-begone?
    Is it the wind at war there, or does the rain storm scourge them?
It is not the wind at war there, it is not the rain that scourges,
It is only Charos passing across them with the dead;
He drives the youths before him, the old folk drags behind,
And he bears the tender little ones in a line at his saddle-bow.
The old men beg a grace, the young kneel to implore him,
'Good Charos, halt in the village, or halt by some cool fountain,
That the old men may drink water, the young men throw the stones
And that the little children may go and gather flowers.'
'In never a village will I halt, nor yet by a cool fountain,
The mothers would come for water, and recognize their children,
The married folk would know each other, and I should never part
    them.'

58   *Taking Leave of the Dead*

COME, brothers, let us kiss the dead man for the last time, giving thanks to God: for he has abandoned his kin and, no longer concerned with things of vanity, of the much-labouring flesh, hastens towards the grave. Where now are relations and friends? Now we are parted from him to whom we beseech the Lord to give rest.

What parting, O brothers? What mourning, what lament, at this present fall? Come therefore to kiss him who but now was with us. For he is for the grave, stone to cover him, to dwell in darkness, to be buried with the dead. All relations and friends, now we are parted from him to whom we beseech the Lord to give rest.

Now life's imposture, the whole festival of vanity dissolves: for the spirit has left the tabernacle: the clay has grown dark, the body's vessel is broken, voiceless, senseless, dead, motionless. Conveying him to the tomb, we beseech the Lord to give him eternal rest.

A flower is our life, a breath, dew, a veritable twilight. Come let us search diligently over the tombs: where is the body's beauty? Where is youth? Eyes and the flesh's form? All like grass withered, all vanished. Come, let us fall with tears before Christ.

Great the weeping and lamentation, great the sighing and constraint, when the soul departs. Hades and waste, the life of transitory things; non-existent shadow, sleep of deceit, the untimely phantom-like struggle of life on the earth. Far let us flee from every sin of the world, that we may inherit celestial glories.

Seeing the dead before us, we are all aware of the final fall: for he has passed away, as smoke from the earth, as a flower has he flourished, as grass been cut off, swaddled in rags, covered with earth. To him who has vanished let us beseech Christ to give eternal rest.

Come, children of Adam, let us see our own image laid in the earth, all comeliness gone, dissolved in the tomb, in the worms' putrescence, spent in darkness, covered with earth. To him who has vanished let us beseech Christ to give eternal rest. . . .

Come to the grave, brothers, let us see the ashes and dust from which we are formed. Where now do we go? What have we become? Who is poor, who rich? Or who in power, who free? And are we not all dust? The face's beauty has rotted, and death has withered every flower of youth.

All the body's organs, so lately alive, fail now; all inactive, senseless: the eyes are sunk, the feet bound, the hands still, the ears shut, the tongue is locked in silence, consigned to the grave. How truly vain is every human concern!

59

THE lad we are burying,
what shall we say of him?
Tall he was as angel,
graceful as a tree,
May was on his shoulder,
spring within his breast,
stars of night and day-star
in eye and on the brow;
fiddle in the field he was,
in the church a candle,
a strong ship in his house.
But the fiddle is broken,
the candle has gone out,
and the lovely ship
is oarless, is oarless.

60   *In the Western Peloponnesus*

Monday 3rd.

LEAVING Andritzena the road at first goes downhill. Barren
mountains, grey, covered with sparse greenery, oaks; from time
to time a fountain. An open space on a slope, like a small inclined
meadow; beyond it, a thicket of shrubs. The road beneath the green
vault; as François entered it ahead of us a flock of goats emerged.
About goats: on the face of a great rock, almost at the top, groups of
goats (I'm always astonished to think how they can maintain themselves on such slopes); they were posed motionless when we passed
them, each in its own posture, as if they had been of bronze.

We go by the side of a river whose waters split into several branches on broad white gravel; it is bordered by leafless shrubs, grey in
colour, lavender, ligaria etc., now and then a sycamore, its white

trunk standing out at a distance. On both sides of the valley through which the river peacefully winds are mountains of medium height, generally russet in colour: it is the Alpheius, which we cross, the water rising to above the knee and coming into the top of my boots, the current taking our horses with it and I spurring mine till by leaps and bounds I get it to the other side. . . .

Travelling in fine sunlight, on the angle of a slope, there are always these tracks through groves of lentisks; here and there swards of grass, now and again a large tree. O art of the designer of gardens! To our right, the mountain; to our left, below the edge of the wood, flows the river, grey on its white bed; on the far side, fields, trees of a russet colour (because of the lack of leaves), and then the mountains. Everywhere the landscape has this quality of simplicity and charm, one smells good smells, the wood's sap penetrates into your muscles, the blue of the sky descends into your spirit, one lives calmly, happily. . . .

Polignia, 9 o'clock at night.

Wednesday 5th February

The day, short and slightly tiring (six hours on the road) was marked by a single episode but that full of charm: the passage of the Jardanus, a river running about an hour and a half from Pyrgos. All night the torrential rain had beaten on the roofs of our lodging and had dripped through on to our heads; none the less, thanks be to God, we set out at 10 o'clock in the morning. The weather cleared up slightly and I took off my back the frightful blanket folded double which was weighing me down horribly; we travelled over the bare plain, under the grey sky, the temperature mild.

Fording the Jardanus. François went forward first, his horse soon lost its footing and began to be taken downstream; Maxime and I crossed side by side; his horse, weaker than mine, was caught by the current; he was carried in up to the hips, and myself only to two-thirds up the thigh.—Sensation of cold water when it comes in over the top of the boots.—Finally we all reached the other side, having dropped the bridles of our animals, which scrambled out as they could.

There was still the baggage, which we waited for. Councils and deliberations; the choice was soon made: to cross none the less. Shepherds showed us a spot, a little lower down, where there was a kind of small raft of branches and islets of vegetation. The baggage was unloaded and carried by hand, and the animals, thus burdenless, swam across. Maxime and François remounted, to help the swimming horses, while I stayed with Dimitri (the cook), Yorgi, and a young shepherd who was helping us; he and I formed the chain. Slipping with my great boots on the muddy banks of the river, I went into the water to the end of the small bridge, where the shepherd, the river coming up to above his knees, carried the baggage to me, which we thus got across piece by piece. While we were occupied in this way, a flock of sheep appeared: consternation, resistance of the horned beasts, that scattered in all directions; the shepherds yelled and dashed after them. Armed with a long reed, I helped to round the animals up; the first were seized by the wool and forced across, the others followed, half jumping, half swimming or splashing. After which we resumed our operations as porters; the bridge collapses under me, and I stay hanging on by a pier, the mechanics having been put out of action by the weight of the sheep. From now on I was content to remain at the foot of the bank, my fellow-porter bringing me the baggage as far as that. . . .

Before reaching Dervish-Tcheleby, enclosures of aloes; they are extremely beautiful, leafy, with their great thick branches bent back.

From the crossing of the river till our arrival, I practised *yelling*; François excelled at this and gave me lessons, and by evening I'd developed a certain power; but I had, as Sassetti said about some horses that trotted badly, a 'broken stomach'.

While we were on the balcony of our house at Dervish-Tcheleby, waiting for our baggage, we saw a masterful black dog bark at two men and chase them off. They were wandering musicians: one of them played a bagpipe and the other accompanied him carrying an immense wallet hanging at his side; they came to us, both covered in those heavy white cloaks of the Greek peasants, so weighty that only in extreme cases does one put one's arms in the sleeves or draw up the hood. The first, a young man of about twenty, wore canvas sandals black from rain, decay, and filth; while the air was escaping from the bladder of his bagpipe he kept glancing from right to left, and from time to time he lowered his mouth to the end of the pipe held in the full leather bag. His companion was not more than twelve years old, he followed him and carried the wallet. At a nearby house a woman gave him something which he put in his canvas bag. When they had played us a tune they went off and the dog began to bark at them again and to pursue them. Why does the vagabond, and above all the musician, seduce me so much? The sight of these wandering existences who seem to be cursed everywhere (though respect is also involved) grips my heart. I have lived something of this life perhaps? O Bohemia! Bohemia! you are the land of my blood! They have, these Bohemians, something better to make than *la chanson de Béranger*. . . .

61   *Olympia*

WE are at Olympia.
In this deserted place of festival there is scarcely anything to hear but the gentle and tender sound of the Aleppo-pines which cover the low Kronos-hill and here and there raise their humble heads among the ruins of the old temple-site.

This friendly valley is so unpretentious that, the enormous echo of its fame in one's heart, one is startled to see it as it actually is. But it has a captivating loveliness. It is a retreat between a low range of hills on the other side of the river—and on this side is separated by small hills from the world. And whoever has dreamt of shutting himself off without hatred from this world, is never to be trusted.

A small idyllic valley for shepherds—an amazing, literal truth!— with a silted-up stream-bed, pine-trees and sparse meadow-land, and then: it was here—the pilgrim cannot deny it—that the aegis-bearing Zeus wrestled with Kronos for the leadership of the world.—That is wonderful and strange.

The slopes on each side of the Alpheios turn to a brown colour. The rays of a warm, clear spring day sun penetrate through to the ruins, to me. Two magpies fly from tree to tree, from column-drum to column-drum. They behave here as if in unchallenged possession. A cuckoo calls and calls from the top of the Kronos-hill. I shall not forget this Olympian cuckoo of the twelfth of April nineteen hundred and seven.

Dusk and coolness descend. Still the sound of gentle wind in the tree-tops is the low, deep music of quietness. It is an eternal whispering breath, a dream-like murmur, as it were an awakening of something that is at the same time wrapped in heavy, wakeless sleep. The vanished life seems sunk within this sleep. It is difficult to make it clear to someone who has never trod this ground how much one murmur differs from another.

It is quite dark. I surrender more and more to the impression of phantom-like contests. It seems as if cries of runners and wrestlers fill the night air. I sense tumult and wild movement; and these hurried, fleeting things work in me like a rhythm, a tune, such as sometimes takes possession of one and is not to be shaken off.

Suddenly from some young shepherd comes the simple sound of a pipe; it keeps me company on my way back.

I climb the Kronos-hill. It smells of pine-resin. A bird sings beautifully and uninterruptedly in the branches. In the shade a fine ilex flourishes. The wounded trunks of the pine-trees with their incised bark have something savage-looking. I pluck a blood-red, anemone-like flower, step over a chain of caterpillars, fifteen to twenty feet long. The windings of the Alpheios seem like those of a God who strives outwards toward Ortygia, beyond the seas, to where Arethusa, the nymph, the beloved, dwells.

The foundations and ruins of the temple-site lie beneath me. There, where the chryselephantine Zeus stood, on the level shrine of the temple of Zeus, a boy plays. It is my son. Perfectly unconcerned, he dances with light happy steps round the spot which bore the image of the God, this world-wonder of art, about which the ancients said that whoever looked on it could never again be completely wretched.

The pines rustle softly and dreamily over me. Sheep-bells, as in the Alps or the Giant Mountains, sound all round. With them comes the murmur of the yellow stream which has channelled a water-course in its broad, sandy bed, and the croak of frogs in the pools of standing water on its banks.

Still the boy skips on the spot of the God-image which, issued from the hand of Phidias, represented the cloud-gatherer, the father of Gods and men; and I think how according to the legend the God struck the shrine with his lightning and in this way expressed his satisfaction to the Master. What Master and what race was that which took lightning for approval! And what art was that which had Gods as critics!

The hills beyond the Alpheios form a kind of half-circle, and as unwittingly my glance searches over it, it strikes me as the arc of an amphitheatre for god-like spectators. Gods and men disputed for the prize on the smooth stadium beneath me.

Thus musing, I go slowly down into the forgetfulness and desertion of the breathing valley: the valley of Zeus, the valley of Dionysos and the Graces, the valley of Hercules, the valley of the sixteen women of Hera, where night and day offerings burned on the altar of Pan, the valley of victors, the valley of ambition, of fame, of worship and glory, the valley of struggle. . . .

And again I step among the grey ruins which cover the lovely field. Everywhere tender green and yellow flowers of May. Yesterday's pair of magpies fly before me here. The columns of the temple of Zeus lie where they have fallen: the huge porous drums have slipped sideways across one another. Over all the smell of flowers and thyme and stone, warm in the genial morning sun. From a young olive-tree, near the temple of Zeus, I break, with uncontrollable desire, and at the same time as furtively as a thief, a sacred branch.

THE SEVEN ISLES

BUT when he saw the evening star above
Leucadia's far-projecting rock of woe,
And hail'd the last resort of fruitless love,
He felt, or deem'd he felt, no common glow:
And as the stately vessel glided slow
Beneath the shadow of that ancient mount,
He watch'd the billows' melancholy flow,
And, sunk albeit in thought as he was wont,
More placid seem'd his eye, and smooth his pallid front.

Morn dawns; and with it stern Albania's hills,
Dark Suli's rocks, and Pindus' inland peak,
Robed half in mist, bedew'd with snowy rills,
Array'd in many a dun and purple streak,
Arise; and, as the clouds along them break,
Disclose the dwelling of the mountaineer;
Here roams the wolf, the eagle whets his beak,
Birds, beasts of prey, and wilder men appear,
And gathering storms around convulse the closing year.

63   *Odysseus arrives at Ithaca*

MEANWHILE Odysseus set out from the harbour by the rough
path that climbed through woodland to the hills where Athene
told him he would find the good swineherd who cared more for his
lord's substance than any other of his serfs.

He found him sitting at the entrance to the farmstead he had built
high up there in a prominent place, a large enclosure with an open
space around it. Unknown to his mistress or to the old Laertes the
swineherd himself had made it for his absent master out of huge
boulders which he'd topped with a hedge of thorns. Outside this he'd

driven in a paling of large close-set stakes, splitting the oak to its dark core to make them. Inside the pound he'd built twelve pig-sties, the one next to the other, each housing fifty fat brood sows. The boars were kept outside: they were fewer in number, for it was on them the suitors feasted, the swineherd having to keep them always supplied with the best of them; and there were now but three hundred and sixty in his care. Four fearsome dogs, bred by the skilful swineherd, always kept guard over them.

The swineherd himself was cutting a pair of boots out of strong ox-hide, shaping them to his feet. Three of his men were out in various places grazing the swine, while he'd sent the fourth into the town with a boar whose slaughter might satisfy the proud suitors' lust for flesh.

Suddenly the loud dogs caught sight of Odysseus and rushed upon him, barking; but he, knowing what to do, dropped his staff and sat down on the ground. Yet even in his own farmstead would he have been savaged had not the swineherd flung his leather from him and rushed through the gate after the dogs, shouting at them and driving them off with stones. Then he spoke to his master, and said: 'Another moment, father, and the dogs would have torn you to bits and an-other disgrace would have been added to the list of griefs and sorrows which the gods have already given me. For here I pass my days, mourning a god-like master and rearing his fat swine for other men to eat, while he perhaps starving and foodless wanders through some foreign land or city—if, that is, he still lives to look upon the light of day. But come, old man, let us go into the hut; and when you've had your fill of food and wine you may tell us where you come from and what you've had to go through.'

With this, the honest swineherd led him into the hut and, spread-ing him a couch of thick brushwood covered with the great thick shaggy goat-skin—his own sleeping-mat—, he made him sit down. Odysseus was full of joy at the way he was received, and he spoke, saying: 'Stranger, may Zeus and the other immortal gods grant you whatever you most desire in return for this warm welcome you have given me.'

64   *The Cave of the Nymphs*

WHAT does Homer obscurely signify by the cave in Ithaca, which he describes in the following verses?

> 'High at the head a branching olive grows
> And crowns the pointed cliffs with shady boughs.
> A cavern pleasant, though involved in night,
> Beneath it lies, the Naiades' delight:
> Where bowls and urns of workmanship divine
> And massy beams in native marble shine;
> On which the Nymphs amazing webs display,
> Of purple hue and exquisite array.
> The busy bees within the urns secure
> Honey delicious, and like nectar pure.
> Perpetual waters through the grotto glide,
> A lofty gate unfolds on either side;
> That to the north is pervious to mankind:
> The sacred south t'immortals is consigned.'

That the poet, indeed, does not narrate these particulars from historical information, is evident from this, that those who have given us a description of the island, have, as Cronius says, made no mention of such a cave being found in it. This likewise, says he, is manifest, that it would be absurd for Homer to expect, that in describing a cave fabricated merely by poetic licence and thus artificially opening a path to Gods and men in the region of Ithaca, he should gain the belief of mankind. And it is equally absurd to suppose, that nature herself should point out, in this place, one path for the descent of all mankind, and again another path for all the Gods. For, indeed, the whole world is full of Gods and men; but it is impossible to be persuaded, that in the Ithacensian cave men descend, and Gods ascend. Cronius therefore, having premised this much, says, that it is evident, not only to the wise but also to the vulgar, that the poet, under the veil of allegory, conceals some mysterious signification; thus compelling others to explore what the gate of men is, and also what is the gate of the Gods; what he means by asserting that this cave of the Nymphs has two gates; and why it is both pleasant and obscure, since darkness is by no means delightful, but is rather productive of aversion and horror. Likewise, what is the reason why it is not simply said to be the cave of the Nymphs, but it is accurately added, of the Nymphs that are called Naiades? Why also, is the cave represented as containing bowls and amphorae, when no mention is made of their receiving any liquor, but bees are said to deposit their honey in these vessels as in hives? Then, again, why are oblong beams adapted to weaving placed here for the Nymphs? . . . Hence, since this narration is full of such obscurities, it can neither be a fiction casually devised for the purpose of procuring delight, nor an exposition of a topical history; but something allegorical must be indicated in it by the poet, who likewise mystically places an olive near the cave. . . . For, neither did the ancients establish temples without fabulous symbols, nor does Homer rashly narrate the particulars pertaining to things of this kind. But how much the more anyone endeavours to show that this description of the cave is not an Homeric fiction, but prior to Homer was consecrated to the Gods, by so much the more will this consecrated cave be found to be full of ancient wisdom.

65   *A Girl and a Woman*

HOW can I ever forget the young girl whom we passed one day at the foot of the Acropolis? Perhaps she was ten, perhaps she was fourteen years of age; her hair was reddish gold, her features as noble, as grave and austere as those of the caryatids on the Erectheum. She was playing with some comrades in a little clearing before a clump of ramshackle shanties which had somehow escaped the general demolition. Any one who has read 'Death in Venice' will appreciate my sincerity when I say that no woman, not even the loveliest woman I have ever seen, is or was capable of arousing in me such a feeling of adoration as this young girl elicited. If Fate were to put her in my path again I know not what folly I might commit. She was child, virgin, angel, seductress, priestess, harlot, prophetess all in one. She was neither ancient Greek nor modern Greek; she was of no race or time or class, but unique, fabulously unique. In that slow sustained smile which she gave us as we paused a moment to gaze at her there was that enigmatic quality which da Vinci has immortalized, which one finds everywhere in Buddhistic art, which one finds in the great caves of India and on the façades of her temples, which one finds in the dancers of Java and of Bali and in primitive races, especially in Africa; which indeed seems to be the culminating expression of the spiritual achievement of the human race, but which today is totally absent in the countenance of the Western woman. Let me add a strange reflection—that the nearest approximation to this enigmatic quality which I ever noted was in the smile of a peasant woman at Corfu, a woman with six toes, decidedly ugly, and considered by everyone as something of a monster. She used to come to the well, as is the custom of the peasant women, to fill her jug, to do her washing, and to gossip. The well was situated at the foot of a steep declivity around which there wandered a goat-like path. In every direction there were thick shady olive groves broken here and there by ravines which formed the beds of mountain streams which in summer were completely dried up. The well had an extraordinary fascination for me; it was a place reserved for the female beast of burden, for the strong, buxom virgin who could carry her jug of water strapped to her back with grace and ease, for the old toothless hag whose curved back was still capable of sustaining a staggering load of firewood, for the widow with her straggling flock of children, for the servant girls who laughed too easily, for wives who took over the work of their lazy husbands, for every species of female, in short, except the grand mistress or the idle English women of the vicinity. . . . There one day I espied the monster with six toes. She was standing in her bare feet, ankle deep in mud, washing a bundle of clothes. That she was ugly I could not deny, but there are all kinds of ugliness and hers was the sort which instead of repelling attracts. To begin with she was strong, sinewy, vital, an animal endowed with a human soul and with indisputable sexual

133

powers. When she bent over to wring out a pair of pants the vitality of her limbs rippled and flashed through the tattered and bedraggled skirt which clung to her swarthy flesh. Her eyes glowed like coals, like the eyes of a Bedouin woman. Her lips were blood red and her strong even teeth as white as chalk. The thick black hair hung over her shoulders in rich, oily strands, as though saturated with olive oil. Renoir would have found her beautiful; he would not have noticed the six toes nor the coarseness of her features. He would have followed the rippling flesh, the full globes of her teats, the easy, swaying stance, the superabundant strength of her arms, her legs, her torso; he would have been ravished by the full generous slit of the mouth, by the dark and burning glance of the eye, by the massive contours of the head and the gleaming black waves which fell in cascades down her sturdy, columnar neck. He would have caught the animal lust, the ardor unquenchable, the fire in the guts, the tenacity of the tigress, the hunger, the rapacity, the all-devouring appetite of the oversexed female who is not wanted because she has an extra toe.

66   *At Zante*

WHYLESTE we laye thus for sixe dayes upon the seae before the towne, I touke greate notis of a little mountayne, the which, as I thought, did ly close to the seae, and semed to be a verrie pleasante place to take a vew of the whole iland and the seae before it. It showed to be verrie greene and playen ground on the tope of it, and a whyte thinge lyke a rocke in the mydle tharof. I tooke suche plesur in behouldinge this hill that I made a kinde of vow or promise to my selfe that assowne as I sett foute on shore I would nether eate nor Drinke untill I had bene on the tope tharof; and in the meane time did labur with tow of my companyons, and perswaded them to beare me company. One of there names was Myghell Watson, my joyner; the other's name Edward Hale, a Cotchman. The day beinge come that we should go a shore, I chalinged my associates with there promise, and gott there good wills to go with me before we wente

into the towne. This hill is called by the Greekes Scopo. It is from the town more than a myle, but I gave our sayleres somthinge to carrie us in the coke boote, as we thoughte to the foute of the hill; but when we weare sett a shore we found it to be almoste tow myles unto it. When we cam to the foute of it, by great fortune we hapened on the ryght waye, the which was verrie narrow and crouked. It was arlye in the morninge, and we weare toulde, 2 or 3 dayes before, that no man muste carrie any weapern with him when he wente a shore, and tharfore we wente only with cudgels in our handes. So, assendinge the hill aboute halfe a myle, and loukinge up, we saw upon a storie of the hill above us a man goinge with a greate staffe on his shoulder, having a clubed end, and on his heade a cape which seemed to hus to have five horns standinge outryghte, and a greate heard of gootes and shepe folloed him.

My frende Myghell Watson, when he saw this, he seemed to be verrie fearfull, and would have perswaded us to go no farther, tellinge us that surly those that did inhabite thare weare savidge men, and myghte easalye wronge us, we hauinge no sordes or dageres, nether any more Company; but I tould him that yf thei weare divers, I would, with Godes help, be as good as my worde. So, with muche adow, we gott him to go to that storie wheare we sawe the man with his club; and than we saw that that man was a heardman. Yeate, for all this, Myghell Watson swore that he would goo no farther, com of it what would. Edward Hale sayd somthinge fayntly that he would not leave me, but se the end. So we tow traveled forwarde, and when we cam somthinge neare the topp, we saw tow horsis grasinge, with packe sadls on ther backes, and one man cominge downe the hill towards us, having nothinge in his handes. Cothe I to my fellow: Nede, we shall see by this man what people they be that inhabit heare. When this man came unto us he lay his hand upon his breste, and boued his head and bodye with smylinge countinance, makinge us a sine to go up still. Yeat than Ned Hall began to diswade me from goinge any further; but I tould him it would not stand with my othe to go backe untill I had bene as farr as I could go. Cominge to the top thare was a prittie fair grene, and on one sid of it a whyte house bulte of lyme, and some square, the whyche had bene the house of an ancoriste, who, as I harde after wardes, Died but a little before our cominge thether, and that she had lived five hundrethe years. Ryghte before us, on the farther side of the greene, I saw a house of som 20 pacis longe, and waled aboute one yarde hie, and than opene to the eaves, which was aboute a yarde more. And I se a man on the inside reatche oute a coper kettell to one that stood with oute the wale. Than saide I to Ned Hale: I will go to yender house and gitt som drinke, for I have greate neede. The wether was verrie hote, and I was fastinge. But Ned Hale tould me that I had no reason to drinke at there handes, nether to go any nearer them. Yeate I wente bouldly to the sid of the house, whear I saw another man drinke, and made a sine to him within that I woulde drinke. Than he touke up the same ketle which had water in it, and offer it me to drinke. And when I did put out my hande to take it, he would not give it me, but sett it further of, and than cam near the wale againe, and lifte up a carpit which lay on the ground, and thar was six bottels full of verrie good wyne, and a faire silver cupe, and he filed that silver boule full of a redeishe wyne, which they do cale Rebola, and he gave it me to drinke; and when I had it in my hande I caled to my frende Nede Hale, who stood a far of, for he was a fraide to come neare. Heare, Nede, cothe I, a carrouse to all our frendes in Inglande. I pray you, cothe he, take heede what you dow. Will you take what drinke they give you? Yeae, truly, cothe I; for it is better than I have as yeat disarved of. When I had give God thankes for it, I drank it of, and it was the beste that ever I dranke. Than he filled me the same boule with whyte Rebola, the which was more pleasante than the other. When I had muche comended the wyne, and tould Ned Hale that he was a foule to refuse suche a cup of wyne, than he come neare the house, and desiered to have som water; so he had the kettle to drinke in. When this was all done, I was so well pleasede with this entertaynmente, that I knew not how to thanke this man. I had no mony aboute me but one halfe Dolor of Spanyshe mony, and that mony is best accepted of in that countrie. I offered to give that peece of silver to this man, but he would not by any means take it. Than I re-

membered that I had tow severall (Seville?) knyfes in my pocket. I
toke one of them and gave it him, and the blad gilded and graven.
When he had taken it oute of the sheathe and louked upon it, he
caled with a loude voyce: Sisto, Sisto! Than another man Came run-
ninge, unto whom he showed but only the hafte of it, and than they
began to wrastell for the knife; but he that I gave it unto kepte it
and leape ower the wale to the side whear I was, and, bowinge him
selfe unto me, he toke me by the hande, and led me aboute by the
ende of that house, and so into a litle cloyster throughe the whyche
we passed into a Chappell, whear we found a preste at mass and wex
candls burninge. He pute me into a pue, whear I satt and saw the
behaveour of the people, for thare weare about 20 men, but not a
woman emongste them; for the wemen weare in a lower chapell by
them selves, yeate myghte they heare and se. Ned Hale cam after,
but hauinge loste sighte of me, at his cominge into the chappell he
kneled Downe neare unto the wemen, but saw them not; but they
saw him, and wondred at his behaveour; for, after I had kneeled
Downe, I stode up in my pue to louk for him, and than I saw tow
wemen put oute there heades and laughed at him—as indeed they
myghte, for he behaved him selfe verrie foolishly. Nether he nor I had
ever sene any parte of a mass before, nether weare we thinge the wyser
for that. This chapell was verrie curiusly paynted and garnished round
aboute, as before that time I had never seene the lyke. Sarvis beinge
ended, we Departed out of the chapell; but presently one cam after
us, who did seme verrie kindly to intreat me to goo backe againe, and
he leed us throughe the chappell into the cloyster, wheare we found
standing eyghte verrie fayre wemen, and rychly apparled, som in
reed satten, som whyte, and som in watchell Damaske, there heads
verrie finly attiered, cheanes of pearle and juels in there eares, 7 of
them verrie yonge wemen, the eighte was Anchante, and all in
blacke. I thoughte they hade bene nones, but presently after I kenewe
they wear not. Than weare we brought into that house wheare
before I had dranke. Clothe beinge layde, we weare requested to sitt
downe, and sarved with good breade and verrie good wyne and egges
the shels of them collored lyke a damaske Rose, and these mad lyke

137

an alla compana (alla campagna) Route, for they keep it in the earthe, because nothinge will thar take salte. My fellow, Ned Hale, would nether eate not drinke anythinge but water, yeat I did eate one egge, bread and cheese and I dranke tow boules of wyne. Whylste we satt there, the Jentelwemen came in, and thre of them came verrie neare us, and louked earnestly upon us. I offered one of them the cup to drinke, but she would not. Then I offered to give him that tended upon us my halfe Dollor, but he would not take any monye. These wemen standing all to gether before us, I thoughte they had bene Dwellers there, because no mony would be taken. I presented my other knyfe, of 2s. price, unto the ould Jentlewoman, the which she was unwilling to take, but at laste she tooke it, and than they all flocked together, and, as it semed to me, they wondered muche at it. When they had well louked upon it, they came altogether towardes me and bowed there bodies, to show ther thankfulnes. So Ned Hale and I Touke our leves and wente awaye verrie merrily; but when we came to the place wheare we lefte our fainte harted frend Myghell Watson, who all this whyle has layen in a bushe, when we had tould him the wonderes that we had sene, and of our kinde entertainmente, he would not beleve us, for he was a shamed, and desiered us to make haste to the towne that he myghte git som vittals; but we mad the less haste for that, and wente to se another monestarie.

67   *Palaeokastrizza,*
                              Easter Sunday. April 20, 1862

I WISH you were here for a day, at least today.... I have been wondering if on the whole the being influenced to an extreme by everything in natural or physical life, i.e., atmosphere, light, shadow, and all the varieties of day and night,—is a blessing or the contrary— and the end of my speculation has been that 'things must be as they may,' and the best is to make the best of what happens.

I should however have added 'quiet and repose' to my list of influences, for at this beautiful place there is just now perfect quiet, excepting only a dim hum of myriad ripples 500 feet below me, all round the giant rocks which rise perpendicularly from the sea: which sea, perfectly calm and blue stretches right out westward unbrokenly to the sky, cloudless that, save a streak of lilac cloud on the horizon. On my left is the convent of Paleokastrizza, and happily, as the monkery had functions at 2 a.m. they are all fast asleep now and to my left is one of the many peacock-tail-hued bays here, reflecting the vast red cliffs and their crowning roofs of Lentish Prinari, myrtle and sage—far above them—higher and higher, the immense rock of St Angelo rising into the air, on whose summit the old castle still is seen a ruin, just 1,400 feet above the water. It half seems to me that such life as this must be wholly another from the drumbeating bothery frivolity of the town of Corfu, and I seem to grow a year younger every hour. Not that it will last. Accursed picnic parties with miserable scores of asses male and female are coming tomorrow, and peace flies—as I shall too. . . .

MISSOLONGHI, DELPHI, ST LUKE

M Y master continued his usual custom of riding daily, when the weather would permit, until the 9th of April; but on that ill-fated day he got very wet, and on his return home his Lordship changed the whole of his dress, but he had been too long in his wet clothes, and the cold of which he had complained, more or less, ever since we left Cephalonia made this attack more severely felt. Though rather feverish during the night, he slept pretty well, but complained in the morning of a pain in his bones, and a head-ache: this did not, however, prevent him from taking a ride in the afternoon, which I grieve to say, was his last. On his return, my master said that the saddle was not perfectly dry, from being so wet the day before, and observed, that he thought it had made him worse. His Lordship was again visited by the same slow fever, and I was sorry to perceive, on the next morning, that his illness appeared to be increasing. He was very low and complained of not having had any sleep during the night. His appetite was also quite gone. I prepared a little arrow-root, of which he took two or three spoonfuls, saying it was very good, but he could take no more. It was not until the 3rd day, the 12th, that I began to be alarmed for my master. In all his former colds he slept well, and was never affected by this slow fever.

His Lordship continued to get weaker, and on the 17th he was bled twice in the morning, and at two o'clock in the afternoon. The bleeding at both times was followed by fainting fits, and he would have fallen down more than once, had I not caught him in my arms. In order to prevent such an accident, I took care not to let him stir without being supported. On this day my master said to me twice, 'I cannot sleep, and you well know that I have not been able to sleep for more than a week': he added, 'I am not afraid of dying: I am more fit to die than many think.' I do not, however, believe that his Lordship had any apprehension of his fate till the day after, the 18th, when he said 'I fear you and Tita (the courier) will be ill by sitting up constantly, night and day.' I answered, 'We shall never leave your Lordship till you are better.' On the 18th he addressed me frequently, and seemed to be rather dissatisfied with his medical treatment. I then said, 'Pray, my Lord, allow me to send for Dr. Thomas,' to which he answered, 'Do so, but be quick. I am only sorry that I did not let you send for him before, as I am sure they have mistaken my disease. . . .' Although his Lordship did not appear to think his dissolution was so near, I could perceive he was getting weaker every hour. His Lordship continued the conversation by saying, 'I now begin to think I am seriously ill: and in case I should be taken away suddenly from you, I wish to give you several directions, which I hope you will be particular in seeing executed.' I answered I would, in case such an event came to pass, but expressed a hope that he would live many years, to execute them himself much better than I could. To this my master replied, 'No, it is now nearly over,' and then added, 'I must tell you all without losing a moment.' I then said, 'Shall I go, my Lord, and fetch pen, ink and paper?' 'Oh, my God, no; you will lose too much time, and I have not it to spare, for my time is now short,' and immediately after, 'Now pay attention.' His Lordship commenced by saying 'You will be provided for.' I begged him, however, to proceed with things of more consequence. He then continued, 'Oh, my poor dear child! my dear Ada! my God, could I but have seen her! Give her my blessing, and my dear sister Augusta and her children: and you will go to Lady Byron and say—Tell her everything —you are friends with her.' His Lordship appeared to be greatly affected at this moment. Here my master's voice failed him, so that I could only catch a word at intervals but he continued muttering something very seriously for some time. I then told his Lordship, in a state of greatest perplexity, that I had not understood a word of what was said: to which he replied—'Oh! my God! then all is lost! for it is now too late. Can it be possible you have not understood me?' 'No, my Lord,' said I, 'but I pray you to try and inform me once more.' 'How can I?' rejoined my master, 'it is now too late and all is over.' I said, 'Not our will, but God's be done,' He answered, 'Yes, not mine be done; but I will try'. His Lordship did indeed make several efforts to speak, but could only repeat two or three words at a time, such as 'My wife! my child! my sister! You know all, you must say all, you know my wishes?' The rest was quite unintelligible. . . . The last words I heard my master utter were at six o'clock on the evening of the 18th, when he said, 'I must sleep now,' upon which he lay down, never to rise again.

69   *Siege of Missolonghi*

IF, as a Greek, our host had any national pride about him, he was imposing upon himself a severe task; for all that he could do was to conduct us among ruins, and, as he went along, tell us the story of the bloody siege which had reduced the place to its present woeful state. For more than a year, under unparalleled hardships, its brave garrison resisted the combined strength of the Turkish and Egyptian armies, and, when all hope was gone, resolved to cut their way through the enemy, or die in the attempt. Many of the aged and the sick, the wounded and the women, refused to join in the sortie, and preferred to shut themselves up in an old mill, with the desperate purpose of resisting until they should bring around them a large crowd of Turks, when they would blow all up together. An old invalid soldier seated himself in a mine under the Bastion Bozzaris (the ruins of which we saw), the mine being charged with thirty kegs of gunpowder; the last sacrament was administered by the bishop and priests to the whole population, and, at a signal, the besieged made their last desperate sortie. One body dashed through the Turkish ranks, and, with many women and children, gained the mountains: but the rest were driven back. Many of the women ran to the sea and plunged in with their children; husbands stabbed their wives with their own hands, to save them from the Turks, and the old soldier under the bastion set fire to the train, and the remnant of the heroic garrison buried themselves under the ruins of Missolonghi.

The Women of Missolonghi

AND it happened that in those days the Turks were besieging Missolonghi, and often all day and sometimes all night Zakinthos trembled from the great cannonade. And it was then that some women of Missolonghi went round begging for their husbands, for their children, for their brothers, who were fighting. At first they were ashamed to come out and they waited for darkness before holding open their hands, because they were not used to it. For they had had servants and on many plains had had goats and cattle and numerous sheep. And so they used to get impatient, looking often out of the window, to see when the sun would set, that they might go out. But when the need became acute, they lost their shame and went round all day.

And when they were tired, they sat down on the shore and often they lifted their heads and listened, because they were frightened lest Missolonghi should fall. And everyone saw them going round, in the streets, at the cross-roads to houses, upper and lower floors, to churches, to chapels, begging. And they received money, and bandages for the wounded. And no one said no to them, because the pleas of the women were usually accompanied by gun-fire from Missolonghi, and the earth trembled beneath our feet. And the poorest took out their mite and gave it and made their cross, gazing towards Missolonghi and weeping. . . .

And I followed the women of Missolonghi, who sat down on the sea-shore; and I was behind a hedge and I watched. And each one produced whatever she had collected and they made a pile. And one of them, reaching out her hand and feeling the shore, cried: 'Sisters, hark if Missolonghi has ever shaken the earth as now. Perhaps she triumphs, perhaps she falls.'

And I began to go, when I saw behind the church an old woman, who had set up small candles in the grass, and she was burning incense and the small candles shone in the greenness, and the incense went up. And she raised her bony hands, passing them through the incense and weeping. And opening and closing her toothless mouth, she prayed. And I felt a great disturbance within me, and I was carried away in spirit to Missolonghi. And I saw neither the castle, nor the camp, nor the lake, nor the sea, nor the earth I trod, nor the sky; pitchblack darkness covered the besieged and the besiegers and all their works and everything that there was. And I raised eyes and hands toward heaven to pray with all the fervour of the soul; and I saw, lit up in the incessant flashing, a woman with a lyre in her hand, who stood in the air among the smoke. And I had just time to marvel at her dress, which was black like the hare's blood, and her eyes . . . when she halted, the woman, among the smoke, and she gazed at the battle; and the thousand sparks that flew into the sky touched her dress and went out. She spread her fingers on the lyre, and I heard her chant:

> At the dawn I took
> the road of the sun
> hanging the just
> lyre from the shoulder;
> and from where it breaks
> until where it sets. . . .

And scarcely had the Goddess finished her words when she vanished, and our people shouted madly because of the triumph, and they and everything else went from me, and my bowels again shook terribly, and it seemed that I had become deaf and blind. And soon I saw in front of me the old woman, who said to me: 'God be praised, Hermit, I thought that something had happened to you. I called you, I shook you, and you heard nothing and your eyes were fixed on the sky, while the earth leapt like bubbles in seething water. Now it is over, and the small candles and the incense are spent. Would you say that our people have triumphed?' And I began to go, with Death in my heart; and the old woman kissed my hand, and, kneeling down, she said: 'How frozen your hand is!'

71   *The Sortie from Missolonghi*, 1827

IT dawned, to reveal what! All the women, loaded, were carrying
their chests with their best embroideries and blankets to the ramparts. This was contrary to the plan, and we foresaw that, each
woman going to her husband, the army would find itself impeded.
Stornaris, also, out of weakness, could not bear to leave anything; the
most important papers he put into two bags and gave them to his
godson Kostas Koutos to take with him, all the rest he put into a
sack, to load them on to the horse. Soldiers and officers together took
one bag each, only to carry cartridges and not to burden themselves
with clothes. Those who had no sword or cutlass put a bayonet on a
pole. All bound the hilts of their cutlasses and swords with braided
cord, to hang them from the arm and at the same time to be able to
use them without difficulty. All strengthened their boots with
Arabian cartridge-belts. . . .

That day, a man from Kravara cut meat from the buttock of a
dead body and ate it. Another heroic soldier went into the church to
pray, while I was going up toward the ramparts. He had just reached
the threshold of the outer door when he fell like a tree to the ground.
I caught him up, I massaged him, I encouraged him by talking of our
sortie. 'Is it certain,' he asked me, 'that we leave?' 'Certain,' I answered, 'Today.' I brought him water; he drank; he got up. 'If we
leave today,' he said to me, 'perhaps I shall last out, otherwise I've
no more strength.'

Night came and I went back to Makris' post, where all were
ready. Dead silence and no word. One teased the other, jokingly.
'Who knows where you will be tomorrow. . . .' One of Stornaris'
officers, Apostolis Tsalakas, a man of fifty-five, soldier since childhood, feeling that he would not save himself and having gold-worked
weapons and some ten thousand gold coins in his belt, took everything off and gave it all to a nephew of his, Panagiotis Sezis, who had

nothing, to buckle on and to arm himself with. As he dressed him and his nephew took the arms, he gave him his blessing, saying:

'My child, these things I have won as a rebel and soldier since childhood. Take them! I have never at any time disgraced them. I give them to you with my blessing. My legs now are too feeble to run over hill and dale. Come, let me kiss you. And use these things for my soul's sake. I shall remain and die here, where the ox will swim in blood after your flight!' . . .

All the armed chieftains and soldiers went and said farewell to their comrades, friends and relations, the wounded and the sick, who with tears of joy parting from them, remained to die fighting. No one complained, for the danger was equal for them and for us. All wished for a happy reunion in the other world. Reaching the Wind-mill, I went and found Kapsalis in the ammunition-store. I told him at what hour he must set fire to it. He answered me: 'I don't need instruction! Only, good luck to you, and when you reach the foot of the mountain, listen and look and you will see where your Kapsalis will blow himself to.' At that moment Tsavelas passed by us and told us to withdraw. He went on to the shore towards Marmatos, to gather together all those who were there.

All the married couples went as pre-arranged to the bridge, like sheep, in silence. Fathers, with cutlasses hanging from one arm, rifles slung from the shoulder, bore child or wife on the other arm and went forward. Many women dressed as men and armed them-selves and as they walked they couldn't be distinguished from the men. Passing along the road by Notis' house, I saw a woman and three other sick Missolonghians lying in the square. The women cried: 'Why do you leave us' as loud as she could; the sick wept. I rebuked her for shouting; she continued. Hurriedly I struck her with the bayonet. I heard a voice I knew: 'Nicholas, would you kill my mother?' 'Yes,' I answered, 'for she will give us away.' I knew the fellow; he was a fearless youth and a hero, our first bugler, Gregory of Missolonghi. With tears I and our friends kissed him, on foot and in haste, but it was impossible to help him. I consoled him, and told him to put his life in God's hand, as we also did. . . .

Kissing the earth, we bade Missolonghi farewell. She had been a paradise to us, and with her we were leaving so many brave men, although we too did not know our fate. . . .

The standard-bearer came out and with the guides, and with Notis, began confusedly to move off, kissing and with sighs bidding farewell to the door of the stronghold and to the steps. Ah, Missolonghi, ah, blood we have given unjustly! . . .

72   *At Delphi*

WE reach the bend of the street. The road continues in a wide curve under huge red walls of rock, and at first one seeks in vain for some spot in this gorge-like Delphic valley for human settlement. From the huge, harsh, red and perpendicular walls of the Phaedriades, the broken ground slopes steeply down above us and seems inaccessible. Everywhere in the Alps are similar scarps on whose heights pasturing goats scramble. There one seldom sees any sign of human life except perhaps a single small hut, while here, on this unlikely building-site, one has to picture a confusion of temples, temple-like treasuries, of priest-quarters, of theatre and stadium, and of countless images in stone and bronze.

We walk slowly along the white road. We startle a large green lizard, which scuttles across the path before us, stirring a cloud of dust. A small donkey, stacked with a mountain of broom, comes towards us; the peasants, it seems, weave baskets of broom to keep cheese in. A mule drags a load of coloured blankets to Kastri, driven by a woman, who, as she goes along, spins industriously from a wad of goat's hair the same thread from which the blankets are made.

With the steep slope of the Delphic temple-site always before me, I cannot help thinking how all the priests of Apollo who once were here, like those of Dionysos, how all these ancient temples, the theatre, the treasuries, the innumerable columns and statues came after and took the place of goats and goat-herds.

The herdsman's life is generally one of solitude. It favours vision-

ary powers. Stillness of the external senses and idleness stimulate the world of imagination, and it would not be hard to find today, perhaps in some Swiss lunatic asylum, a peasant-girl, crazed with religious phantasy, who was overcome by similar things, who uttered 'with raving mouth' similar things as overcame and were uttered by the first seers, the Sibyl or her successors at Delphi. This latter considered herself to be either the wedded wife of Apollo, or his sister, or she declared herself his daughter.

We climb the steep road within the temple-site. Everywhere among the foundations of former temples, treasuries, altars, statues, the camomile flowers in large clumps, as at Eleusis or on the Acropolis. The stone of the old road is smooth and only with difficulty do we mount without slipping.

I rest not far from that jutting-out rock, called the Sibyl's Stone. The ceaseless humming of bees sounds among the hot scented clumps of camomile in which I lie. Who would dare to assert that every detail of the immense past of this rocky platform was present before him? The cthonic spring, the intoxicating vapours issuing from the fissure in the rock, gush forth, they say, no more, and already in the time of the great Periegetes the daimons had left the Oracle. Will they ever come back again? And if they do come back, will the Oracle, like a long unused instrument of divine speech, sound out anew?

Meanwhile, the architectural remains do not excite me greatly. In this huge mountain-setting art had indeed in comparison always a pygmy character. Surpassing all in wild, unyielding majesty nature reigns here, and when out of forbearance or from divine command she tolerated also the settlement of the human ants who, not without daring, nestled here, yet the grandeur of her silence, the nobility of her speech still dominated, present beneath, behind, over and in everything.

One thinks of Apollo, one thinks of Dionysos; but in these surroundings it is not of their image in stone and bronze that one thinks; rather one thinks of the true idol, the primitive image of wood, of which no trace has come down to us. Here and there one beholds Gods, luminous, immaterial, visionary; chiefly, however, one recognizes them in their actions. Here the Gods are invisibly present; and so also, like them, do the daimons people nature invisibly.

Is the cthonic spring really dried up? Have the daimons really left the Oracle? Are most of them dead, as they say that the great Pan is dead? And is the great Pan really dead?

I believe that every other spring of pre-Christian life is dried up rather than the Pythian; I believe that the great Pan has not died, either from the decadence of contemporaries, still less from the millennial curse of the Christian priesthood. And here among these sun-cracked ruins, the mystery which is said to be quite dead, and the daimons and the Gods and that Pan himself who is reported extinct, are all present.

Among the 'many streams which our earth upward sends' many still today rise at Delphi, and, as once in the herdsman Koretas, still provoke agitation and inspiration in the soul of man, even if we esteem this inspiration but little, and, generally speaking, do not wish to make that profound dedication with which sacred intoxication is linked.

This Parnassus and this her red ravine are springs: springs of natural streams and of the inexhaustible silver streams of the Greek soul which flows through the millenniums. It is one aura and spirit which surrounds these springs, and another which surrounds the ups and downs of the stream of Greek life. Strange, how the source of streams and their cradle are most close to what is most primitive and immemoriably ancient: the most primitive and immemoriably ancient in what is everlivingly young. One cannot call such sources Greek alone, for most of them, in contrast to the streams which they feed, are without name.

Opposite, on the other side of the ravine, not unlike the call of the horns of Uri echoes from the wall of rock the sound of a bagpipe, played by an invisible goatherd who climbs with his goats over the rocks. Herdsmen dwelt and still today dwell round these blessed springs. Plato called the soul a tree, whose roots are in the head of man and which from there with trunk, branches and leaves rises into the Heavens. I deem the world of the senses to be part of the soul, to be her roots, and I place in the human mind a metaphysical seed from which the tree of Heaven, with trunk, branches, leaves, blossoms and fruit, grows.

Now it seems to me that the senses of the herdsman, the senses, let us say, of the hunter-herdsman, are the most noble and the most ancient roots of all, and that the life of the herdsman and the hunter on the mountains is the richest soil for such roots, and thus the best food for man's metaphysical seed.

73   *The Source of Blessing*

OUR greatest blessings come to us through madness, when it is sent as a divine gift; for the prophetess at Delphi and the priestesses at Dodona being mad have done many good things both private and public for Greece, but few or none when in their right minds.

74   *The Power of Music*

GOLDEN lyre, possessed by Apollo and the violet-tressed Muses, the foot hears you, brightness begins; singers obey your notes when on trembling strings you sound the dance's prelude; you curb the deathless flame's strong thunderbolt; the eagle, king of birds, sleeps on God's sceptre, wings folded, while a dark cloud falls over his bending head and seals his eyelids: asleep, his supple back heaves, spelled by your quivering song. Even the terrible War-God, dropping his sharp uncouth spears, in slumber melts his heart; with the skill of Leto's son and the rich-breasted Muses, your shafts charm even the sacred Powers.

All unloved of God, on earth and in the tumultuous sea, shudders when it hears the voice of Pieria's daughters, as he too who lies in Hell, God's enemy, hundred-headed Typhon, nursed in the famous

Cilician cave, though now on his shaggy breast lie Kyme's cliffs and Sicily, held fast by Heaven's pillar, snow-clad Etna, which year-long suckles the sharp frost. From its depth belch forth pure founts of unapproachable fire and by day its rivers roll down lurid smoke-streams, and by night the red flame hurls in its stride resounding rocks into the deep sea below. And the beast spouts terrible founts of fire, marvellous to see, marvellous even to hear of from those who have seen what brute is bound beneath Etna's dark-leaved heights and the plain, while his bed, furrowing his outstretched back, goads him.

75   *Among the Ruins*

DELPHI is I suppose one of the most spectacular places on God's good earth: sheer rock-face of Parnassus soaring upwards to end in eagle-crags and, further back, white ridges of snow; below, the deep valley, loaded with olive trees, with a stream winding down the bottom to the jutting inlet of sea away in the distance. How much they knew about atmosphere, those old ones, bringing their gods to rest in such places as this. We wandered over the ruins, with the blood-red poppies spurting up between cracks in the stone, and everywhere anemones and blue grape-hyacinths. Odd that this place once controlled the destiny of a world. Perhaps it still does. Historically, the real fount of inspiration must have degenerated here into a kind of closed shop, sacerdotalism and priest-craft. It must have become like the Vatican, with the rich bringing gifts, the cities of Greece building their treasuries to fill with offerings to the god—i.e. to the priests, who must, incidentally, have maintained a very fine news-service, a highly efficient Reuter. Strange how the pattern repeats itself. First there is the genuine inspiration, the revelation of the mystery, with great dynamic force. An actual spiritual teaching. This at Delphi was as likely as not Orphism. The mysteries were held by the initiates and sown into the community. Then gradually the inner fire goes, the initiates become a caste, holding behind closed doors the letter of the law, imposing superstition, stamping out any new revelation. And so strong are the conservative forces in man that the actual decay can last over centuries, through the sheer weight of inertia and man's longing to have all the problems taken off his shoulders and decided for him by a body of officials, to surrender, using Dostoievsky's terms, his freedom in return for worldly peace of mind and partial happiness. Babylon, Delphi, Rome—and many other places besides. The creative life is formalized, given a hierarchy, a set of dogmas, an authority. Ossification. Until a new people, barbarians probably, but full of energy, come and destroy the suffocating structure and set the blood flowing again. Then all that remains are a few broken stones, a ruined theatre, a stadium full of vanished eyes which once watched the fine bodies of long-disappeared athletes. Sitting in the afternoon sun looking down on the stadium I tried to bring back to life the sweating, cheering, excited crowd which once gazed at the spectacle in front of them. But I could not. All was too silent, a death-hush full of unseen presences, with only, high above, the eagles circling and circling in the blue vault with scarcely a flicker of their wing-tips, and, on the road below, an old woman leading her loaded donkey up the hill into the village. Apollo; the Pythia who, drunk with the burnt laurel-leaves, spoke the God's word; Delphi itself, the world's navel—all sunk, sunk and silent. Odd that after two thousand years a Greek poet should try to bring Delphi once more to life. It is deeply moving, this effort of the Greeks to keep their old gods, this effort of a Gemistos Plethon, of a Sikelianos, to name two who above others have tried. It is deeply moving, but can it be? There is a wisdom in polytheism that we have ignored—we begin at last to realize that. Extreme monotheism has crippled much life; it has assumed uniformity where in fact there is diversity; it has meant that all ideals, all expressions of vitality which seem to contradict or to bear no relation to this one central ideal have been suppressed or denied. But can you, because of that, restore the old gods? I doubt it. Yet you can at least, and you must, learn to respect all those expressions of life of which they after all were but the names.

76

THE lord whose oracle is at Delphi neither speaks nor conceals, but indicates with a sign.

77   *The Last View*

TODAY, looking down from above, as for instance from the theatre, it is as if you have beneath you a descending sea-bed where everything is reduced to the same level: the pieces of marble, the cut stone, the rocks which years ago rolled down from Parnassus and where the Sibyl once sat: the bed of a quiet shallow sea full of these pebbles which each of us, according to his nature, deciphers: a polygonal wall so living that your hand instinctively repeats the movement of the mason who cut and fitted the stone; a bending of thumb and forefinger as they raise a dress with a grace such as that you saw yesterday in a Greek village; a living thigh, as the knee bends for a woman to descend from the chariot; a Sphinx's head with the eyes neither open nor closed; the smile, which they call archaic— but that isn't really adequate—of a Hercules or a Theseus: some such fragments of a life which was once complete, disturbing fragments, close to us, ours for one moment, and then mysterious and un-approachable as the lines of a stone licked smooth by the wave, or of a shell in the depths.

78   *The Monastery of St Luke*

UPON the Brow of this Hill, on the South-East side, is situated the Convent of St Luke, sirnamed Stiriotes, from this Hill so called also. They do not mean St Luke the Evangelist; but another, a Hermite of this Desart: which we found in the Office we saw, and they use in their Church; where the Title of Stiriotes is given him.

This is one of the finest Convents in all Greece, and consists ordinarily of above a Hundred and fifty Persons; of which some they call Hieromonachie; who are in Orders, and only attend upon the Service of God, and some other Employment in their Cells, as knitting of Caps, and other necessary Affairs. The Seniors of these have a young one to wait on them, whom they teach to write, and read, and to say his Office. If he have any Ingenuity, he proceeds to understand to say their Liturgies, &c. The others are called Caloyers; and are employed about all servile and necessary Offices about the Convent; some of them tilling the Ground, others keeping the Sheep; and are commonly seen up and down in the Fields, about that business; only Sundays and Holy-days they meet all together in the Church. Out of the Seniors, the Abbots, whom they call Hegoumenoes, are chosen every second Year. The present Abbot is named Gregoria; who is a good ingenious Man, and understands the antient Greek indifferently well. The Valley round about them belongs to the Convent, and bears good Wine, Oyl, Corn, and Honey. They have several little Huts up and down, where the Caloyers lodge near their Business; and these they call Metochia, the same word, which the antient Greeks used for Colony. Out of this they have a considerable Revenue: but of late are so impoverished by some scarce Years, that they have been forced to sell their Church-plate, to pay the Turk his dues; which is Two hundred Dollars a Year, or about fifty Pounds English. The rest of their Livelihood is Charity; which cannot be much in Money, out of the Misery that poor People are brought into. They have been likewise, some Years ago, much molested by the Turks; who came in companies, plundred them, misused them, and some of them they killed; so that the Convent was well near destroyed: and, at last, they were forced to flee to Constantinople, to complain of the unsupportable Violences, against their Privileges, obtained even from the Turks themselves. Upon which they had a Turk granted them, to protect them from the like Outrages; whom they are obliged to maintain, and pay.

We had the Company of the Hegoumenos a good while; and among other things we asked him, Who was the Founder of their

Convent? Who told us, That it was the Emperour Romanus, Son to Constantine the Seventh, and Grand-Son to Leon, called the Philosopher: and shewed us an old Book, that spake of the Building of it; and carried us down into a Vault of the Church, and shewed us two Tombs; which, he said, were the Tombs of this Emperour, and his Empress. . . . The Convent it self seemeth to have been built out of more antient ruins; and I observ'd many Pillars of grey Marble lying up and down there, and other antient hewn Stones. Their Accommodation for themselves and Strangers, is indifferent good, considering the Country; and they receive them with as great Civility, and Kindness, as the Grand Charter-house, near Grenoble, in the Alps, doth: though they want their great Revenues, and Prosperity. They sent for a good Lamb from the Fold, and killed it for us; and beside, with Rice, Chickens, good Olives, Cheese, Bread, and Wine, they gave us a most hearty and Christian Welcome. Their Cells are little arched Rooms of Stone, and every one hath one to himself. Their manner of living is the same with all the Greek Monks, using severe Fasting in their Lents, and never eating Flesh at any time. They rise three hours before day to their Morning-Service: Three hours after Sun-rising, is their Communion-Service; and two hours before night, their Evening-Service, or Vespers. They have other Books also, they read between, at set Hours, in private. . . . They eat all together in a Hall; round which are long Tables of white Marble, where they sit according to Seniority; and at the upper end is a little one, where the Hegoumenos sits alone in a Chair. They have several Offices, and Ceremonies, before and after Dinner. At that after Dinner I was present, when I returned this way, and is thus: When all have dined, and are risen, before they depart the Room, there is a piece of Bread brought in a dish, and a cup of Wine set upon the Hegoumeno's Table; which by Prayers he seems to Consecrate, like the Sacrament; and then brings it round the Hall: first the Bread; of which every one breaketh a Crumb, as they stand ranked from one end of the Hall to the other, on each side. Then the Wine is brought in like manner, and every one drinketh of it round. After which some Prayers and Thanksgivings are said; and then every one de-

parteth to his Cell. The next day, after Morning-Service, the Hegoumenos carried us into a kind of Buttery, as I may call it, and made us
breakfast with him, with Bread and Honey, and Olives, good Wine
and Aqua Vitae. He told us then, amongst other things, That the
Ambassadour of France, Monsieur de Nantuille, was there several
days, and would fain have had the Roman Mass said in their Church.
But they told him, It was a thing they could by no means grant, it
being contrary to their Rites. But he yet pressing them, they at last
absolutely refused it; letting him know, that if such a thing should be
done, they could no more say their Liturgy in that Church. At which
the Ambassadour was very much offended, being a great Zelot for
the Roman Church, who made it his Business every where to per-
swade the Greeks, that their Belief is the same with the Latines, some
few Punctilioes only excepted. But they then had had no News of the
Council held by the Patriarch, and some of the Bishops by his contrivance; and the Doctrine of Transubstantiation was altogether
unknown to them, as I before said. . . .

There is an Hermite, that liveth a Mile and half off, whom I saw
not this time; but when I last came that way, the April ensuing, we
went to his Hermitage, descending from the Convent, doen the Hill
Southwards; first passing a little River in a pleasant Plain, well
planted with Vineyards and Olive-trees; and among them, little
Houses, where the Caloyers come sometimes for Recreation, in the
Summer. After this we mounted by a steep Rock, by an easie Ascent,
in a way cut out of the Rock, and large enough for two carts to pass
by one another; on the top of which we discerned the antient Ruins of
a Castle, and a Town. This I believe to be that, Pausanias calleth
Bulis, in the Confines of Phocis and Boeotia, seven Stadia, or almost a
Mile from the Port. . . . Near this Harbour the Convent hath a
Metochy, or Farm; and in the Harbour they fish, and lade the Corn
they can spare, to transport it to the Neighbouring Parts. Thence we
turned to the left hand, upon a Ridge of craggy Rocks, about half a
Mile, which brought us to the Cell of the Hermite.

The Hermitage is situated upon the South-East-side of a Rock; and
is a little House, with a pretty Chapel, or Oratory, at the upper end of

a large Garden, most pleasant by Nature, without much Assistance either of Cost, or Art. It is only hedged about with such Shrubs, and Bushes, as the Soil beareth, the upper side which is fenced by the Rock, only excepted. But Nature is here profuse in curious Plants; of which I gathered about half a hundred, that grow not ordinarily in England, in and about the Garden.... Something below his House, descending towards the lower side of his Garden, is a Fountain of very good Water; and beyond that a River, that runneth down from the high Cliffs of the Helicon, making a natural Cascade, at such a convenient distance, that it affordeth great Pleasure to the Eyes, without the least Offence to the Ears: until, at last, with all the murmurs of Applause a Poet in his most charming Contemplations can fansie, it passeth by this happy Place, where Peace and Innocency seem to dwell; far out of the reach of the Hate or Flattery of inconstant Fortune; to which, even those Rocks, and the vast Stones that lie in its Channel, seem to comply, and, while Men seem dumb, make their Praises mount aloud to Heaven. A prodigious height round about, one discovereth the Helicon's white Tops, still covered with Snow; which this poor Hermites aged Head seemeth, in epitome, to resemble. He followeth the Steps of St John Baptist, in the Wilderness; not cloathed in Hypocritical Rags; but with a decent long Garment, of a brown Hair-colour, dyed of that hue with the Skins of Wallnuts; and not much differing from the rest of the Caloyers. But his Life is most severe. His ordinary food is Bread and Herbs, and his drink Water; and that only on Sunday, Tuesday, Thursday, and Saturday. Sometime upon Saturday, Sunday, and great Holy-days, he will eat a little Honey and Bread; but hardly ever drinketh Wine, but that of the Holy Sacrament. The time that he spendeth from his Devotions, he employeth in writing Books of their Liturgies. He hath a Companion, or Servant, that doth him all necessary Offices; but useth not such severity as himself. His employment, at spare time, is chiefly in making Crosses; which he carveth with admirable Curiosity. The Work is hollow, and so fine, that it is beyond Belief; and hath represented upon it the principal Parts of our Faith, as the Nativity, Annunciation, &c. but especially the Death and Passion of our Saviour. For one of these I offered Ten Dollars; but he would not part with it, hearing we made no use of them in our Devotions in England. . . .

After I had discussed sometime with this good Old Man, whom they esteem a Saint, I was conducted below his Garden, between it and the River, to another Hutt; where two other Caloyers live, and look to a Garden, well planted with Beans and Pease; and another just by it, furnished with four or five hundred Stocks of Bees. A Place near as pleasant as the other above; being just upon the Banks of the River; which I esteem to be that, which Pausanias calleth Heraclitus. . . . The good Caloyer presently went, and took a Stock of Bees, and brought me a Plate of delicate white Honey-combs, with Bread and Olives, and very good Wine: To which he set us down in his Hutt, and made us a Dinner, with far greater satisfaction, than the most Princely Banquet in Europe could afford us. For the Quiet and Innocency of their Life, the natural Beauty of the Place, the Rocks, Mountains, Streams, Woods, and curious Plants, joyn'd with the Harmonious Notes of Nightingales, and other Birds, in whole Quires, celebrating, and as it were, welcoming that forward Spring, to speak the truth, so charmed my melancholik Fancy for a time, that I had almost made a Resolution never to part with so great a Happiness, for whatever the rest of the World could present me with. But, in conclusion, it prov'd too hard a Task for me, so soon to wean myself from the World.

79   *The Church of St Luke and Mosaic Decoration*

THE church of the monastery is the largest that the Byzantines left in Greece, built, they say, after the plan of St Sophia of Constantinople. Entering one is greeted by such splendour that one wonders how a fine building like this came into being among such wild mountains. I do not know how many masons and builders and workmen and other craftsmen came from Constantinople and set the foundations and worked for years to bring it to completion. The walls are built with ancient marble found scattered round about and it is because of this that you see a number of plaques with ancient inscriptions and carvings, put in upside down by the Christian masons.

Inside, the church is decorated like a palace. To the height of ten feet or so from the ground it is veneered with a rare marble of many colours, red, green, blue. All above this up to the ceiling is adorned with mosaic. There is not a nook or cranny which is not covered by mosaic and gold, even where the eye cannot see. The floor again is coloured marble with such lovely patterns that you are ashamed to walk on it. The columns also are of precious marble.

Whoever enters such a church feels its majesty. But the artist above all will be moved. Most artists admire the building, finding its form so perfect that they overlook the mosaics. But, since my craft called for it, it was the mosaics that drew my attention.

This art is very difficult. It needs great skill and even greater patience, for the artist who works in mosaic is forced to present whatever he has in mind by placing cube against cube. And as such detail cannot be achieved with mosaic as it can with the brush, the artist is forced to make his design as simple as possible, in order to carry it out. The same applies to colours, since they cannot be mixed as the painter mixes them: they must be decided upon beforehand and arranged in such a way that they appear harmonious when seen from a distance. For this reason decoration in mosaic is brilliant and simple, with thick and sharp colours.

Artists who wish to decorate a church in a remote place first of all build in a corner of the court-yard the furnace for baking the mosaic. These sheets of mosaic are of glass glazed with many colours, half a centimetre thick. Then these sheets are broken by a pointed hammer, made specially for the purpose, and are split into tiny pieces of different shapes, most of them square like dice, and are put into boxes. Each colour needs three or four kinds of mosaic, ranging from dark to light. Gold mosaic is made in a special way. A sheet of white glass is spread out and after the gold leaf is stuck on, it is covered with a thin layer of glaze and baked in the oven. Then it is split like the other mosaic. To do the actual work, the wall is first plastered with a kind of cement. Then the chief artist takes the design which he has already prepared and stamps it on the fresh plaster, and then roughly draws in the colour. On this basis the craftsmen plant the cubes of mosaic, checking their work against the finished design which the chief artist has prepared for them on paper. On face and hands the work is done with thin cubes. The craftsmen fill in the main lines of the design and all the parts which require special attention, the apprentices fill in the gold ground and the costumes, and the chief artist adds the last touches to the face and throws a glance over the whole work, changing whatever needs correction.

80   *In the Monastery of St Luke*

IN the monastery of St Luke, of all
   the Stiriote women who had gathered
to dress the Epitaphio, and of all
the mourners who until the dawn of Easter
Saturday had stayed awake, which could think—
so gently they lamented!—that the dull
enamel underneath the flowers was flesh
of dead and anguish-wracked Adonis?
                                        For the rose—
concealed pain, and the Funeral Lament,
and the spring airs which entered the church door,
had to the Resurrection miracle
raised up their minds, and as anemones
upon the hands and feet they saw Christ's wounds,
so covered was he with deep-scented flowers!...

But that same night of Saturday, just as
from the Holy Door one candle-flame was passed
to all the others, and from the Sacred
Altar light spread wave-like to the porch, all
shuddered as through the 'Christ is risen' broke
suddenly a voice: 'Georgina, Michael!'...

And there, the hero of the village, the girls'
idol, Michael, whom all thought lost at war,
at the church door was standing; with wooden leg
he stood, and did not pass into the church,
for, candles in the hand, all were gazing
at him, were gazing at him, the dancer who
used to shake the Stiriote threshing-floor,
at his face, and at his leg, nailed it seemed
upon the threshold, not advancing more! . . .

And then—let the verse be my witness, this
simple and this sincere verse—from the pew
in which I stood I saw the mother, tearing
from her head her handkerchief, fall swiftly down
and clasp the leg, the soldier's wooden leg—
I saw it as my verse describes, this simple,
this sincere verse—and from her deepest heart
call out: 'My darling one. . . . My Michael!'. . .

And then—let the verse be my witness, this
simple and this sincere verse—behind her
all who since the eve of Easter Thursday had
gathered, quietly, mistily to mourn
the dead and flower-hid Adonis, now loosed
such terror-struck and violent cry, that as
I stood up in the pew, darkness filled my eyes! . . .

ARTA, EPIROS, SULI, METEORA, THESSALY

THERE were five-and-forty masons, and sixty workmen more,
Who toiled to build the tower-pile upon the bridge of Arta;
The whole day through they built it up, and at night it tumbled
down.
The builders groaned and fretted, and ever made lament;
The workmen they were merry, to have earned a new day's wage.
It fell on one fine Sunday—it was a high feast-day—
The master-builder laid him down to take a little sleep,
And in his sleep he had a dream—a vision as he slumbered—
Unless a victim perished the pile would never hold.
And neither rich nor poor man, nor any one on earth,
Save his, the master-builder's, wife, would make the foundation
stand.
He called out to a labourer to go and do his bidding:
'Now go and tell thy mistress, the mistress of the house,
To dress herself and deck herself, put on her golden gauds,
Put on her gauds of silver, put on her silken gown—
Now swiftly speed and swift return and swiftly tell her thus.'
He went and found her where she sat at sewing and at song.
'Now greet thee well, my mistress, the mistress of the house,
The master-builder sends me, bids you put on the gold,
Put on the gauds of silver, put on your silken gown,
And come to feast with us. . . .'
She dressed herself, she decked herself, put on her gauds of gold,
Put on her gauds of silver, put on her silken gown;
And there she went to find them, whereas they sat at meat.
'Now greet thee well, my mistress, the mistress of my house,
My wooing-ring has fallen down—the first I ever wore—
And therefore did I send for thee to come and pick it up.'
Then, as they let her down into the midst of the tower-pile,
One heaped in earth upon her, another heaped in lime,
And he, the master-builder, he struck her with his mallet.

'Three sisters were we once, and all three of us were slain.
There was one killed in the church, and one in the monastery,
And the third, the fairest of the three, upon the bridge of Arta.
Now as my hands do tremble may its pillars tremble too,
And as my heart is throbbing, so may the bridge throb too!'

82   *In the Epiros*

FROM Delvino onwards the road rises abruptly from mountain to
mountain, from ridge to ridge, ribbon-like, over-hanging, with
steep climbs.

All round, the mountain-sides supporting the bare, treeless peaks
are green with wild ilex and oak.

Lower down, thick shady plane-trees cover the ravines.

Crystal waters utter their cool song sweetly in the deep valleys.

From bush to bush, in white-flowering myrtle and in the thick
wild shrubs the playful speech of the stonechat fills the quiet mountain
dawn with joy.

At each new bend, as the road climbs higher, the sky opens wider;
eyes embrace beautiful, ever-expanding worlds.

Plains and mountains, rivers and seas dream in the blue light.
They level out in the distance. They mingle with the boundless sky.

High, terribly high. The great contentment which the sensitive
traveller experiences in these high blue solitudes is doubled by the
secret feeling of delight that no ugliness of the human crowd reaches
here.

The motionless mountain silence prompts with a certain secret
pleasure in the soul the happiness of complete isolation. Something
which seems outside life. Something therefore like the longing for
eternal peace. The thrice-blessed non-existence! . . .

One embraces life more completely on the heights. Perhaps
because one comes closer to God.

We go on.

Now we cross a sun-dazzled stretch with open, limitless horizon above the mountain-mass.

We turn back and descend into a small green valley.

Then we climb once more into the mountains. To other mountains and to other sun-dazzled stretches, and to other sharp peaks.

A mountain-world. And only mountain. And again mountain. The mountains dominate to the horizon beneath us.

Ravine, valley, are lost, are assimilated in the boundless, many-branched mountain-mass.

High mountains, shadowing mountains, wooded mountains, mountain-shapes like petrified waves in space, in a blue, mystical light.

Somewhere round here was the religion of ancient Greece born. Dodona, Io, Zeus the Thunderer. . . .

One experiences more deeply the mystery of the world's birth, seeing from these heights the god-created crown of the mountains of Epiros waving bluely and dipping up and down in space.

A poor little mountain-village to our left, upon a projecting rock.

Thatched huts. Small houses covered with grassy tiles which shine silver in the sun.

The village of Garthikaki.

Such a caressing sound has the name of this isolated little mountain-village that one would say it takes something from the call of the partridges which fill the surrounding rocks with joy.

At the foot of the mountain-village, goat-folds. He-goats and she-goats. Bleatings and bells. Kitsos and the shepherdess Mosco. Daphnis and Chloe. Pan, the Great Pan, who never dies up here. Deathless, incorruptible Life. . . .

83   *Ioannina*
                                    May 11, 12, 13, 1849.

THREE days passed at Ioannina, but with constant interruptions from showers. The mornings are brilliant, but clouds gather on

Mitzikeli about nine or ten, and from noon to three or four, thunder and pouring rain ensues. The air is extremely cold, and whereas at Parga I could only bear the lightest clothing, I am here too glad to wear a double capote, and half the night am too cold to sleep.

Apart from the friendly hospitality of the Damaschino family, a sojourn at Ioannina is great pleasure, and were it possible, I would gladly pass a summer here. It is not easy to appreciate the beauty of this scenery in a hasty visit; the outlines of the mountains around are too magnificent to be readily reducible to the rules of art, and the want of foliage on the plain and hills may perhaps at first give a barren air to the landscape. It is only on becoming conversant with the groups of trees and buildings, picturesque in themselves, and which combine exquisitely with small portions of the surrounding hills, plain, or lake, that an artist perceives the inexhaustible store of really beautiful forms with which Ioannina abounds.

During these days time passed rapidly away, for there was full employment for every hour; one moment I would sit on the hill which rises west of the city, whence the great mountain of Mitzikeli on the eastern side of the lake is seen most nobly: at another, I would move with delight from point to point among the southern suburbs, from which the huge ruined fortress of Litharitza, with many a silvery mosque and dark cypress, forms exquisite pictures: or watch from the walls of the ruin itself, the varied effects of cloud or sunbeam passing over the blue lake, now shadowing the promontory of the kastron or citadel, now gilding the little island at the foot of majestic Mitzikeli. Then I would linger on the northern outskirts of the town, whence its long line constitutes a small part of a landscape whose sublime horizon is varied by mountain forms of the loftiest and most beautiful character, or by wandering in the lower ground near the lake, I would enjoy the placid solemnity of the dark waters reflecting the great mosque and battlements of the citadel as in a mirror. I was never tired of walking out into the spacious plain on each side of the town, where immense numbers of cattle enlivened the scene, and milk-white storks paraded leisurely in quest of food: or I would take a boat and cross to the little island, and visit the monastery, where that most wondrous man Ali Pasha met his death: or sitting by the edge of the lake near the southern side of the kastron, sketch the massive, mournful ruins of his palace of Litharitza, with the peaks of Olytzika rising beyond. For hours I could loiter on the terrace of the kastron opposite the Pasha's serai, among the ruined fortifications, or near the strange gilded tomb where lies the body of the man who for so long a time made thousands tremble! It was a treat to watch the evening deepen the colours of the beautiful northern hills, or shadows creeping up the furrowed sides of Mitzikeli.

And inside this city of manifold charms the interest was as varied and as fascinating:—it united the curious dresses of the Greek peasant—the splendour of those of the Albanians: the endless attractions of the bazaars, where embroidery of all kinds, fire-arms, horse-gear, wooden-ware, and numberless manufactures peculiar to Albania were exhibited—the clattering storks, whose nests are built on half the chimneys of the town, and in the great plane-trees whose drooping foliage hangs over the open spaces or squares:—these and other amusing or striking novelties which the pen would tire of enumerating, occupied every moment, and caused me great regret that I would not stay longer in the capital of Epirus. And when to all these artistic beauties is added the associations of Ioannina with the later years of Greek history, the power and tyranny of its extraordinary ruler, its claim to represent the ancient Dodona, and its present and utter melancholy condition, no marvel that Ioannina will always hold its place in memory as one of the first in interest of the many scenes I have known in many lands.

84   *Aquarelle on the Lake of Yannina*

TOWARDS sunset the bare, treeless, bronze Mitzikeli opposite lights up and flames from the lake's edge to the peak above.

The sun now has almost sunk behind the mountains and bathes, shakes its golden mane in the dreaming lake.

The lake, spell-bound, as if wearing on its mother-of-pearl back the rose-pale tearful laughter of the beautiful Phrosini, drowned by

Ali Pasha in its depths, breathlessly stretches out and sighs with voluptuousness in the glowing shivers and the blush of sunset.

Horses now with carts come down from the town to drink and cool themselves in the water.

Half-hidden behind the mountains the sun shoots flaming tassels of light through the thick-leaved, full-grown willows at the lake's edge.

The waters of the lake catch fire. Rose-red now they reflect in their depths strange interminglings of brown horses, belly-deep in the water, and of swarthy riders set like mythical centaurs on their backs.

Carriages and carts, boats and wagons roll down, sink into the red lake, horses and spoked wheels thresh the waters.

Thus strangely and curiously lit up in the mysterious hour of sunset, all together—lake-edge trees, rushes swaying gently, carriages, carts, wagons, the bronze horses and the swarthy centaurs—form in the sunset-flamed waters a fantastic, composite picture, giving unearthly appearance to the beautiful landscape.

And when at last the sun, late in the evening, takes the last reflections of twilight with it towards the obscure darkness, before the lights of Yannina are lit—the Mohammedan verger from the top of the needle-like minaret has spread impressively, mournfully over the leaden sleep of the lake his religious mystery—in the blue shadows at the lake's edge, in the evening stillness, wake the first timid notes of the zither, tuning up beneath the thick willows to accompany the immortal songs of Yannina.

85 *The Saga of Suli*

NOW all through the eighteenth century the Pashas of Yannina had been trying to subdue the little republic of Suli in the wild mountains of Thesprotia, some fifty miles to the south-west. They had never succeeded, and the Suliots had stolen from them about sixty villages, from which they exacted tribute and produce. At the time when Ali was made Pasha of Yannina the Suliots were particularly active and annoying, for they were in the pay of Ibrahim and of Catherine of Russia as well. Ali knew perfectly well that the Suliots would not be easy to conquer, but decided all the same to attack them.

Suli itself was a natural fortress in some of the most spectacular scenery in the Balkans. The settlement consisted of a few villages on a plateau about two thousand feet above the river Acheron, the Black River, which flowed through a deep chasm full of forbidding rocks and woods, 'one of the darkest and deepest of the glens of Greece'. A cultivated English traveller of the period let himself go in his descriptions of 'a spot which Mythology had selected as the scenes of her wildest fantasies', and exulted in the 'perpendicular rocks, broken with every form of wild magnificence', and 'the huge precipices like the ruins of a disjointed world'. His romantic but not inaccurate phrases, foaming with adjectives, tumbled forth like a cataract—if the woods were gloomy and the mountains wild, the chasms were terrific and the magnificence awful. A topographer, writing more calmly, conveys in his different way an impression of equal value: 'The river in the pass is deep and rapid, and is seen at the bottom falling in many places in cascades over the rocks, though at too great a distance to be heard, and in most places inaccessible to any but the foot of a goat or a Suliot.' If in its wilder aspects Suli might be called Dantesque, it had also some resemblances to the craggy, wooded landscapes we see in Chinese paintings: there were thickets of ilex and holly-oaks, great numbers of birds, especially storks and eagles, and in marshy places a profusion of yellow irises. The villages on the plateau itself, which could only be reached by one steep and narrow passage three miles long, had even something gentle and domesticated in their appearance, for there were cultivated terraces planted with corn and vegetables and fruit trees, and amongst them stood the houses, small square buildings with pitched roofs and two storeys, the lower used as a store or stable, and the upper containing two or three rooms.

As for the people, perhaps 12,000 in number, they had a character and traditions of their own. They had probably been in Suli since the time of Scanderbeg, were Christians, and had at one time been concerned in a plot to free Greece from the Turks. In general, they had many points in common with the other mountaineers of Greece. They were principally concerned to maintain the freedom of their little confederation, and to aid in its defence they thought their first duty. Males were conscripted and trained in arms from the age of ten, and they were of course experts in guerilla war-fare, skirmishes and sorties and stratagems, sudden attacks and quick retreats. They were renowned for their courage, as Byron noted:

> Oh! Who is more brave than a dark Suliote,
> In his snowy camese and his shaggy capote?
> To the wolf and the vulture he leaves his wild flock,
> And descends to the plain like a stream from the rock.

It was said of them that to show how brave they were they would send only a small force against a large one, while against a small force they would go in great numbers, because by that means they would be able to take more prisoners and loot. So much did they value personal courage that the women had precedence, when they went to draw water at the well, according to the acknowledged bravery of their husbands. The women themselves were brave, and in time of war would carry food and ammunition, attend to the wounded and sometimes take part in the actual fighting. There were no written laws in Suli or courts of law, and differences were settled by the heads of clans. There was an excellent rule that men, owing to their tendency to start fighting, must never interfere in any quarrel, but the women were encouraged to act as peacemakers. On feminine frailty the Suliots were just as hard as the Turks and the Albanians, and on the slightest suspicion of adultery women were sewn up in sacks and thrown over the cliffs into the Acheron. When the men had nothing better to do they used to look after their flocks and sheep. They never engaged in trade, but would live, like the Klephts, by brigandage, or upon the tribute paid to them in money or kind, rice or maize, by their sixty subject villages in the plains below. Like Klephts and Skipetars, they were known for their love of dancing and singing, their activity, their quickness in difficult country, their straight

shooting, and in particular for their extraordinarily keen eyesight—
it was even said that they could see in the dark, like cats. . . .

It was in the spring of 1790 that Ali decided to launch his first
attack on Suli. He sent an army of 3000 men but they were able to
achieve nothing, for the Suliots simply retired to their almost im-
pregnable heights; the attackers had to content themselves with
looting the villages in the plain that were known collectively as
Parasuli; and then, as a result of Suliot sorties from above, they had
to retire to Jannina. Ali's attention after this being engaged by other
matters, he decided to wait a little before making a second attack. . . .

. . . It was in July 1792 that Ali launched his second attack on Suli.
He made his men such a forceful speech that some of them broke
their scabbards in token of their determination to conquer, and the
whole army set out, part of it under the command of Ali's eldest son
Mukhtar and part under a general called Pronio Aga of Paramythia,
eighty-five years old, of gigantic stature and with a long snow-white
beard, who had with him his eleven sons, all between the ages of
thirty and sixty and as tall and strong as their father.

At first the attack went well, for Ali's army managed to overcome
the Suliot outposts. But the Suliots, who probably had no more than
1500 men in arms, put up a desperate resistance. None of them was
more heroic than Moscho, the wife of Tzavellas and mother of Photo:
she distributed ammunition, organized and armed the women,
rushed out with them to stop some of the men retreating, and then
led an attack on some of the enemy who were climbing up. In a
fortified tower near the entrance to the pass sixteen of the defenders
had all been killed, and amongst them she came upon the body of
her favourite nephew.

'I may have arrived too late to save your life,' she cried, 'but I'll
get my own back for your death!'

And off she went to lead another attack. Part of Ali's army had
managed to enter one of the ravines, and when Moscho and the
Suliot women discovered this they rolled rocks down on the middle
of the invading column, which cut it in half, caused a panic, and
enabled their menfolk to attack the front half. After the fighting had

lasted ten hours the invaders retreated in disorder, some of them throwing away their arms and equipment in order to escape more easily over the rocks, some hiding in the woods, and some making for the plain as fast as they could. . . .

When Mukhtar came back from Adrianople Ali put him in charge again of the operations against Suli, where he tried no sensational feats, but contented himself with strengthening his position. The Suliots had done what they could for themselves in the way of re-victualling and fortification, but their hardships and the incessant nervous strain had begun to tell on them, they were suffering from disease as well, and tended to quarrel among themselves. Mukhtar managed to occupy the banks of the Acheron and cut off their water supply, so they had to depend on rain-water, and when that ran short they let down over the cliffs big sponges on ropes weighted with lead and got what they could that way. At this time, when they so badly needed heartening, they were pulled together by the influence of an extraordinary man, a monk called Samuel, nicknamed 'Last Judgment' Samuel, who had appeared as if from nowhere to lead them. He has been neatly, if insufficiently, described as 'a man of wild enthusiastic character, who ran about animating the citizens, with a bible in one hand and a sword in the other, cutting off heads and explaining prophecies'. Simple people said he had been sent from God, and suspicious ones asserted that he was a distinguished foreign officer in disguise, but everybody agreed that he was extremely energetic and had become the life and soul of the resistance. He seemed to be everywhere at once, now firing a gun, now making a speech, then darting through the enemy lines on missions to Parga, Paramythia, and Preveza. On Kunghi, one of the highest points of Suli, he built a fort.

In September Ali launched his grand final attack on Suli. Veli was in command, and by treachery managed to get 200 of his men into Suli at night. The Suliots suffered great losses, and only had two forts left, Kako-Suli and Kunghi, which 'Last Judgment' Samuel had built. Photo, who had managed to escape from Yannina, led an attack from Kunghi. The fighting went on for seven hours, and stones were used as well as sabres and muskets. Seven hundred of the enemy were killed, while the Suliot losses only amounted to eleven, including three women. But it was all in vain. There was no water left, and the Suliots agreed to enter into negotiations with Veli to determine the conditions of their surrender.

Three days later Photo and Dimo Draku set out for Parga with two thirds of the Suliots, while the rest went towards Preveza. But 'Last Judgment' Samuel refused to surrender; with five other men he stayed at Kunghi, and blew up the fort as the enemy approached. . . .

The other party, about 1000 in all, had reached a monastery on a mountain called Zalongo, when they were attacked by another division of Ali's army. The gates of the monastery were forced open and a massacre began. About sixty women and children managed to escape up the mountainside, and when they reached the top the women, working themselves up into a frenzy of defiance, began to sing the old Suliot songs and dance the old Suliot dances, ever increasing in pace and fervour as they gradually drew nearer to the edge of a precipice: then with a final cry of triumph they threw themselves over. It was perhaps the most sensational act in the whole history of Suli.

86   *The Saints of the Rocks of the Meteora*

THE earliest inscription is across a small piece of ancient stone and reads: 'Jeremia 1192 A.D.'.

The first men who lived deep in these caves or in the ravines of the Meteora, each on his own, were anchorites. Then, there were no great churches, only chapels. They had neither companions, nor earthly ties, nor written theology. Chrysobuls refer explicitly to an anchorite community founded at the base of the Meteora rocks on the model of Mount Athos: 'A little church of the Archangels hewn in the rock.' Amid the holes and caves in the rocks man sought God, the Truth the world denied.

It was then, in 1335, that Athanasius came to the Meteora. 'Being persecuted, there arrived in the Thebaid the hermit Athanasius, the truly immortal', says the saint's contemporary biographer, 'accompanied by his spiritual father, the elder Gregorius'. Athanasius was a hesychast. His biographer names the brilliant teachers who had initiated him. They were Gregory of Sinai, Daniel the Hesychast, and Gregory Palamas. They were three shining lights, torchbearers of Orthodoxy whom he had known as a monk in the Skete of Magoula on Mount Athos, the Holy Mountain. From the first he had learnt the difficult psychology of the hermit, the perils of individualism, the deadly sin of despair. The Sinaite was a wonderful teacher, true to the maxims of the first hermits. He taught him the value of advice, the reality of punishment, how to cease fasting when the body refuses to comply; the acceptance of prophecy without consequent ruin, the substance of pure prayer:

'Arise from love of the world and love of pleasure, lay aside cares, strip your mind, renounce your body; for prayer is nothing other than estrangement from the world, visible and invisible. For what have I in heaven? Nothing. And what have I desired on earth beside Thee? Nothing but to cling constantly to Thee in prayer without distraction. To some wealth is pleasant, to others glory, to others possessions, but my wish is to cling to God and to put the hope of my salvation in Him.'

From Palamas he was to learn acceptance of the Word, tenacity in ideas, the admission of the divine co-existence within mankind in history. He was to ally prayer and thanksgiving: 'Five days of the week he would pray alone and silently in the Grotto of Stylos and weave wool, while on Sundays and Feast Days he would come down to the little church to give thanks and to congregate.'

Thus it came about that the first small monastery was founded and the first cells built. 'And at the expense of a certain magnate of the Trivalli he raised a small church of Christ.' He now had fourteen companions with him and the date was probably 1350. They were cruel implacable years when the terrible second civil war had just ended and two suspicious co-Emperors were reigning in Constantinople. In Thessalonica, a hard inter-class conflict had broken out.

Bitter theological dissension shook the Empire to its foundations, the mystic vision of the Orthodox East being once more attacked by the lucid rational thought of the West. Gregory Palamas was the leading figure in this debate: 'By his doctrine of the uncreated light and divine energy he gave an indestructible foundation to the traditional mystical teaching of the Orthodox Church. The Orthodox East found its final and systematic expression and also its theological and philosophical justification in his works. Gregory expressed and grounded the doctrine of the Deity in the created world, the mystical communion between man and God and the possibility of man's overcoming his creaturely limits through grace, without any pantheistic confusion or any compromise of the absolute nature of the Divine.'

87   *The First Step*

OUR first step is to seek a retired habitation, lest through eyes or ears we receive incitements to sin and imperceptibly become accustomed to it, and impressions and forms of things seen or heard abide in the soul causing destruction and loss; and in order that we may be able to continue in prayer. For thus we should overcome previously formed habits, in which we lived alienated from the commandments of Christ—this entails no small struggle, to overcome one's accustomed mode of life, for habit strengthened by lapse of time gains the strength of nature—and we shall be able to rub out the stains of sin by toiling in prayer and assiduous meditation upon the will of God; to which meditation and prayer it is impossible to attain in a crowd, which distracts the soul and introduces worldly cares. Whoever in a crowd could fulfil the precept: 'If any man will come after me, let him deny himself'? (Luke ix. 23). For we must deny ourselves and take up the Cross of Christ, and thus follow him. But to deny oneself means complete forgetfulness of the past and retirement from one's own will, in which it is very hard, almost impossible, for a man to succeed when he lives in promiscuous intercourse. Indeed mixing in such a life impedes even the taking of one's cross and following Christ. For preparedness to die on Christ's behalf, and the mortification of one's members that are upon the earth, and to stand in battle array to meet every danger that comes upon us for the name of Christ, and to be indifferent towards this present life—this is to take up one's cross; the obstacles put in the way of which by the intercourse of common life we see to be great.

88   *Meteora*

THE scenery of Meteora is of a very singular kind. The end of a range of rocky hills seems to have been broken off by some earthquake or washed away by the Deluge, leaving only a series of twenty or thirty tall, thin, smooth, needle-like rocks, many hundred feet in height; some like gigantic tusks, some shaped like sugar-loaves, and some like vast stalagmites. These rocks surround a beautiful grassy plain, on three sides of which there grow groups of detached trees, like those in an English park. Some of the rocks shoot up quite clean and perpendicularly from the smooth green grass; some are in clusters; some stand alone like obelisks: nothing can be more strange and wonderful than this romantic region, which is unlike anything I have ever seen before or since. In Switzerland, Saxony, the Tyrol, or any other mountainous region where I have been, there is nothing at all to be compared to these extraordinary peaks....

On the tops of these rocks in different directions there remain seven monasteries out of twenty-four which once crowned their airy heights. How anything except a bird was to arrive at one which we saw in the distance on a pinnacle of rock was more than we could divine; but the mystery was soon solved. Winding our way upwards, among a labyrinth of smaller rocks and cliffs, by a romantic path which afforded us from time to time beautiful views of the green vale below us, we at length found ourselves on an elevated platform of rock, which I may compare to the flat roof of a church; while the monastery of Barlaam stood perpendicularly above us, on the top of a much higher rock, like the tower of this church. Here we fired off a gun, which was intended to answer the same purpose as knocking at the door in more civilized places; and we all strained our necks in looking up at the monastery to see whether any answer would be made to our call. Presently we were hailed by someone in the sky, whose voice came down to us like the cry of a bird; and we saw the face and grey beard of an old monk some hundred feet above us peering out of a kind of window or door. He asked us who we were, and what we wanted, and so forth; to which we replied, that we were travellers, harmless people, who wished to be admitted into the monastery to stay the night; that we had come all the way from Corfu to see the wonders of Meteora, and, as it was now getting late, we appealed to his feelings of hospitality and Christian benevolence.

'Who are those with you?' said he.

'Oh! most respectable people,' we answered; 'gentlemen of our acquaintance, who have come with us across the mountains from Mezzovo.'

The appearance of our escort did not please the monk, and we feared that he would not admit us into the monastery; but at length he let down a thin cord, to which I attached a letter of introduction which I had brought from Corfu; and after some delay a much larger rope was seen descending with a hook at the end to which a strong net was attached. On its reaching the rock on which we stood the net was spread open: my two servants sat down upon it; and the four corners being attached to the hook, a signal was made, and they began slowly ascending into the air, twisting round and round like a leg of mutton hanging to a bottle-jack. The rope was old and mended, and the height from the ground to the door above was, we afterwards learned, 37 fathoms, or 222 feet. When they reached the top I saw two stout monks reach their arms out of the door and pull in the two servants by main force, as there was no contrivance like a turning-crane for bringing them nearer to the landing-place. The whole process appeared so dangerous, that I determined to go up by climbing a series of ladders which were suspended by large wooden pegs on the face of the precipice, and which reached the top of the rock in another direction, round a corner to the right. The lowest ladder was approached by a pathway leading to a rickety wooden platform which overhung a deep gorge. From this point the ladders hung perpendicularly upon the bare rock, and I climbed up three or four of them very soon; but coming to one, the lower end of which had swung away from the top of the one below, I had some difficulty in stretching across from the one to the other; and here unluckily I looked down, and found that I had turned a sort of angle in the precipice, and that I was not over the rocky platform where I had left the horses, but that the precipice went sheer down to so tremendous a depth, that my head turned when I surveyed the distant valley over which I was hanging in the air like a fly on the wall. The monks in the monastery saw me hesitate, and called out to me to take courage and hold on; and, making an effort, I overcame my dizziness, and clambered up to a small iron door, through which I crept into a court of the monastery, where I was welcomed by the monks and the two servants who had been hauled up by the rope. The rest of my party were not admitted; but they bivouacked at the foot of the rocks in a sheltered place, and were perfectly contented with the coffee and provisions which we lowered down to them.

89   *The Plains of Thessaly*

May 17, 1849.

A LOVELY scene! as the sun rises over the immense extent of verdure, which soon becomes animated with rural bustle. It will be difficult at a future period to recall, even to memory, the indescribable clearness and precision of this Greek landscape, far more to place it on paper or canvas. We start early, and trot quickly over green roads, which cross the wide level from village to village. There are buffali ploughing; and there are strange waggons, with spokeless wheels of solid wood, drawn by oxen; and great caravans of horses carrying merchandise from Saloniki to the mountains—the lading tied in sacks of striped cloth. With some there are whole families migrating, children, puppies, and fowls, mingled in large

panniers. The men wear black capotes, the women white, and dress their long plaited hair outside a white handkerchief. There are great gray cranes too, the first I ever saw enjoying the liberty of nature. These birds seem made for the vast plains of Thessaly: how they walk about proudly by pairs, and disdain the storks who go in great companies! Now and then there is a vulture, but there is too much society for them generally. As for jackdaws and magpies, they congregate in clouds, and hover and settle by myriads.

We come to the Peneus once more—now a great river. Giant, white-stemmed abeles, in Claude-like groups, are reflected in its stream; herons are peering and watching on its banks; and immense flocks of brown sheep are resting in the shade of the trees.

90   *Winter*

BEWARE the first months of the year, all bad, ox-skinning days, with cruel frosts when the north wind blows over earth, blows over horse-breeding Thrace to the wide sea, and churns it up, while earth and forest howl.

On many a high-leafed oak, on many a thick pine it falls, fells them in mountain hollows to the rich earth, while the huge wood roars, and beasts, those even with pelts of fur, shudder, tail between the legs, for the wind pierces their shaggy breasts.

Through ox-hide it goes unhalted, through the goat's long hair, the old man buckles like a wheel before it.

But not the sheep's fleece, thick with wool, does that keen blast pierce, nor a girl's fine skin, who, not learned in love yet, keeps indoors with her mother, and bathes her delicate body and with oil anoints it, and goes to her bed in an inner room.

On a winter's day, when the boneless Polypus gnaws his foot in a fireless house, a sorry dwelling, for the sun shows him no grazing-ground, but over Africa circles, over its people and its cities, and scarcely shines on the Greeks:

Then horned and unhorned beasts of the wood chatter pitifully and fly through copse and dale, seeking only shelter in thick brake or hollow rock.

Like a crutch-supported man, like one back-broken and ground-ward staring, they wander to escape the white snow.

Then put on, as I have bid, soft coat and full-length shirt—weave the thick woof into thin warp. This put on, that your hairs stir not, do not rise on your body.

Lace up the well-fitting, ox-hide boots, thickly felt-lined; and when the season of frost comes, stitch with ox-sinew skins of firstling kids together, to keep your back from the rain, and wear a felt hat, to keep the ears dry.

For when the north wind descends, dawn is chill, and a wheat-nourishing mist from the starry sky spreads over earth, over fields of the fortunate:

Sucked from ever flowing rivers and raised high by the tempest-uous gale, sometimes towards evening it turns to rain, and sometimes, when the north blast of Thrace piles the thick cloud, to wind.

91   *Mount Ólympos*

OLYMPOS and Kissavos,
two mountains were at strife,
which of them should make the rain,
which should make the snow.
Kissavos, it made the rain,
Ólympos the snow.
Ólympos thereon turned round
to Kissavos and said:
"Don't scold me, brother Kissavos,
trod by Turkish feet:
I am ancient Ólympos
known throughout the world;
two and forty peaks are mine,
two and sixty springs.
For every peak a banner is,

for every branch a klepht.
An eagle on my highest peak
pecks at a hero's head:
'Head, how come you to this plight?'
'Peck on, O bird, feed
on my youth, my manhood gorge
until it fills you:
your wings will grow a span's length,
cubit long your claws.
I was an Armatole
in Louros, Xeromeros;
twelve years through I was a klepht
on Ólympos and Khasia.
Sixty Agas have I killed,
burnt their houses down;
Turks, Albanians, that I've slain—
you cannot count them, bird.
But my own turn came at last
to perish in the fight.' "

92   *On Olympos*

I CLIMBED up through the cedars and followed the stream to its
source under a huge rock in the middle of the gorge—a place
which the shepherds had called Palavós, the Babbling Fool. From
here on directions should have been unnecessary. I could see the
whole upper gorge mounting the eastern face of Olympos; willow,
beech and walnut trees gave way to gigantic firs almost black against
the white stone, climbing the steepest ridges that led up to the tight-
bunched, starry summits of which one never lost sight, though they
looked still more remote from here than from the sea. For seven
more hours they remained vertiginous and inaccessible, while the
path climbed and the gorge grew shallower and then divided into a
vast fan of gullies, between two of which, pointing on a high spur, I

caught sight of the gable of the Alpine Club Refuge; I reached it at one o'clock. A well-built house of stone was an incongruous thing at six thousand feet, with the precipitous gorge in full view all the way down to the coast, and the white, wide, concave wall of rock with its summits shooting into the air, yet from that same wall the long limbs of the mountain descended with other peaks all round like hospitable arms. I tried the door of the refuge; it was locked, but the weather was fair and I had no need of a roof. On the dry stones under the big, straight, jutting trunks I ate a midday meal and fell asleep. At three that afternoon the fog floated up in small, white puffs like water-lilies through the ravine. Leaving my rucksack under a tree, I set off up the steep ridge for a horizon in the middle of the sky.

The great firs thinned out and the packed boulders of the ridge grew smaller and looser, while the sky became hazy and more and more white clouds floated upward from the sea. The going was steep but so regular that I did not think to scan with any great care the terrain of the main eastern wall to my right. In two hours I reached the top of the Skala peak, not quite three hundred feet lower than the highest summits that rose one beyond the other in a straight line directly to the north. Now at last I was only separated from the top of Olympos by a small col—but in a matter of minutes everything around me was invisible in the dark fog rising from the lower zones of air. There was a swirling wind in the grey-brown light, and then a dim, pyramidal shape loomed through the mist in front of me: another peak called Skolió to the west. It was five; there was a chance the cloud would lift towards sunset and from there I might have a view of all three summits, the Stepháni and the Great and Lesser Mýtikas. So I crossed to the Skolió along the edge of a precipice and there waited for Olympos to reveal itself behind the thick, milky element pouring steadily up the nearest visible brim of the cliff beneath me. Then in the space of a few seconds the rim extended farther and farther out into the fog, and suddenly a dark depth dropped across the air to one long, jagged mass of stone, fissured and split from top to bottom into a series of black points while moment by moment the cloud lifted off them. The whole wall plunged for thousands of feet into a world of menacing, slimy ledges, one beneath the other slanting too steeply for hand or foot, to a point where one could see no more. Down there it was night already; here there was still time to climb higher.

I made my way back along the precipice to the Skala peak, descended into a narrow col, then began to mount up a steep slope while the fog came down again and covered everything but the next handhold and a small circle of brownish-yellow stone tilted up against the surrounding whiteness. At last I could see the edge of the stone circle all round me with nothing beyond.

I had only one desire now: to stay till the fog should clear and I could see the sunset from the summit; somehow or other I would find my way down to the refuge in the dark. The fog did clear after a few minutes, only to show me I had climbed the wrong peak; a few feet higher, a few yards away across another chasm, rose the top of the Great Mýtikas, and now the sun was setting. Under a heavy bank of clouds the last watery rays slanted ever so slightly upward from the other side of Greece. On one side was the vertical drop into that dank, inhuman cirque I had seen from the Skolió, and on the other the eastern wall of the mountain facing the Aegean. I decided to go straight down it, instead of returning to the Skala and descending by the long ridge I had come up in the afternoon. It was growing dark so fast it was hard to see what hazards this might entail, and I started down again, taking a little extra care where to place each foot. Soon I needed my compass with its luminous dial. Seeing nothing but the black outline of the earth around and above me, I could not take one route and avoid another but only keep on in a straight line down the mountain. I realized my stupidity when I reached the edge of an unexpected precipice in the dark. There was no knowing its height; it took an hour to climb to the nearest place where I could traverse to an easier slope. Even then I could only continue in the same straight line, following the compass, and once again before I knew it I was lying on a narrow ledge, feeling with one hand a new cliff falling away on the other side. A few feet off I could just make out the shape of a fir tree, its top level with the ledge; uncertain whether I could climb back again to some other traverse, I stood up and jumped. My outstretched arms clasped a whipping, bending, stinging mass of branches and tightened round the trunk, which only swayed backwards and forwards as I climbed down to another ledge where it grew, and from which I was unable to find an exit for what seemed like a very long time. And so down three thousand feet of precipices, which would have been insignificant by day, during the next four hours.

It was midnight when I reached the slope above the refuge and stumbled in the dark upon the rucksack under the tree.

I woke up next morning thinking of water; the two gullies slanting on either side of the refuge were filled with perpetual snow and ice. Beneath, in the gully to the south, was a spring which flowed with a thin trickle during the morning hours, and here I filled my canteen before setting off again, this time with my rucksack. Higher than this there were no more springs on Olympos, as I remembered many times that morning when I would have given much to drain my canteen of its last drop on the hot stone and little cliffs which last night's descent had made familiar. While the hours wore on, high overhead the Skala and the two peaks of the Mýtikas and the Stepháni next to it preserved, it seemed for ever, that brilliant, sharp remoteness I had first noticed from the shore. It was like climbing a gigantic stair, mounting so slowly I hardly noticed it growing narrower, nor the twisted pinnacles that rose like baroque columns out of the slope, one above the other, closer and closer on either side, until the whole vast eastern wall had become a precipitous couloir between a forest of pinnacles of which the highest was the Mýtikas itself. Now it was like a stair inside a tower. I climbed more and more slowly.

The first moments at the top came less as a surprise than as a sense of something justly fulfilled. The level space around me was only a few feet wide but long enough to lie down on, with several irregular, flat slabs forming, as it were, miniature terraces beneath. I stood on the easternmost edge and all at once my thirst vanished with the cool touch of wind as I breathed the upward rush of tingling air. I ate an apple and needed nothing more during a long afternoon. Once the fog blew up out of the ravine and for some time I was left alone in the middle of the white air with a small Swiss flag painted on a square of metal that swivelled round and round the top of a rod planted permanently and neatly in the rock. While the cloud lightened and moved, there stood forth one by one the Lesser Mýtikas which I had climbed yesterday, and the Skala and Skolió, to the north the Stepháni and Profit Ilias. The mist withdrew over the sea, soft and blue 9,580 feet below, and the sun came out from the clouds and the intimate sky smiled on the hills of Macedonia and the peaks of the Grammos and the Pindos, on Athos rising across the sea, on Parnassos further south, and on both sides of the summit the immense, brown, shadowy, undulating uplands of Olympos, spacious and warm and kindly as if fingers of sunlight had formed their shape. There were winds everywhere, but it was possible to take shelter on these narrow but comfortable slabs of stone, still warm under a cloudless sky: for the setting of the sun the Greek uses a verb meaning to reign in splendour. . . .

93   *The Thracian Worship of Dionysos*

THAT the original home of Dionysos-worship was in Thrace, that his cult, popular among many of the Thracian peoples, was particularly honoured among the southernmost of the Thracian stocks who were best known to the Greeks and lived on the coast between the mouths of the rivers Hebros and Axios and in the mountainous country behind—to all this the Greeks themselves bore frequent and manifold witness. The god whose name the Greeks knew in its Greek form 'Dionysos' had, it appears, among the numerous and divided Thracian peoples various appellations of which those most familiar to the Greeks were Sabos and Sabazios. The Greeks must have known and remarked on the nature and worship of the god at an early period of their history. They may have met with him in Thrace itself. At all periods they had an extensive and varied inter-

course with this country and must in the early days of their wanderings have passed through it on their way to their future home. They
may have had further opportunities of knowing it from the Thracian
races or tribes who, according to a few isolated legends, had dwelt in
primitive times in certain localities of Central Greece. The ethno-
graphical material of these legends was regarded as founded on fact
by the great historians of the fifth and fourth centuries.

The cult of this Thracian divinity differed in every particular from
anything that we know of from Homer as Greek worship of the gods.
On the other hand, it was closely related to the cult paid by the
Phrygians, a people almost identical with the Thracians, to their
mountain-mother Kybele. It was thoroughly orgiastic in character.
The festival was held on the mountain tops in the darkness of night
amid the flickering and uncertain light of torches. The loud and
troubled sound of music was heard; the clash of bronze cymbals; the
dull thunderous roar of kettledrums; and through them all penetrated the 'maddening unison' of the deep-toned flute, whose soul
Phrygian *auletai* had first waked to life. Excited by this wild music,
the chorus of worshippers dance with shrill crying and jubilation.
We hear nothing about singing: the violence of the dance left no
breath for regular songs. These dances were something very different
from the measured movement of the dance-step in which Homer's
Greeks advanced and turned about in the Paian. It was in frantic,
whirling, headlong eddies and dance-circles that these inspired companies danced over the mountain slopes. They were mostly women
who whirled round in these circular dances till the point of exhaus-
tion was reached; they were strangely dressed; they wore *bassarai*,
long flowing garments, as it seems, stitched together out of fox-skins;
over these were doeskins, and they even had horns fixed to their
heads. Their hair was allowed to float in the wind; they carried snakes
sacred to Sabazios in their hands and brandished daggers or else
thyrsos-wands, the spear-points of which were concealed in ivy-
leaves. In this fashion they raged wildly until every sense was wrought
to the highest pitch of excitement, and in the 'sacred frenzy' they fell
upon the beast selected as their victim and tore their captured prey

limb from limb. Then with their teeth they seized the bleeding flesh and devoured it raw.

It is easy enough, by following poets' descriptions and plastic representations of such scenes, to elaborate still further the picture of this nocturnal festival of fanatic enthusiasm. But, we must ask, what was the *meaning* of it all? We shall get nearest to the truth if we will exclude as far as possible all theories imported from unrelated provinces of thought and fix our attention solely on what, for the participants, was the result of it all—the result anticipated and consciously proposed by them, and therefore the recognized object, or, at least, one of the recognized objects of these strange proceedings. The participators in these dance-festivals induced intentionally in themselves a sort of mania, an extraordinary exaltation of their being. A strange rapture came over them in which they seemed to themselves and others 'frenzied', 'possessed'. This excessive stimulation of the senses, going even as far as hallucination, was brought about, in those who were susceptible to their influence, by the delirious whirl of the dance, the music and the darkness, and all the other circumstances of this tumultuous worship. This extreme pitch of excitement was the result intended. The violently induced exaltation of the senses had a religious purpose, in that such enlargement and extension of his being was man's only way, as it seemed, of entering into union and relationship with the god and his spiritual attendants. The god is invisibly present among his inspired worshippers. At any rate, he is close at hand, and the tumult of the festival is to bring him completely into their midst. There are various legends about the disappearance of the god into another world and his return thence to mankind. Every second year his return is celebrated, and it is just this Appearance, this 'Epiphany' of the god, that gives the reason and the motive of the festival. The Bull-God, in the most ancient and primitive form of the belief, appeared in person among the dancers, or else the imitated roaring of a bull produced by hidden 'Mimes of Terror' served to suggest the invisible Presence. The worshippers, too, in furious exaltation and divine inspiration, strive after the god; they seek communion with him. They burst the physical barriers of their soul. A magic power takes hold of them; they feel themselves raised high above the level of their everyday existence; they seem to *become* those spiritual beings who wildly dance in the train of the god. Nay, more, they have a share in the life of the god himself; nothing less can be the meaning of the fact that the enraptured servants of the god call themselves by the name of the god. The worshipper who in his exaltation has become one with the god, is himself now called Sabos, Sabazios. The super-human and the infra-human are mingled in his person; like the frenzied god he throws himself upon the sacrificial animal to devour it raw. To make this transformation of their nature outwardly manifest, the participants in the dance-festival wear strange dress: they resemble in their appearance the members of the wild *thiasos* of the god; the horns they set on their heads recall the horned, bull-shaped god himself, etc. The whole might be called a religious drama, since everything is carefully arranged so as to suggest to the imagination the actual presence of the mysterious figures from the spirit world. At the same time, it is something more than mere drama, for it can hardly be doubted that the players themselves were possessed by the illusion of living the life of a strange person. The awe-inspiring darkness of night, the music, especially that of the Phrygian flute, to which the Greeks attributed the power of making its hearers 'full of the god', the vertiginous whirl of the dance—all these may very well, in suitably disposed natures, have really led to a state of visionary exaltation in which the inspired person saw all external objects in accordance with his fancy and imagination. Intoxicating drinks, to which the Thracians were addicted, may have increased the excitement; perhaps they even used the fumes derived from certain seeds, with which the Scythians and the Massagetai knew how to intoxicate themselves. We all know how even today in the East the smoke of hashish may make men visionaries and excite religious raptures in which the whole of nature is transformed for the enthralled dreamer. 'Only when thus possessed did the Bakchai drink milk and honey out of the rivers; their power ceased when they came to themselves again,' says Plato. For them the earth flowed with milk and honey, and the air was filled with the sweet odours of Syria. Hallucination was accompanied by a state of feeling in which pain itself was only an added stimulus to sensation or in which the visionary became completely insensible to pain, as is not unusual in such states of exaltation.

Every detail confirms the picture of a condition of wild excitement in which the limitations of ordinary life seemed to be abolished. These extraordinary phenomena transcending all normal experience were explained by saying that the soul of a person thus 'possessed' was no longer 'at home' but 'abroad', having left its body behind. This was the literal and primitive meaning understood by the Greek when he spoke of the 'ekstasis' of the soul in such orgiastic conditions of excitement. This ekstasis is a 'brief madness', just as madness is a prolonged ekstasis. But the ekstasis, the temporary alienato mentis of the Dionysiac cult was not thought of as a vain purposeless wandering in a region of pure delusion, but as a hieromania, a sacred madness in which the soul, leaving the body, winged its way to union with the god. It is now with and in the god, in the condition of enthousiasmos; those who are possessed by this are ἔνθεοι; they live and have their being in the god. While still retaining the finite Ego, they feel and enjoy to the full the infinite powers of all life.

In ekstasis the soul is liberated from the cramping prison of the body; it communes with the god and develops powers of which, in the ordinary life of everyday, thwarted by the body, it knew nothing. Being now a spirit holding communion with spirits it is able to free itself from Time and see what only the spiritual eye beholds—things separated from it in time and space. The enthusiastic worship of the Thracian servants of Dionysos gave birth to the inspiration mantikê, a form of prophecy which did not (like prophecy as it invariably appears in Homer) have to wait for accidental, ambiguous and external signs of the god's will, but on the contrary entered immediately into communion with the world of gods and spirits and in this heightened spiritual condition beheld and proclaimed the future. This power belonged to men only in ekstasis, in religious madness, when 'the God enters into men'. The Mainads are the official exponents of this mantikê of inspiration. It is simple and intelligible enough that the

Thracian cult of Dionysos, which was throughout a means of stimulating men to a condition of extreme exaltation that they might enter into direct communion with the spirit-world, also encouraged the prophesying of inspired seers, who in their rapt exaltation and frenzy became clairvoyant. Among the Thracian Satrai there was a tribe called the Bessoi who produced *prophetai*, and these were in charge of an oracle of Dionysos situated on the top of a high mountain. The prophetess of this temple was a woman who gave prophecies like the Pythia at Delphi, that is to say, in a state of rapt ecstasy. This, at least, is what Herodotos says, and we have many other accounts of Thracian *mantikê* and its close connection with the orgiastic cult of Dionysos.

ATHOS

AND there is another Hille, that is clept Athos, that is so highe, that the Schadewe of hym rechethe to Lempne (Lemnos), that is an Ile; and it is 76 Myle betwene. And aboven at the cop of the Hille is the Eir so cleer, that Men may fynde no Wynd there. And therefore may no Best lyve there; and so is the Eyr drye. And Men seye in theise Contrees, that Philosophres som tyme wenten upon theise Hilles, and helden to here Nose a Spounge moysted with Watre, for to have Eyr; for the Eyr above was so drye. And aboven, in the Dust and in the Powder of the Hilles, thei wroot Lettres and Figures with hire Fingres: and at the zeres end thei comen azen, and founden the same Lettres and Figures, the whiche thei hadde writen the zeer before, withouten ony defaute. And therfore it semethe wel, that theise Hilles passen the Clowdes and joynen to the pure Eyr.

WE steered for a tall square tower which stood on a projecting marble rock above the calm blue sea at the S.E. corner of the peninsula; and rounding a small cape we turned into a beautiful little port or harbour, the entrance to which was commanded by this tower and by one or two other buildings constructed for defence at the foot of it, all in the Byzantine style of architecture. The quaint half-Eastern half-Norman architecture of the little fortress, my out-landish vessel, the brilliant colours of the sailors' dresses, the rich vegetation and great tufts of flowers which grew in crevices of the white marble, formed altogether one of the most picturesque scenes it was ever my good fortune to behold, and which I always remember with pleasure. We saw no one, but about a mile off there was the great monastery of St Laura standing above us among the trees on the side of the mountain, and this delightful little bay was, as the sailors told us, the scarricatojo or landing-place for pilgrims who were going to the monastery.

We paid off the vessel, and my things were landed on the beach. It was not an operation of much labour, for my effects consisted principally of an enormous pair of saddle-bags, made of a sort of carpet, and which are called khourges, and are carried by the camels in Arabia; but there was at present mighty little in them: nevertheless, light as they were, their appearance would have excited a feeling of consternation in the mind of the most phlegmatic mule. After a brisk chatter on the part of the whole crew, who, with abundance of gesticulations, all talked at once, they got on board, and towing the vessel out by means of an exceeding small boat, set sail, and left me and my man and the saddle-bags high and dry upon the shore. We were somewhat taken by surprise at this sudden departure of our marine, so we sat upon two stones for a while to think about it. 'Well,' said I, 'we are at Mount Athos; so suppose you walk up to the monastery, and get some mules or monks, or something or other to carry up the saddle-bags. Tell them the celebrated Milordos Inglesis, the friend of the Universal Patriarch, is arrived, and that he kindly intends to visit their monastery; and that he is a great ally of the Sultan's, and of all the captains of all the men of war that come down the Archipelago: and,' added I, 'make haste now, and let us be up at the monastery lest our friends in the brig there should take it into their heads to come back and cut our throats.'

Away he went, and I and the saddle-bags remained below. For some time I solaced myself by throwing stones into the water, and then I walked up the path to look about me, and found a red mulberry-tree with fine ripe mulberries on it, of which I ate a prodigious number in order to pass away the time. As I was studying the Byzantine tower, I thought I saw something peeping out of a loophole near the top of it, and, on looking more attentively, I saw it was the head of an old man with a long grey beard, who was gazing cautiously at me. I shouted out at the top of my voice, 'Kalemera sas, ariste, kalemera sas (good day to you, sir); ora kali sas. . . .' he answered in return, 'kalos orizete. . . .' So I went up to the tower, passed over a plank

that served as a drawbridge across a chasm, and at the door of a wall which surrounded the lower buildings stood a little old monk, the same who had been peeping out of the loophole above. He took me into his castle, where he seemed to be living all alone in a Byzantine lean-to at the foot of the tower, the window of his room looking over the port beneath. This room had numerous pegs in the wall, on which were hung dried herbs and simples; one or two great jars stood in the corner, and these and a small divan formed all his household furniture. We began to talk in Romaic, but I was not very strong in that language, and presently stuck fast. He showed me over the tower, which contained several groined vaulted rooms one above another, all empty. From the top there was a glorious view of the islands and the sea. Thought I to myself, this is a real, genuine, unsophisticated live hermit; he is not stuffed like the hermit at Vauxhall, nor made up of beard and blankets like those on the stage; he is a genuine specimen of an almost extinct race. What would not Walter Scott have given for him? The aspect of my host and his Byzantine tower savoured so completely of the days of the twelfth century, that I seemed to have entered another world, and should hardly have been surprised if a crusader in chain-armour had entered the room and knelt down before the hermit's feet. The poor old hermit observing me looking about at all his goods and chattels, got up on his divan, and from his shelf reached down a large rosy apple, which he presented to me; it was evidently the best thing he had, and I was touched when he gave it to me. I took a great bite: it was very sour indeed; but what was to be done? I could not bear to vex the old man, so I went on eating a great deal of it, although it brought the tears into my eyes.

96   *Of the Road from Laura*

THERE are so many little rills everywhere run trickling down the stony rocks as one would think all the hill to be nothing but water within; hence they haue many little Turkish mills, some large built especially those near their Monasteryes, for their convenience and dayly use. In some places next the sea these rivolets make a large river and not passable without bridges, as in two or three places from Laura to Ibero.

About two houres from Laura towards Ibero there is a great stream gushing out an Alabaster rock. Athanasius saw the V.M. there, did not beleiue it was she, till he striking the rock and this water gushing confirm'd his faith that it was her indeed. There is a little grotto aboue and below a keosk where we were entertain'd by the ecclesiarches who accompanyed us, and a great wax candle was set up before the V.M. picture which allwayes stands there.

There are many castles or towers standing at distance from the Monasteryes, near the sea. They are useless for defence since Guns have been invented; but formerly they might haue signified something, at least a refuge to the Moncks if invasions suddain should be made. We saw several houses couer'd with wood, which was hollowed in like tiles but lay'd the length of the tree.

I look't narrowly for Bel. Bupraestis, but perhaps it was not the time for I found it not (Apr. 1677). The place, to one that loves solitude and plants, may well be cal'd what they now name ἐπίγειος παράδεισος, yet unequal, passing steep ascents and descents, craggy stony way.

97   *The Ascetics of Athos*

ACCORDING to the definition of the Danish philosopher Kierkegaard, man may take three attitudes in the face of life:
The aesthetic.
The ethical.
The religious.
The man with the aesthetic attitude wants to enjoy life as it passes. His desire is to live each fleeting moment, and he has a flexible soul, able to pass quickly from one moment to the next. Love-affairs, not marriages. Acquaintances, not friendships. Temporary employment, not a career. It is just a touch on the circle of life. The man with the ethical attitude stands in contrast to this fickle and changing

person. Devotion, faith. Married life, not affairs. Friendships, not acquaintances. Dutiful work, not temporary employment. His life is endless labour and worry.

The man with the religious attitude is above the other two. His purpose is not limited. It is not comparable to other human purposes. It is in contrast to them.

His life is one of passion, paradox, and pain. It is in continual struggle, outside the environment of men, in endless movement, like the fish on the shore. . . . Pascal said that it is the Christian's duty to live the struggle of the Lord at Gethsemane. And the Danish philosopher judges that without the struggle and the passion there is no faith. The man who takes the religious attitude attempts a passionate leap beyond the other two attitudes, to rest in the paradox, the immeasurable, the tragic.

This third attitude should characterize naturally the ascetic life. But it is not altogether possible. Men who become monks introduce the three attitudes into the monasteries. There are monks on Athos—and they are the majority—who worship only the form. The divine for them is the melody, the holy scripts, and the ceremonial. Then there are those who become monks for ethical reasons. Because they have found that life in society is an ugliness, where colossal powers are wasted on transient things, on unnecessary things, on nothing, they have decided that their abstinence from such a struggle and their inactivity on Athos is a protest, is itself ethical.

But the third category? The tragic and the paradox of Kierkegaard? It is the poor hermit who has claims to that. He lives in the barren and rocky district of Athos known as the Wilderness. Completely alone, he carves small crosses which he will sell, while the rain enters his thunder-shaken cave. His possessions are his little bag, his cup and his knife. He denies himself the luxury of a church. He has no icons other than those he sees in his visions. Men he does not see. His cell is a hole in a cave or hollow of a rock which covers him. For the sailor who looks up from the sea below, the hidden eagles-nests high on the crags are terrifying. Nevertheless, within these are men who eat nothing but greens, who all their life have moved on a narrow path cut out of the rock, hanging over the abyss. Some never come down from there. Their every step is a trial and a danger. This method they have found to kill the flesh. Others impose on themselves heavy punishments, wearing, for instance, big weights, according to the practice of hermits from the time of Athanasios of Athos, or building on the precipice or otherwise inviting pain and danger. Those who leave their holes, go and present themselves every so often waxen and skeleton-like at the monastery of Laura, to get bread; and those who do not go out, end their life there and leave their bones among the rocks, for earth is a luxury.

This is the passionate leap.

98   *Monastic Life*

MONASTIC life is called the art of arts and the science of sciences; for it does not introduce us to the perishable things of this world which drive the mind from what is best and engulf it; but it promises us wonderful and unspeakable treasures which the 'Eye hath not seen, nor ear heard, neither have entered into the heart of man'. Hence, 'We wrestle not against flesh and blood, but against principalities, against powers, against the rulers of the darkness of this world.'

If therefore present existence is but darkness, let us flee from it, let us flee with resolve, having nothing in common with the enemy of God; for 'whosoever . . . will be a friend of the world is an enemy of God'. And who can help the enemy of God? Therefore let us imitate our fathers and, like them, let us seek the treasure in our hearts and, having found it, let us hold fast to it in doing and guarding—for which task we were appointed in the beginning. But if some other Nicodemus appears and begins to argue, saying: 'How can anyone enter his own heart and do and dwell therein?'—as that one said to the Lord: 'How can a man enter the second time into his mother's womb, and, being old, be born', let such a one also hear: 'The wind bloweth where it listeth.' But if, even amidst the events of active life, we display such doubts through lack of faith, how can we enter into the mysteries of contemplative life? For active life is the approach to contemplation.

99   *The Way of Silence*

BY means of silence you must thoroughly cleanse the mind, and give it constant spiritual exercise; for as the eye is turned upon sensory objects and marvels at what it sees, so the pure mind turns to intelligible things, and is ravished by spiritual contemplation, and it becomes hard to tear it away. And in the measure that by means of silence it is stripped of the passions and purified, so it becomes worthy of spiritual knowledge. Then the mind is perfect, when it tramples down its own knowledge and is united with God. Having thus attained kingly rank, the mind cannot now bear to be impoverished and is not dragged down by false desires, even if all the kingdoms of the world are offered it. Thus, if you wish to reach such heights of virtue, be heedless of all men, and hasten to leave the world and follow eagerly the path of the saints; and wear unkempt garments and soiled attire, and eat modestly, and be of a simple disposition, and of plain speech, and walk without arrogance, and be unpretentious in your voice, and live in scarcity, and be despised by all. And above all guard your mind, and preserve sobriety, and patience in strait circumstances, and keep unharmed and unchanged the spiritual blessings you have acquired. And give careful attention to yourself, not to accept any of the pleasures that seek to insinuate themselves. For although silence quietens the passions of the soul, they are wont to rage more vexingly and acutely, and to force those who have them to sin, just as bodily wounds, being chafed and scraped, become hard to cure. For an idle thought may separate the mind from the recollection of God, the demons assaulting it and the senses concurring with them. For only great struggle and fear can guard the soul. Therefore you should separate from the whole world, and tear the soul from its sympathy for the body, and become cityless, homeless, without possessions, heedless of money, unburdened, without dealings, ignorant of human affairs, humble, compassionate, good, gentle, quiet, ready to welcome in the heart the impressions of divine knowledge as they are produced. For as Basil the Great teaches us, it is not possible to write in wax unless first the letters previously engraved on it are erased. Such did the saints achieve: separated entirely from the habits of the world and preserving heavenly wisdom undulled within them, they shone with divine laws, having mortified their 'members which are upon the earth' (Col. iii.5) through their pious deeds and thoughts, and through their fear of God and yearning for him. For by constant prayer and the study of the divine Scriptures the intellectual eyes of the soul are opened and they see the Lord of the powers. Then there is great joy; and a keen desire burning in the soul, and the body also ravished by the spirit, the whole man becomes spiritual. Such become those who practice blessed silence and the strict life, and who, having withdrawn from every human consolation, in solitude converse clearly with our Lord in heaven alone.

100   *Monk's Life on Athos*

ND a small axe I had and I cut and cleared away pine-trees, holm-oaks, and in their place olives I planted, and pear-trees, and here apples, and here, for my delight, almonds, and then cabbages and leeks and garlic. And I rejoiced in the earth as you rejoice in money. I stood in a garden of graces, in a true paradise of love. And often I went down and gathered limpets, shells, crabs and sometimes prawns; and I was more happy with these things than with all my lordships and all my lordly banquets and all my ladyships. . . .

Towards God I was all gratitude, my heart beat with unspeakable happiness, the place full of scents, the trees of fragrance, birds flying round, you chanting to them, they responding to you, earth offering flowers and lilies to the eyes' delight—I burn at the recollection, am torn with regret: birds charming the ears, you happy, and again and again falling to praise God: hearing, sight, touch, smell gratified, giving thanks and praise to God. You are bored in your cell? Go out and walk, stroll through the blessed solitude: go to the spring, go down to the lovely sea-shore, go into the caves, cells of the old ascetics, divine palaces; only do not forget the 'Kyrie Eleison', lest the springs of mercy close.

101   *The Perfect Contemplative*

SOLITARY, one who is unmixed with the world,
    and continually speaks with God alone.
Seeing, he is seen, loving, he is loved,
and becomes light glittering unspeakably.
Praised, he feels himself more poor.
and being close, yet goes a stranger.
O miracle strange in every way and inexplicable.
For immense richness, I exist penniless,
and having as I think nothing, possess much,
and I say I thirst, in the midst of waters.

102   *The Vigil of St Stephen and the Bishop*

HIEROTHEOS, at one time bishop of Koritsa in Albania, . . .
    now, in retirement, lived in a cottage and garden at St Anne's,
and had become an old man without losing alertness, humour, and
the air of one used to taking the lead. . . . He loved his garden like
any old peasant, and like a peasant expected it to feed him in return
for his attention. Devoted to the duty imposed on him by the church,
he was at the beck and call of any monastery for annual festivals or
special occasions. In high summer the Mountain is a paradise under
its trees and beside the fountains, but it is a blistering land of rocky
rises and descents for man and mule. Winter turned the Mountain
into an enemy. Winds howled down precipices, raced across rocks,

raised thunderous seas. Snow isolated colonies of men from other countries. Within the limits of a mule's powers, Hierotheos passed from place to place in answer to a call for his presence. Vigils averaged fourteen hours, the present one would last seventeen; through them he sat enthroned, apparently beyond bodily needs. He was as careless of money as he was of the weather, and gave it away, together with the splendid fruit and vegetables he grew. Fifteen years later a selfless old man continued the same life. In his eighties he became a small man still shrinking, inclined to mumble, and not always easy to follow. The monks openly spoke of a saint among them. . . .

A veiled deacon glided up to the bishop, and bowed over and over before him, until touching the floor with the knuckles of both hands. He asked him to bless the vigil now to begin. It was the outside world's 6 p.m., but not time for a general move to church. Instead, we filed into another room for a soup and fish supper, tramping straight from supper into church for great vespers, which turned into matins towards midnight when I was called out of church with the visiting monks for raki, jam, and coffee. The chandeliers had been lighted and the corona swayed; but otherwise there had been no unusual ceremonial. Hierotheos remained motionless throughout, on his throne, pastoral staff in hand. We returned to a glowing scene. Hierotheos, now in magnificent vestments, descended from throne to pavement to venerate, before exposing St Stephen's relics; for the First Martyr's right hand is one of the two relics of that saint in this church. He paced over to the long sparkling rood-screen, halting where the golden candle-light poured over the wealth of his apparel, and there raised the flashing silver hand, enclosing the yellowed bones; turned it about before our scores of watching eyes; raised it yet higher to tempt our gaze upwards; and at last laid it back in the reliquary before the gates. The monks then advanced in turn to kiss St Stephen's ikon attached to the south-east pillar, then the smaller ikon of the day, also a St Stephen, next to cross to the reliquary to press their lips to the two relics, after removing hat and veil. As they raised their heads, a priest signed the cross on their foreheads in oil from the ikon lamps.

A handsome chair was placed to face the screen. Hierotheos seated himself, attended by priests and deacons, who settled a scarlet mitre on his head. The chanting swelled; the heavenly dance symbolized in rocking corona and swaying chandeliers passed in light and shadow across the pavement, found, lost, and re-found the silver-sheeted ikons, the silver lamps, reddened and warmed the double-headed eagles buckling the corona together, and redeemed the crudity of the ostrich eggs suspended from it. The slender wax tapers, held against their music by the veiled chanters, caused bearded mouths to open in a pool of honey-coloured light. Hours later dawn began entering palely through the snow-glazed windows, ever making a way more strongly into the building, devouring more of the mystery. Monks who had remained in church since early evening filled the same places, one or two hanging from the arms of their stalls like dead soldiers from wire entanglements. . . .

The lesser and greater entrances of the Liturgy had taken place. After the lesser, expressing the entry of the Saviour of Man into the world on His mission of teaching, the Gospels had been elevated to the announcement 'Wisdom, O believers', and the congregation at last rested in the stalls listening to the epistle.

Later the cherubic hymn had risen from the choirs, to be interrupted by the 'great entrance', when the holy gifts were borne into the sanctuary. The slow-moving procession now symbolized the passage of the Saviour of Man to His Passion and death. The hymn continued in the choirs. Chalice and paten were set in the altar in secret; in secret the clergy fanned the holy elements with the aer, the veil which has covered them; in secret the priest elevated the paten with the words: 'Holy things to the holy'.

It was broad daylight when, in a final lively scene, seniors, juniors, and laymen, the monastic labourers and the meek, shuffling poor received the blessed bread from Hierotheos on his throne; and other wine-wetted bread was distributed among the devout in the north choir. So concluded a vigil which continued from 6 p.m. until 11 a.m., an exercise and discipline and joy drawing a hundred and fifty men together.

The Monk and The Sea

COMING out from the first even-song, I went down to the beach and gazed at the waves, at the emerald hills, the blue shadow of an Aegean island opposite me, to free myself. It was a blessed sunset. The sea, somehow still, had so controlled her movement that it had become rhythmical. Distant her breath sounded, harsh, but ordered and joyful. In measured time the wave leapt and fell like snow, stirring the pebbles. A young monk came out alone to go for his walk on the deserted sands, after the even-song. His slender build, in his Byzantine dress, was very clearly outlined on the whiteness of the sand, in the sunset. He was still young. If he went back into the world, he would have, for good or for evil, a human history. Here it was not possible. He was a monk. He would grow old, he would learn the texts by heart, he would die—that was his life. I followed him as he went and even his walk seemed to me strange. Was not a walk an activity? Did it not require a past and a future? He bent and gazed at the pebbles which the sea had worked on, giving to some an extraordinary smoothness and an unexpected symmetry. He picked up one and threw it into the waves. Then a second. Then he skimmed the third a little further. And he continued this melancholy pastime, throwing the pebbles with a certain skill, a skill, however, slack with weariness. It seemed to me that the sea grew more lively and began to play with the young monk. Like a lovely animal moved by the instinct of sport, it leapt and seized and swallowed the stone of the young monk and again it seemed to raise up its front legs to beg another, and as it grasped it so increased its low cry of content. Creation, truly, was playing. Never had I seen so close at such a moment of intimacy and of play, life and the monk together. I heard their secret conversation, the rebuke and the apology, the call and the refusal. 'Come,' she said to him. 'There is time yet to mend your fault. I have tempests. I have roads. I have worlds. I have peoples. I have beauty and triumph. Make up your mind!' And she flung at his feet foam of her waves, rose-coloured, blue and opal, marvellously worked, treasures of shape and colour.

As upright and motionless he gazed out at her, the monk threw a final pebble. Then he moved off. With slow measured step, with the movement of custom and submission, he went back to the monastery. He went to find again that of which I have spoken. He hurried back to the chain of formulas repeated each day without change, to begin once more his slow preparation for death. And I who a short while ago had witnessed the dark and severe even-song, felt at that moment how if creation and her laws are something undying and can in no way be cheated or subdued, yet the decision of the man who succeeds in scorning them like this man, preparing his death, is something which deserves at very least respect. You may find it terrible and loathe it. But you cannot despise it. That was the impression I had when, after their momentary game, I saw the two enemies separate.

104   *Monk of Athos*

SINNER and monk on Athos' holy ground
Me daily Satan burns and hell devours:
A traveller forever lost and drown'd,
A damnéd soul that sighs away the hours.
Without, the isles in sapphire seas are bound,
And Daphnis-Heaven upon Earth-Chloë showers
His genial radiance: shoots spring from the ground
And swarming creatures suck the sap that pours
From her warm breast. Olympus, Pelion,
The island peaks, the headlands every one,
Kassandra's magic lake, each thing appears
In bridal dress. But I? Ah, I do nought
But cry 'Have mercy, Lord' and wash with tears
The painted Christ that Panselenus wrought.

The End of an Age

IN the *Corpus Eremiticum*, a work of the Early Fathers, there is the following story. Some strangers come to a hermit and ask him what experiences he has as a hermit. The man, who is in the course of fetching water from a cistern, draws up the bucket and asks the strangers to take a look down into the well. What do they see there? The strangers look into the depths and answer, 'Nothing!' After a while the strangers look down once more into the depths; the hermit again puts his question, and this time the strangers answer, 'Ourselves, our faces.' The hermit says, 'When I was busy, the well was restless. Now there is peace, and one can see what one is. That is the experience of being an anchorite.'

It may well be that Athos is the true home of anti-Faust. Faust, who only feels himself to be alive when he is actively searching and in a *state of unrest*, counts for nothing here. When we decided 500 years ago to abandon the way of Athos, it was he, Doctor Faustus, who emerged from the darkness, a universal figure: the shadow in the grey frock coat confronting Gretchen, the disquietened soul; reflected in her eyes he perceives his own image, as in second sight.

Doctor Faustus, the researcher, became the typical figure of his age, usurping the place of king and ruler. Rightly, for the man of science was to outlive the kings and wield more power than any of them. He became the mediator between God and the new age. . . .

On Mount Athos they believe that events might have taken quite another direction. And perhaps it is true that ours was not the only possible way. If only we had not accepted the strenuous burden of progressive science, which has thrust us out into space, urged us to explore the mystery of origins through historical research, and tried to drown the voice of our true concerns in the din of the machine age! Could it be that this thirst for knowledge is vastly overrated, this science of ours, this monster idol of the West? For gradually we are coming to see that we are tied to the spokes of a revolving wheel, which turns and turns without taking us anywhere.

Faust is a symbolic romance, whose hero is *the scientist, the discoverer, as tool and prey to the devil.* Faust is the *savant* caught in the wheel; a mild and kindly gentleman who touches off the most monstrous explosion. He is the scientist sold to the devil for his intellectual greed. He must go on and on, and no one but the devil can lead him. What does the devil stand for? He is emptiness; the end in itself. . . .

This is the old legend. Goethe's *Faust* begins in the same way. But where does it end? Strangely enough, it ends here, with faith reconquered, at the foot of this holy mountain of the anchorites.

106   *On Freedom*

WE all suffer here on earth and seek freedom, but few there are who know the meaning of freedom and where it is to be found.

I too want freedom and seek it day and night. I learnt that freedom is with God and is given of God to humble hearts who have repented and sacrificed their wills before Him. To those who repent the Lord gives His peace and freedom to love Him. There is nothing better in the world than to love God and one's fellow-man. In this does the soul find rest and joy.

O all you peoples of the earth, I fall on my knees to you, beseeching you with tears to come to Christ. I know His love for you. I know and therefore I cry to the whole world. If one does not know a thing, how could one speak of it? . . .

I am an old man awaiting death. I write the truth for love of God's people over whom my soul grieves. If I should help but a single soul to salvation I will give thanks to God; but my heart aches for the whole world, and I pray and shed tears for the whole world, that all may repent and know God, and live in love, and delight in freedom in God.

O all you peoples of the earth, pray and weep for your sins, that the Lord may forgive them. Where there is forgiveness of sins there is freedom of conscience and love, even if but a little.

The Lord does not desire the death of a sinner, and on him who repents He bestows the grace of the Holy Spirit, which gives peace to the soul and freedom for the mind and heart to dwell in God. When the Holy Spirit forgives us our sins we receive freedom to pray to God with an undistracted mind, and we can freely think on God and live serene and joyous in Him. And this is true freedom. . . .

THE AEGEAN
AND THE ISLANDS

AS the sapphire and the aquamarine from the turquoise, so differ the waters of the Aegean from the flat blue of the Mediterranean whole. Sail from Italy or Egypt. And as the rose-tinted shores of the islands and promontories rise incarnate from the sea, a door shuts the world behind. Earth's emotion diffuses a new essence. Who are we to cut the water and cleave the air with prow and funnel?

Those who sit at home with their anthologies, their Homers and Byrons, have long grown impatient of the hackneyed eulogy. Travellers, on the other hand, know that the Greek poet has not lived who can hackney the Greek sea itself. How lies it apart? What magnet to our stifled love hold this blue, these tawny cliffs and always the mountains framing the distance? Why does the breeze blow with a scent of baking herbs which the misty shores echo in their colours? What is this element, hybrid of air and water, physical as a kiss, with which the night enfolds us? The islands float past, forming and re-forming in good-bye, gleaming golden white against the sharp blues, or veiled in the odorous haze of evening. A silver sheen overspreads the sea as the ship moves north; the sky grows mild, hung with stationary clouds. Through the straits, all day across the Marmara brings the shadowy cones of the Princes' Islands, and the mirage of Constantinople. Then down again beside the rich soil and undulating ranges of Anatolia, to the bay of Smyrna, Rhodes, and below, in the corner, Cyprus. At the foot lies Crete; on the west, Corfu. This is the radiance of the elusive essence; Byzantium, the key-stone of its arc. From the southern boundary of Albania to the Asia Minor littoral, the entity is definite as Great Britain or the islands of Japan. Within it, the divinity of earth moves to the brink of tangibility. And if, in the first migrations, its custody was vouchsafed a people in whom the quest of the divine, which distinguishes man from beast, was already conscious, small wonder that this people has played a significant part in the general evolution of civilization.

Sea

I WALK, at noon, along a deserted Thracian sea-shore, after a refresh-ing autumnal bathe. And the sea is to me as a beloved woman whom I have made mine and whose embrace I have just left. I sit now on the old familiar beach beneath a huge oak-tree whose leaves flutter in the breeze and murmur ceaselessly. I gaze at the sea before me sparkling like a queenly robe of golden stars, and I am spell-bound. To the left I watch the sea dressed in warm sensual blue colours, full of passion, and I think of a woman of many ways who somewhere I have known. Then I look for the first time carefully away into the distance on the right and I make out, on that sea be-loved so many centuries, the noble shape of a tall island whose name men have known and heard like music since ancient times. And I also had heard it and had seen it on the map. . . .

Another day, another ash-grey afternoon on strange beaches. It was cloudy and I stood at the sea's edge watching the swollen waters and the south wind blew madly as if wanting to carry me off. I was seized by that inexplicable fear at feeling alone in the world and without any other person. I feel as perhaps the earth, circling in chaos, feels, isolated from other bodies also circling in chaos, with no link between them. Then I am uprooted from society and become something lost in the world, and I shudder. Then I would wish a loved voice say to me: 'And if you are alone in the world, I also am: come with me.' But that ash-grey afternoon I heard no voice and I went on walking at the sea's edge until my restlessness became sorrow, until my sorrow became sentimentality.

Again a sun-bathed noon. I stood on the upper part of the shore and down there on the sands I saw a girl with short dress, raised hair, bare feet, washing in the sea some eastern rugs. Some were thrown down on the sand, some piled on a small wall a bit higher up. A seventeen-year-old lad, handsome, bare-foot, stood behind the wall with his hands in his pockets and looked now at the sea, now at the girl. I stood on the shore above and saw in the distance sea and island,

and below me the lovely beach. I watched the bare-foot girl go knee-deep into the sea, wash the rugs and come out again, and water dripped from the black hem of her dress and her legs were wet. The lad, when he saw that I watched, withdrew slowly a little towards the fishing boats drawn up on the sand. The girl finished her work; she sat on the wall and picked up her black stockings; to put them on, she raised one leg upon the other, drawing up her dress so her naked leg showed, and every now and then she raised her head towards me to see if I was looking. The sea sparkled with all her splendour in the morning sun. The girl stood, picked up her petticoat from the ground, passed it over her dress, loosened her dress and slipped on the petticoat, and did the dress up again, looking at me the whole time. Then with raised arms she set her hair straight. She left her breasts half uncovered in front. Slowly, from behind, with his hands in his pockets, as if indifferent, came the young lad, the poor young lad who, just adolescent, was sick with his first desire for a woman's body. The girl, as soon as she saw him, called him to come and collect the things in a small cart which stood close by. And she put on her shoes and again arranged her hair a little, and she walked a bit on the wall for me to see her, and then she slowly came up the slope to-wards me. The lad went over to the small cart, but instead of putting the rugs in he lay down in it, with his feet dangling over the edge, resting on the sand. He watched us and some hidden resentment and jealousy rose from him. The girl, continuing to climb, stared at me as I stood motionless on the upper part of the shore. The sea shone in the midday sun. The girl felt that she had two men in her power, ready. But nothing disturbed me except the young lad sick with hidden desire. And the voluptuous sea laughed as if indifferent; but she was not indifferent, but with irony pricked on the devilish desires.

109   *Greek Mariners*

I SAILED from Smyrna in the *Amphitrite*, a Greek brigantine, which was confidently said to be bound for the coast of Syria, but I knew that this announcement was not to be relied upon with positive certainty, for the Greek mariners are practically free from the stringency of ship's papers, and where they will, there they go. However, I had the whole of the cabin for myself and my attendant, Mysseri, subject only to the society of the Captain at the hour of dinner. Being at ease in this respect, being furnished, too, with plenty of books, and finding an unfailing source of interest in the thorough Greekness of my Captain and my crew, I felt less anxious than most people would have been about the probable length of the cruise: I knew enough of Greek navigation to be sure that our vessel would cling to earth like a child to its mother's knee, and that I should touch at many an isle before I set foot upon the Syrian coast; but I had no invidious preference for Europe, Asia, or Africa (I was safe from all danger of America), and I felt that I could defy the winds to blow me upon a coast that was blank and void of interest. My patience was extremely useful to me, for the cruise altogether endured some forty days, and that in the midst of winter.

According to me, the most interesting of all the Greeks (male Greeks) are the mariners, because their pursuits and their social condition are so nearly the same as those of their famous ancestors. You will say that the occupation of commerce must have smoothed down the salience of their minds; and this would be so, perhaps, if their mercantile affairs were conducted according to the fixed business-like routine of Europeans; but the ventures of the Greeks are surrounded by such a multitude of imagined dangers, and (from the absence of regular marts, in which the true value of merchandize can be ascertained) are so entirely speculative, and besides are conducted in a manner so wholly determined upon by the wayward fancies and wishes of the crew, that they belong to Enterprise, rather than to Industry, and are very far indeed from tending to deaden any freshness of character.

The vessels in which war and piracy were carried on during the years of the Greek Revolution, became merchantmen at the end of the war, but the tactics of the Greeks, as naval warriors, were so exceedingly cautious, and their habits as commercial warriors are so wild, that the change has been more slight than you might imagine. The first care of Greeks (Greek Rayahs) when they undertake a shipping enterprise, is to procure for their vessel the protection of some European power. This is easily managed by a little intriguing with the dragoman of one of the embassies at Constantinople, and the craft soon glories in the ensign of Russia, or the dazzling Tricolour, or the Union Jack. Thus, to the great delight of her crew, she enters upon the ocean world with a flaring lie at her peak; but the appearance of the vessel does no discredit to the borrowed flag: she is frail, indeed, but she is gracefully built, and smartly rigged; she always carries guns, and, in short, gives good promise of mischief and speed.

The privileges attached to the vessel and her crew by virtue of the borrowed flag are so great as to imply a liberty wider even than that which is often enjoyed in our more strictly civilized countries, so that there is no good ground for saying that the development of the true character belonging to Greek mariners is prevented by the dominion of the Ottoman. These men are free, too, from the power of the great Capitalist—a power more withering than despotism itself to the enterprises of humble venturers. The capital employed is supplied by those whose labour is to render it productive; the crew receive no wages, but have all a share in the venture, and in general, I believe, they are the owners of the whole freight; they choose a captain, to whom they intrust just power enough to keep the vessel on her course in fine weather, but not quite enough for a gale of wind; they also elect a cook and a mate. The cook whom we had on board was particularly careful about the ship's reckoning, and, when, under the influence of the keen sea-breezes, we grew fondly expectant of an instant dinner the great author of pilafs would be standing on deck with a quadrant in his hands, calmly affecting to take an observation. But then, to make up for this, the captain would be exercising a controlling influence over the soup, so that all in the end went well. Our mate was a Hydriot, a native of that island rock which grows nothing but mariners and mariners' wives. His character seemed to be exactly that which is generally attributed to the Hydriot race; he was fierce, and gloomy, and lonely in his ways. One of his principal duties seemed to be that of acting as counter-captain, or leader of the opposition, denouncing the first symptoms of tyranny, and protecting even the cabin-boy from oppression. Besides this, when things went smoothly, he would begin to prognosticate evil, in order that his more light-hearted comrades might not be puffed up with the seeming good fortune of the moment.

It seemed to me that the personal freedom of these sailors, who own no superiors except those of their own choice, is as like as may be to that of their sea-faring ancestors. And even in their mode of navigation they have admitted no such an entire change as you would suppose probable; it is true that they have so far availed themselves of modern discoveries as to look to the compass instead of the stars, and that they have superseded the immortal gods of their forefathers by St Nicholas in his glass case, but they are not yet so confident either in their needle, or their saint, as to love an open sea, and they still hug their shores as fondly as the Argonauts of old. Indeed, they have a most unsailor-like love for the land, and I really believe that in a gale of wind they would rather have a rock-bound coast on their lee than no coast at all. According to the notions of an English seaman, this kind of navigation would soon bring the vessel on which it might be practised to an evil end. The Greek, however, is unaccountably successful in escaping the consequences of being 'jammed in', as it is called, upon a lee shore.

These seamen, like their forefathers, rely upon no winds unless they are right astern, or on the quarter; they rarely go *on* a wind if it blows at all fresh, and if the adverse breeze approaches to a gale, they at once fumigate St Nicholas, and put up the helm. The consequence of course is, that under the ever-varying winds of the Aegean they are blown about in the most whimsical manner. I used to think that Ulysses with his ten years' voyage had taken his time in making Ithaca, but my experience in Greek navigation soon made me understand that he had had, in point of fact, a pretty good 'average passage'.

Such are now the mariners of the Aegean: free, equal amongst themselves, navigating the seas of their forefathers with the same heroic and yet childlike spirit of venture, the same half-trustful reliance upon heavenly aid, they are the liveliest images of true old Greeks that time and the new religions have spared us. . . .

We were nearing the isle of Cyprus, when there arose half a gale of wind, with a heavy chopping sea. My Greek seamen considered that the weather amounted, not to a half, but to an integral gale of wind at the very least; so they put up the helm, and scudded for twenty hours. When we neared the main land of Anatoli, the gale ceased, and a favourable breeze springing up, soon brought us off Cyprus once more. Afterwards the wind changed again, but we were still able to lay our course by sailing close-hauled.

We were at length in such a position, that by holding on our course for about half an hour, we should get under the lee of the island, and find ourselves in smooth water, but the wind had been gradually freshening; it now blew hard, and there was a heavy sea running.

As the grounds for alarm arose, the crew gathered together in one close group; they stood pale and grim under their hooded capotes like monks awaiting a massacre, anxiously looking by turns along the pathway of the storm, and then upon each other, and then upon the eye of the Captain, who stood by the helmsman. Presently the Hydriot came aft, more moody than ever, the bearer of fierce remonstrance against the continuing of the struggle; he received a resolute answer, and still we held our course. Soon there came a heavy sea that caught the bow of the brigantine as she lay jammed in betwixt the waves; she bowed her head low under the waters, and shuddering through all her timbers, then gallantly stood up again over the striving sea with bowsprit entire. But where were the crew? — It was a crew no longer, but rather a gathering of Greek citizens;— the shout of the seamen was changed for the murmuring of the people—the spirit of the old Demos was alive. The men came aft in a body, and loudly asked that the vessel should be put about, and that the storm be no longer tempted. Now, then, for speeches:—the Captain, his eyes flashing fire, his frame all quivering with emotion— wielding his every limb, like another and a louder voice—pours forth the eloquent torrent of his threats, and his reasons, commands, and his prayers; he promises—he vows—he swears that there is safety in holding on—safety, *if Greeks will be brave*! The men hear and are moved, but the gale rouses itself once more, and again the raging sea comes trampling over the timbers that are the life of all. The fierce Hydriot advances one step nearer to the Captain, and the angry growl of the people goes floating down the wind; but they listen, they waver once more, and once more resolve, then waver again, thus doubtfully hanging between the terrors of the storm and the persuasion of glorious speech, as though it were the Athenian that talked, and Philip of Macedon that thundered on the weather-bow.

Brave thoughts winged on Grecian words gained their natural mastery over Terror; the Brigantine held on her course, and reached smooth water at last.

110   *Aegean Melancholy*

WHAT linking of soul to the halcyons of the afternoon!
 What calm in the voices of the far-off land!
The cuckoo in the trees' mantilla,
and the mystic hour of the fishermen's supper,
and the sea on the accordion playing
the long lament of the woman,
the lovely woman who bared her breast
when she remembered the cradles
and lilac sprinkled the sunset with fire!

With caique and the Virgin's sails
sped by the winds they are gone,
lovers of the lilies' far country;
but how here night attends on sleep
with murmuring hair on shining throats
or on the big white shores;
and how with Orion's gold sword
is scattered and spilled aloft
dust from the dreams of girls
scented with mint and basil!

Where at the cross-road the ancient sorceress stood
burning the winds with dry thyme
lightly, in the hand a pitcher with the waters of silence,
easily, as though they entered Paradise,
delicate shadows stepped. . . .
And from the crickets' prayer fermenting the fields
lovely girls with the moon's skin have risen
to dance on the midnight threshing-floor . . .

O signs that pass in the depths
of the mirror-holding water—
seven small lilies which sparkle.

When Orion's sword returns
it will find poor bread under the lamp
but life in the stars' embers;
will find generous hands linked together in space,
abandoned sea-weed, the shore's last children,
years, green stones. . . .

O green stone—what storm-prophet has beheld you
halting the light at the birth of day,
the light at the birth of the two eyes of the world!

111   *Aegean Even-Song*

THE sun falls behind the city of Syra. . . . Silence reigns over all,
not a single breath of air stirs; over all an indolent warmth
spreads and the sea, drowned, is still. Sailing ships rest where they
happen to be with folded wings, like birds resting on the water.

When the wind-blown, wave-rocked, deep-sounding current of
the Aegean, whose mood directs the life and expression of the islanders, quietens, everything takes on another look, a new look. Then at
all points, clear, large, rising up and approaching in silence, the islands
which circle the horizon appear, as if some mass were performed,
something great consummated in nature.

223

Unpaintable, unsingable, inexpressible then is the dance of the Nymphs of the Aegean, crown of flowering passion. Tinos, a warm, violet pile, copying the inimitable Hymettos during the most intense moments of its life, the last caresses of the Sun. A joining blue line of sea links Tinos and Mykonos. Mykonos, a most gentle pink, like a faded April rose. Another, more open joining line of sea and then Naxos, velvet, dark red burning fire. Holy Delos swimming in motionless water. A wonderful necklet of flowers circling the sky with its central flower the small isle of Pharos, a gold branch of an acacia. . . .

In the still city of Syros, gay blue-white, rose-white cottages shine as they climb one on the shoulders of the other up to the top of the two cones of the mountains, to gaze with bright eyes at the shapes of men sitting near the quay dark and voiceless, as if they followed lazily the liturgy or were simply cattle resting. . . .

From the sky new, fresh caresses everlastingly descend, passionate kisses of air, intangible but of extreme clarity. A most bright apple-gold crown grows, dry and yet moist is the red powder spilled. Now Tinos, dark violet and fresh with dew. Now Mykonos burning like Hymettos. Now Paros, faded violets. Now the little isle of Pharos, dark-coloured. Now the sea . . . drawing in, drinking the colours, lit up, white, like thick milk, rolled gold its surface.

Here everywhere and on all sides, from the depths of the Aegean, from the bowels of those magic soils, crumbled as if ready to be shaped into many forms, rises to the light the race of men, created under the maternal caresses of these holy dwellings of the Gods. Here only skies and earth and winds and sea and colour forever caress the senses, like a mother a beloved child; they nourish the mind with tenderness like a natural flower, flower above the visible animal world of earth. Body and soul, heart and mind open like beautiful flowers and like a bunch of flowers give out rich perfume. . . .

And there is one moment more, when the sea, as if the sun, dropped into her depths, gave light from within, all milk on which gold flows, trembles and sparkles like a mirage; and there is still another, a final moment, when all the sea is hot burning violet, waters smell and all is an ecstasy as the moon, suddenly appearing, holds back her rays in the motionless air, a huge, startled face which regards the boundless passion with an air of elusive mockery.

. . . O God of Greece. Once only have my lips moved in prayer, once only have they uttered a petition, that such be the hour and such the sight when my worshipping eyes close, when but one way of expressing this holy enchantment remains, to bend and kiss the native soil, to rise up and cross myself in deep reverence, worshipping the soil and the waters and the colour and the sky of holy Greece.

112   *On Aegina*

AT Niko's little taverna in the square on the waterfront music was being played on a violin and a zither. From the bare white walls the fierce faces of heroes looked down on us and the clouds of gunfire smoke, bellying about the ships in the print of the battle of Navarino, seemed still to be stirring balefully in the drifts of cigarette smoke that circled the hanging lamp. The rattle and scrape of the music bored into the subconscious with its insistent rhythms.

Like the alchemist's season of dissolution the company dissolved into black confusion of drunkenness. In this melting of our separate elements there was only a little despair at the loosening of all control. The unpremeditated experiment proceeds in happiness and knows no real anxiety. When Costa danced with his black curls bobbing over his forehead, subtly fusing all the frieze movements of archaic painting into the flowing motion of his dance, there came a brief season of white and purification. His suppleness was so fluid, so graceful when he kicked off his shoes for the freedom of his bare feet, that he held one's gaze fixed in a pure white delight of indelible memory. Then, for a little while the mood hovered in the blue season while the man with the goat's eyes danced himself into inviolable isolation. With intricate steps he spun himself a cocoon of concentration and abstraction. His was pure dancing, an exercise in self-expression, the extemporized variation of an individual upon a theme. And suddenly there was an explosion in the party, the alchemic components burst into red and the elixir streamed forth. Costa leaped upon the shoulders of the goat man, yellow haired Dionysios swung the caique boy up onto his and the two couples danced a wild, twirling improvization at one another. The boys swayed upon the men's shoulders, their arms outstretched and their fingers clicking like castanets. In pure and liquid gold the elixir poured over us and we were possessed at last by the magic revelation.

All next day I carried the exaltation of that moment like a secret source of illumination within me. There was a new brightness and purity to colour, a new clarity in the atmosphere and a new beauty in all I saw. The sea was running hard, and the white horses herded by the rocks at the harbour mouth. Spray flashed up and splashed across the northern mole sending cold shafts through the warm sunshine. The brown nets were laid out for mending in the shelter. Miles upon miles of nets were spread out in stripes of fading umber half covering the quay. The fishermen sat crosslegged to mend them or stretched a torn section between their toes and hands. Or they stood coiling them with those beautifully flowing movements of theirs, one feeding the long net to another who paid it out in coils. They worked quietly and concentratedly but there was one to every group who sat with his shuttle idle in his lap and told a long involved story while the others listened as they worked. Behind them the town was bright in the clear sunlight. Like mild explosions the palm fronds tossed in the wind between the speckled pantiles of the roofs. All the length of the quay the storm-bound caiques were moored, rocking an echo to the turbulence of the gulf. Their hulls were painted with greens and blues in miraculous gradations from viridian to Nile green and from a deep ultramarine to the innocent face of the sky. Sometimes one among them was white like a seagull or even some mystic bride of the sea.

Above all that clear bright scene was an empty space where the wind tore by. An arched space that was bounded by the hard bright sky and the blazoned track where the sun passed overhead. At midday the heat was cast on the quay like a pall and the men carried their nets back to the store. The quay became no more than a geometric abstraction bleached by the sun and the wind. Six last men carried a net in long loops slung from their shoulders. They walked heavily along the moles as though along an archaic frieze. A boy running barefoot darted towards the pigeons scavenging on the quay. The white birds rose in a startled flutter, wheeled round and settled again behind him.

113 *Syra: A Transmitted Reminiscence*

I saw it in its earlier day—
Primitive, such an isled resort
As hearthless Homer might have known
Wandering about the Aegean here,
Sheds ribbed with wreck-stuff faced the sea
Where goods in transit shelter found;
And here and there a shanty-shop
Where fez-caps, swords, tobacco, shawls,
Pistols, and orient finery, Eve's—
(The spangles dimmed by hands profane)
Like plunder on a pirate's deck
Lay orderless in such loose way
As to suggest things ravished or gone astray.

Above a tented inn with fluttering flag
A sunburnt board announced Greek wine
In self-same text Anacreon knew,
Dispensed by one named 'Pericles'.
Got up as for the opera's scene,
Armed strangers, various, lounged or lazed,
Lithe fellows tall, with gold-shot eyes,
Sunning themselves as leopards may.

Off-shore lay xebecs trim and light,
And some but dubious in repute.
But on the strand, for docks were none,
What busy bees! no testy fry;
Frolickers, picturesquely odd,
With bales and oil-jars lading boats,
Lighters that served an anchored craft,
Each in his tasselled Phrygian cap,
Blue Eastern drawers and braided vest;
And some with features cleanly cut
As Proserpine's upon the coin.
Such chatterers all! like children gay
Who make believe to work, but play.

I saw, and how help musing too.
Here traffic's immature as yet:
Forever this juvenile fun hold out
And these light hearts? Their garb, their glee,
Alike profuse in flowing measure,
Alike inapt for serious work,
Blab of grandfather Saturn's prime
When trade was not, nor toil, nor stress,
But life was leisure, merriment, peace,
And lucre none and love was righteousness.

114   *The Festival of the Madonna at Tinos*

IT was a fine starry night, and the thousands of little oil lamps
which decorated the church and its steeple rivalled the lights of the
celestial hemisphere in their twinklings. Patience, assisted now and
again by an ingenious push, enabled us to get inside and witness the
weird sights in the church—men and women were there grovelling on
their knees; cripples, blind and halt, were imploring the favour of the
Madonna; further on, a woman, after standing ominously still for a
while, as if contemplating the scene, was suddenly seized with

religious frenzy. She shrieked, she threw her arms about, and was carried out in wild hysteria. This frenzy was most infectious, and presently the whole church was full of hideous yells and maddened suppliants who are supposed when in this state to be under the special influence of the Deity. There is something which carries one's mind back to Antiquity in the way these crowds are lodged. In olden days no inns existed on Delos, and at the festivals places of shelter were found near and in the temple. Now in Tinos the old custom of *incubatio* is continued, for when invalids aspire to a perfect cure they must sleep in the church for a night at least. . . .

Up in the gallery of the church crowds were collected, with their beds, their carpets, and their cooking utensils; for this portion of the church had been given up as a lodging house to those who were lucky enough to find room. Luckier still were those who could find a few inches of ground on which to lay their bed down in the vault beneath, for in the 'evresis' they think they breathe sacred air. This vault or crypt is low, but higher than a tall man's stature, and the denseness of the atmosphere was intensely stifling. Close to us as we entered were three blind men, holding on to one another, groaning and striking their breasts; behind them was a sinister form, which barked, as it were, not able to speak, and wriggled at my feet like a fish. Further on was a poor girl, in the last stage of consumption, leaning for support on her sister. . . . An old man on all fours hindered our progress; and close to him a madman stood, still for the time being, but ominously so. A damsel stretched on the knee of her mother was relating, like Ophelia, in subdued and mysterious voice, some secret of her distraught brain, whilst her mother offered up a never-ceasing prayer to the all-healing Madonna for the recovery of her child's intellect.

It was piteous to look at a noble form leaning against the wall: she had a Greek type of countenance; her hair was black, and hung in rich tresses down her back; her eyes were almond-shaped, her nose straight; she seemed like a sister of the Caryatides, but, alas! like them, she was deaf. I advanced and found myself before a hole which led into an inner vault, and thence another opened out, but I could stand no more. Sick and faint, I reached the open air after a struggle with the pilgrims who were eagerly pushing in with their little tin phials they had bought outside to fill with water from the sacred stream. Others, too, were buying consecrated oil from the priests, which they poured into the eyes of their children, and which they were going to take home in little tins to their friends who could not come. . . .

Down in the town quite another scene greeted us. Those pilgrims who had effected their cure or done their devotions were enjoying themselves vastly in the cafés. Dancing was the order of the night; those curious weird dances of the Greek islands, for example, the συρτός, a wavy line of five or six women, hand in hand, and led by a pocket handkerchief held by one man, whose acrobatic executions were wonderful to behold. Then there was the rapid dance performed by rows of men with their arms around each other's shoulders, four steps backwards, four forwards, with pointed toe, first slowly, with the pace increased till I was almost dazzled by its rapidity.

A man, a noted dancer, performed for the benefit of the others who are tired: he turned somersaults in his white fustanella; he brandished knives in an alarming manner as he rushed to and fro; altogether he was a terrible performer, an Albanian Greek from the mainland mountains, they said.

Early in the morning of the great day . . . fresh steamers discharged crowds of sickly-looking individuals, for the night had been rough and a perfect hurricane was blowing. . . .

The sea of men rolled beneath me, for I had secured a seat for the occasion on a balcony; as it went past it looked like a carpet sparkling with every colour—gold-embroidered tunics, snow-white fustanella, gorgeously embroidered skirts and vests from Asia sparkling with gold and silver coins, rich furs, and the more humble green and blue dresses of the islanders, mingled with a tinge of gaudy parasols and tall hats from the more civilized Athens. It was a sight to rivet and dazzle one. '"Ἔρχεται, ἔρχεται!' ('It comes!') was heard on all sides in a dull murmur; the procession was coming, and the crowd solemnly divided so as to make a passage for the priests,

On the steps of the sanctuary the priests were marshalled, in rich vestments, carrying banners round the holy icon; then as a breath of wind disturbs a pool so did the advent of the procession disturb the almost breathless crowd below. Everyone made the sign of the cross and lowered his head in silence as it passed; and then when it was gone the murmur and the noise again increased—the sacred ceremony was over.

The Death-Wails of Mykonos

115

THE bells of Mykonos were tolling mournfully, to tell of the death of the young man; and I shuddered involuntarily now that I knew that my desire was to be realized. I was to be present at a *moerologia* over the dead.

'The women are preparing the corpse now; by ten o'clock all will be ready,' Mrs Monk gaily suggested as we were discussing some eggs and boiled milk for breakfast. 'The moerologista Zachara is engaged to sing, and no one is better suited than she for her occupation.'

We then talked about these women: how they practise their dirges when working in the fields; how they have certain verses and certain stock ideas for nearly every emergency; and how by constant practice it comes quite easily to them to make impromptu verses about the special case in question. A few years ago they used to send to Mykonos from all the islands round when a death occurred at which a special honour was desired to be shown to the deceased magnate; but lately this custom has been abandoned. It must have been a weird sight to see the woman dressed in the peculiar costume of Mykonos, the tall makramadas head-dress, on her way to a neighbouring island to sing her wail. . . .

In answer to my enquiries Mrs Monk told me how they treated a corpse in Mykonos: the funeral takes place as soon as possible after death—generally within a few hours—the dead body is washed in water and wine, then the deceased is wrapped either in a shroud or dressed in his best clothes and placed on a bier in the middle of the outer reception room of the house, his face is turned towards the east, his hands across his breast, and his feet are bound together with black bands; and at his head and feet stand two lamps adorned with coloured ribands. The bier is covered with flowers, out of which the wax-like face of death peers in hideous contrast.

When everything was prepared the kinsmen and friends of the deceased man were summoned to attend the lamentation by the bellman and amongst the others I wended my way to the house of mourning, feeling heartily ashamed of myself for intruding on their grief; but at the same time I was fortified by the consciousness that the Mykoniotes were flattered at the notice taken of their custom.

The moerologista Zachara came in shortly after we arrived; the kinswomen were all seated round the corpse; the afflicted widow and her children were groaning audibly on the divan, and had their hair down ready for the customary tearing and shaking. The entrance of Zachara was the signal for the commencement of that demonstrative grief in which the Greeks love to indulge: they all set to work to sing in mournful cadence about the merits of the deceased, keeping time with their feet and beating their knees with their hands; then suddenly, with a fearful shriek, the widow went off into an ecstasy of grief. She tore her hair, she lacerated her cheek, she beat her breast, she scratched her bare arms, until at length two or three women rushed forward to restrain her in her extravagant grief; her poor little children lay crouching in a corner, terrified beyond measure at what was going on and screaming with all their might.

At length Zachara, who hitherto had taken no part in the proceedings, but had stood in a statuesque attitude with a well-feigned face of poignant grief, as if contemplating the misery before her to inspire her muse, now rushed forward, fell on the corpse, kissed it, and rose to commence her dirge in that harsh and grating voice which the Greeks love, but which is so distasteful to Western ears. Thus she began:

I yearn to mourn for the dead one
Whose name I dare not say,
For as soon as I speak of the lost one
My heart and voice give way.

As she reached the end of this stanza her voice trembled, she paused for a moment, as if to regain her composure, during which time nothing was heard but stifled sobs.

Who hath seen the sun at midnight?
Who hath seen a midday star?
Who hath seen a bride without a crown
Go forth from her father's door?
Who hath seen the dead returning
Be he king or warrior brave?
They are planted in Charon's vineyard,
There is no return from the grave.

This was Zachara's prologue, and after it the grief and lamentations were renewed with fresh vigour. So far doubtless, many of the mourners had heard before on similar occasions, for it was one of her stock pieces; after this she had to deal with the special case of the deceased. She sang of the loneliness of the living, of the horrors of death, and in that strange language of hyperbole she wondered how the sun could venture to shine on so lamentable a scene as the present. During all this time the widow, the kinswomen, and the children were wild with grief. Nature at length asserted herself and demanded a pause, during which the company refreshed themselves with raki, biscuits, figs, and other small refections which had been laid out on a table in the corner of the room.

Then the tide of grief flowed on again; in fact, a Greek lament is one of the most heart-rending scenes that can be witnessed. . . .

116   *Delos*

ON charts they fall like lace,
    Islands consuming in a sea
Born dense with its own blue:
And like repairing mirrors holding up
Small towns and trees and rivers
To the still air, the lovely air:
From the clear side of springing Time,
In clement places where the windmills ride,
Turning over grey springs in Mykonos,
In shadows with a gesture of content.

The statues of the dead here
Embark on sunlight, sealed
Each in her model with the sightless eyes:
The modest stones of Greece,
Who gravely interrupted death by pleasure.

And in harbours softly fallen
The liver-coloured sails—
Sharp-featured brigantines with eyes—
Ride in reception so like women:
The pathetic faculty of girls
To register and utter a desire
In the arms of men upon the new-mown waters,
Follow the wind, with their long shining keels
Aimed across Delos at a star.

117   *On Naxos*

START at dawn on the eastern side and leave the village stirring
    in the twilight. You are nearly breasting the final shoulder of
Koronos when the sun leaps up from behind Ephesus, red and huge

over the mountain of Samos. Dawn had been purely Homeric with streaming rays, flushed and quiet except for the gathering riot of birdsong coming from the valley gardens below. So many birds greeting the day together make it hard to tell them apart, but nightingales and larks sing out above the rest. Then into the pearly foredawn, comes this leaping sun, Helios springing from his couch, and the distant coast of Asia Minor is shadowed violet. In a few minutes you have crossed the shoulder and are again in shadow. But not for long. The sun hurries behind you and lights the western islands which now come into view. You are so high among the early goat bells where bracken grows among the opening rock roses that Paros and Anti-Paros and all the islands to the north and south of them appear like blue clouds sailing low down in the pale sky. There is no division between the sea and sky, just a gradation of many palest blues and a gathering sheen as the sea reaches the shore far below you. Now you are on the tops, the rocky moorlands where every day the movement of the sun is undisguised and inexorable. The views of the sea are so wide that the poet who likened God's mercy to its breadth must have been here before you. Remote, silvered and opalescent, the lovely shapes of the other Cyclades are scattered before you. To eastwards you can trace the route of Dionysus' triumphant sail and see the coast of Asia Minor where the pirates would have taken him.

On these high slopes the goats amble and graze. Their bells sound from far off. Their blacks and browns and whites fleck the grey rock. Ever preoccupied, their ignorance of time makes their motions peaceful to watch. One wonders why it is that the expression of their orange eyes should be so suspicious. The herdsmen seem as though in a trance of waiting. Drenched in sunlight they sit motionless or walk so unhurriedly it seems they scarcely move of their own volition. It is an existence wholly of daydream and must have been the chief nursery of myth. Pan and the nymphs are the very essence of a shepherd's midday reveries and the reflective notes of the pipe are the music of those hourless, passive days.

As you come down the further side you begin to meet the people coming up to their high fields. Greetings are quietly exchanged; you are still under the quiet spell of the dawn which people instinctively hesitate to violate. Soon you enter the lanes in between fields and orchards and suddenly you see people at work picking fruit or hoeing in their gardens. Their clothes give them protective colouring so that they seem like the cicadas in the trees, only visible when one's vision is directed right upon them and rightly focused. And as you go on through mile upon mile of this wealth of fertility you marvel at the spilling cornucopia harvests piled about the villages. Dionysus was created of all this and you can recognize him in the radiant lemons hanging on the trees, in the brilliance of the red peppers and in the sensuous purple of the egg plants.

At last you reach Naxia again and are greeted by the great marble doorway standing on its islet. It is a magnificent size as it stands up to the winds. Now Boreas, the north wind of summer thrashes the dark sea to a wild white foam and the door-way frames the remote sky which the wind has polished to a hard bright blue. Little boys bathe on the crescent of yellow sand, diving with shrill shouts from the black broken rocks. It is a lovely place where fields of golden stubble sweep back from the blue sea and the black rocks of the shore. Here it must have been that Dionysus found Cretan Ariadne asleep and worn out with her love for the faithless Theseus. Here that he first loved her and took her up beside him in his panther-drawn car of triumph.

118   *Patmos*

NEAR is
And difficult to grasp, the God.
But where danger threatens
That which saves from it also grows.
In gloomy places dwell
The eagles, and fearless over
The chasm walk the sons of the Alps

On bridges lightly built.
Therefore, since round about
Are heaped the summits of Time
And the most loved live near, growing faint
On mountains most separate,
Give us innocent water,
O pinions give us, with minds most faithful
To cross over and to return.

So I spoke, when more swiftly
Than ever I had expected,
And far as never I thought
I should come, a Genius carried me
From my own house. There glimmered
In twilight, as I went,
The shadowy wood
And the yearning streams of
My homeland; no longer I knew those regions;
But soon, in a radiance fresh,
Mysteriously,
In the golden haze,
Quickly grown up,
With strides of the sun,
And fragrant with a thousand peaks,

Now Asia burst into flower for me, and dazzled
I looked for one thing there I might know, being unaccustomed
To those wide streets where down
From Tmolus drives
The golden-bedded Pactolus,
And Taurus stands, and Messogis,
And full of flowers the garden,
A quiet fire; but in the light, high up
There blossoms the silver snow
And, witness to life immortal,

On inaccessible walls
Pristine the ivy grows, and supported
On living pillars, cedars and laurels,
There stand the festive,
The palaces built by gods.

But around Asia's gates there murmur,
Extending this way and that
In the uncertain plain of the sea,
Shadowless roads enough;
Yet the boatman knows the islands.
And when I heard
That of the near islands one
Was Patmos,
I greatly desired
There to be lodged, and there
To approach the dark grotto.
For not like Cyprus,
The rich in wellsprings,
Nor any of the others
Magnificently does Patmos dwell,

Hospitable nonetheless
In her poorer house
She is,
And when, after shipwreck or lamenting for
His homeland or else for
The friend departed from him,
A stranger draws near
To her, she is glad to hear it, and her children,
The voices of the hot noonday copse,
And where the sand falls, and the field's
Flat surface cracks, the sounds—
These hear him, and lovingly all is loud
With the man's re-echoed lament. So once

She tended the God-beloved,
The seer who in blessèd youth

Had walked with
The Son of the Highest, inseparable, for
The bearer of thunder loved the disciple's
Ingenuousness, and the attentive man
Saw the face of the God exactly
When over the mystery of the vine
They sat together at the banqueting hour
And in his great soul, calmly foreknowing,
The Lord pronounced death and the ultimate love, for never
He could find words enough
To say about goodness, then, and to soothe, when
He saw it, the wrath of the world.
For all things are good. After that he died. Much could
Be said of it. And the friends at the very last
Saw him, the gladdest, looking up triumphant,

Yet they were sad, when now
The evening had come, amazed,
For the souls of these men contained
Things greatly predetermined, but under the sun they loved
This life and were loath to part from
The visible face of the Lord
And their homeland. Driven in,
Like fire into iron, was this, and beside them
The loved one's shadow walked.
Therefore he sent them
The Spirit, and mightily trembled
The house, and God's thunderstorms rolled
Distantly rumbling above
Their heads foreknowledge bowed, when deep in thought
Assembled were the heroes of death,

Now that, departing,
Once more he appeared to them.
For now the kingly one extinguished
The day of the sun and broke
The straightly beaming, the sceptre,
Divinely suffering, yet of his own free will,
For it was to come back when
The time was due. To have done so later
Would not have been good, and the work of men
Abruptly broken off, disloyally, and from now on
A joy it was
To dwell in loving Night and in fixed,
Ingenuous eyes to preserve
Abysses of wisdom. And low down at
The foot of mountains, too, will living images thrive,

Yet dreadful it is how here and there
Unendingly God disperses whatever lives.
For only to part from the sight
Of their dear friends
And far across the mountains to go
Alone, when doubly
Perceived, heavenly spirit before had been
Unanimous; and not predicted was this,
But seized them by the hair, on the instant,
When suddenly the God
Far off in haste looked back
At them, and vowing,
So that he would stay, from now on goldenly
Bound fast as to ropes,
Calling the evil by name, they linked hands,

But when thereupon he dies
To whom beauty most adhered, so that
A miracle was wrought in his person and

The Heavenly had pointed at him,
And when, an enigma to one another
For ever, they cannot understand
One another who lived together
Conjoined by remembrance, and not only
The sand or the willows it takes away,
And seizes the temples when even
The demigod's honour and that of his friends
Is blown away by the wind, and the highest
Himself averts his face
Because nowhere now
An immortal is to be seen in the skies or
On our green earth, what is this?

It is the sower's cast when he scoops up
The wheat in his shovel
And throws it, towards clear space, swinging it over the threshing-
    floor.
The husk falls at his feet, but
The grain reaches its end,
And there's no harm if some of it
Is lost, and of the speech
The living sound dies away,
For the work of gods, too, is like our own,
Not all things at once does the Highest intend.
The pit bears iron, though,
And glowing resins Etna,
And so I should have wealth
With which to form an image and see
The Christ as he truly was,

But if someone spurred himself on
And, talking sadly, on the road, when I was
Defenceless, attacked me, so that amazed I tried
To copy the God's own image, I, a servant—

In anger visible once I saw
The Lord of Heaven, not that I should be something, but
To learn. Benign they are, but what they most abhor,
While their reign lasts, is falsehood, and then
What's human no longer counts among human kind.
For they do not govern, the fate
It is of immortals that governs, and their work
Proceeds by its own force and hurrying seeks its end.
For when heavenly triumph goes higher
The jubilant son of the Highest
Is called like the sun by the strong,

A secret token, and here is the wand
Of song, signalling downward,
For nothing is common. The dead
He reawakens whom coarseness has not
Made captive yet. But many timid eyes
Are waiting to see the light.
They are reluctant to flower
Beneath the searing beam, though it is
The golden bridle that curbs their courage.
But when, as if
By swelling eyebrows made
Oblivious of the world
A quietly shining strength falls from holy scripture,
Rejoicing in grace, they
May practise upon the quiet gaze.

And if the Heavenly now
Love me as I believe,
How much more you
They surely love,
For one thing I know:
The eternal Father's will
Means much to you. Now silent is

His sign on thundering heaven. And there is one who stands
Beneath it his whole life long. For Christ lives yet
But all the heroes, his sons,
Have come, and holy scriptures
About him, and lightning is explained by
The deeds of the world until now,
A race that cannot be stopped. But he is present in it. For known
To him are all his works from the beginning.

Too long, too long now
The honour of the Heavenly has been invisible.
For almost they must guide
Our fingers, and shamefully
A power is wresting our hearts from us.
For every one of the Heavenly wants sacrifices, and
When one of these was omitted
No good ever came of it.
We have served Mother Earth
And lately have served the sunlight,
Unwittingly, but what the Father
Who reigns over all loves most
Is that the solid letter
Be given scrupulous care, and the existing
Be well interpreted. This German song observes.

119   *The Revelation of St John on Patmos*

AND I saw a new heaven and a new earth: for the first heaven
and the first earth were passed away; and there was no more
sea. And I John saw the holy city, new Jerusalem, coming down from
God out of heaven, prepared as a bride adorned for her husband.
And I heard a great voice out of heaven saying,

'Behold, the tabernacle of God is with men, and he will dwell with
them, and they shall be his people, and God himself shall be with
them, and be their God. And God shall wipe away all tears from their

eyes; and there shall be no more death, neither sorrow, nor crying, neither shall there be any more pain: for the former things are passed away.'

And he that sat upon the throne said,

'Behold, I make all things new.' And he said unto me, 'Write: for these words are true and faithful.'

And he said unto me,

'It is done. I am Alpha and Omega, the beginning and the end. I will give unto him that is athirst of the fountain of the water of life freely. He that overcometh shall inherit all things; and I will be his God, and he shall be my son. But the fearful, and unbelieving, and the abominable, and murderers, and whore-mongers, and sorcerers, and idolators, and all liars, shall have their part in the lake which burneth with fire and brimstone: which is the second death.'

And there came unto me one of the seven angels which had the seven vials full of the seven last plagues, and talked with me, saying,

'Come hither, I will show thee the bride, the Lamb's wife.'

And he carried me away in the spirit to a great and high mountain, and showed me that great city, the holy Jerusalem, descending out of heaven from God, having the glory of God: and her light was like unto a stone most precious, even like a jasper stone, clear as crystal; and had a wall great and high, and had twelve gates, and at the gates twelve angels, and names written thereon, which are the names of the twelve tribes of the children of Israel: on the east three gates; on the north three gates; on the south three gates; and on the west three gates. And the wall of the city had twelve foundations, and in them the names of the twelve apostles of the Lamb. And he that talked with me had a golden reed to measure the city, and the gates thereof, and the wall thereof. And the city lieth foursquare, and the length is as large as the breadth: and he measured the city with a reed, twelve thousand furlongs. The length and the breadth and the height of it are equal. And he measured the wall thereof, a hundred and forty and four cubits, according to the measure of a man, that is, of the angel. And the building of the wall of it was of jasper: and the city was pure gold, like unto clear glass. And the foundations of the wall of the city were garnished with all manner of precious stones. The first foundation was jasper; the second, sapphire; the third, chalcedony; the fourth, an emerald; the fifth, sardonyx; the sixth, sardius; the seventh, chrysolyte; the eighth, beryl; the ninth, a topaz; the tenth, chrysoprasus; the eleventh, a jacinth; the twelfth, an amythyst. And the twelve gates were twelve pearls; every several gate was of one pearl: and the street of the city was pure gold, as it were transparent glass. And I saw no temple therein: for the Lord God Almighty and the Lamb are the temple of it. And the city had no need of the sun, neither of the moon, to shine in it: for the glory of God did lighten it, and the Lamb is the light thereof. And the nations of them which are saved shall walk in the light of it: and the kings of the earth do bring their glory and honour into it. And the gates of it shall not be shut at all by day: for there shall be no night there. And they shall bring the glory and honour of the nations into it. And there shall in no wise enter into it any thing that defileth, neither whatsoever worketh abomination, or maketh a lie: but they which are written in the Lamb's book of life.

And he showed me a pure river of water of life, clear as crystal, proceeding out of the throne of God and of the Lamb. In the midst of the street of it, and on either side of the river, was there the tree of life, which bore twelve manner of fruits, and yielded her fruit every month: and the leaves of the tree were for the healing of the nations.

And there shall be no more curse: but the throne of God and of the Lamb shall be in it; and his servants shall serve him: and they shall see his face; and his name shall be in their foreheads.

And there shall be no night there; and they need no candle, neither light of the sun; for the Lord God giveth them light: and they shall reign for ever and ever. And he said unto me,

'These sayings are faithful and true: and the Lord God of the holy prophets sent his angel to show unto his servants the things which must shortly be done. Behold, I come quickly: blessed is he that keepeth the sayings of the prophecy of this book.'

The Old Ships

I have seen old ships sail like swans asleep
Beyond the village which men still call Tyre,
With leaden age o'ercargoed, dipping deep
For Famagusta and the hidden sun
That rings black Cyprus with a lake of fire;
And all those ships were certainly so old
Who knows how oft with squat and noisy gun,
Questing brown slaves or Syrian oranges,
The pirates Genoese
Hell-raked them till they rolled
Blood, water, fruit and corpses up the hold.
But now through friendly seas they softly run,
Painted the mid-sea blue or shore-sea green,
Still patterned with the vine and grapes in gold.

But I have seen,
Pointing her shapely shadows from the dawn
And image tumbled on a rose-swept bay,
A drowsy ship of some yet older day;
        And, wonder's breath indrawn,
Thought I—who knows—who knows—but in that same
(Fished up beyond Æaea, patched up new
—Stern painted brighter blue—)
That talkative, bald-headed seaman came
(Twelve patient comrades sweating at the oar)
From Troy's doom-crimson shore,
And with great lies about his wooden horse
        Set the crew laughing, and forgot his course.

It was so old a ship—who knows, who knows?
—And yet so beautiful, I watched in vain
To see the mast burst open with a rose,
And the whole deck put on its leaves again.

121   *The Women of Smyrna*

AS you move through the narrow streets of the city at these
times of festival the transom-shaped windows suspended
over your head on either side are filled with the beautiful descendants
of the old Ionian race; all (even yonder empress throned at the
window of that humblest mud cottage) are attired with seeming
magnificence; their classic heads are crowned with scarlet and laden
with jewels or coins of gold—the whole wealth of the wearers;—
their features are touched with a savage pencil, hardening the outline
of eyes and eyebrows, and lending an unnatural fire to the stern,
grave looks, with which they pierce your brain. Endure their fiery
eyes as best you may, and ride on slowly and reverently, for, facing
you from the side of the transom that looks longwise through the
street, you see the one glorious shape transcendent in its beauty;
you see the massive braid of hair as it catches a touch of light on its
jetty surface—and the broad, calm, angry brow—the large eyes
deeply set, and self-relying as the eyes of a conqueror, with all their
rich shadows of thought lying darkly around them,—you see the
thin fiery nostril, and the bold line of the chin and throat disclosing
all the fierceness, and all the pride, passion, and power that can live
along with the rare womanly beauty of those sweetly turned lips.
But then there is a terrible stillness in this breathing image; it seems
like the stillness of a savage that sits intent and brooding day by day
upon some one fearful scheme of vengeance, and yet more like it
seems to the stillness of an Immortal whose will must be known and
obeyed without sign or speech. Bow down!—Bow down and adore
the young Persephonie, transcendent Queen of Shades!

122   *Rhodes of the Knights and the Turks*

THE chivalrous relics at Rhodes are very superb. I know of no
buildings, whose stately and picturesque aspect seems to corre-

spond better with one's notions of their proud founders. The towers and gates are warlike and strong, but beautiful and aristocratic: you see that they must have been high-bred gentlemen who built them. The edifices appear in almost as perfect a condition as when they were in the occupation of the noble knights of St John; and they have this advantage over modern fortifications, that they are a thousand times more picturesque. Ancient war condescended to ornament itself, and built fine carved castles and vaulted gates: whereas, to judge from Gibraltar and Malta, nothing can be less romantic than modern military architecture; which sternly regards the fighting, without in the least heeding the war-paint. Some of the huge artillery, with which the place was defended, still lies in the bastions; and the touch-holes of the guns are preserved by being covered with rusty old corslets worn by defenders of the fort three hundred years ago. The Turks, who battered down chivalry, seem to be waiting their turn of destruction now. In walking through Rhodes one is strongly affected by witnessing the signs of this double decay. For instance, in the street of the knights, you see noble houses, surmounted by noble escutcheons of superb knights, who lived there, and prayed, and quarrelled, and murdered the Turks; and were the most gallant pirates of the inland seas; and made vows of chastity, and robbed and ravished; and, professing humility, would admit none but nobility into their order; and died recommending themselves to sweet St John, and calmly hoping for heaven in consideration of all the heathen they had slain. When this superb fraternity was obliged to yield to courage as great as theirs, faith as sincere, and to robbers even more dexterous and audacious than the noblest knight who ever sang a canticle to the Virgin, these halls were filled by magnificent Pashas and Agas, who lived here in the intervals of war, and, having conquered its best champions, despised Christendom and chivalry pretty much as an Englishman despises a Frenchman. Now the famous house is let to a shabby merchant, who has his little beggarly shop in the bazaar; to a small officer, who ekes out his wretched pension by swindling, and who gets his pay in bad coin. Mahometanism pays in pewter now, in place of silver and gold. The lords of the world have run to seed. The powerless old sword frightens nobody now—the steel is turned to pewter too, somehow, and will no longer shear a Christian head off any shoulders. . . .

We went out upon the lines of fortification, through an ancient gate and guard-house, where once a chapel probably stood, and of which the roofs were richly carved and gilded. A ragged squad of Turkish soldiers lolled about the gate now—a couple of boys on a donkey; a grinning slave on a mule; a pair of women flapping along in yellow papooshes; a basket-maker sitting under an antique carved portal, and chanting or howling as he platted his osiers; a peaceful well of water, at which knight's chargers had drunk, and at which the double-boyed donkey was now refreshing himself—would have made a pretty picture for a sentimental artist. As he sits, and endeavours to make a sketch of this plaintive little comedy, a shabby dignitary of the island comes clattering by on a thirty-shilling horse, and two or three of the ragged soldiers leave their pipes to salute him as he passes under the Gothic archway.

The astonishing brightness and clearness of the sky under which the island seemed to bask, struck me as surpassing anything I had seen—not even at Cadiz, or the Piraeus, had I seen sands so yellow, or water so magnificently blue. The houses of the people along the shore were but poor tenements, with humble court-yards and gardens; but every fig-tree was gilded and bright, as if it were in a Hesperion orchard; the palms, planted here and there, rose with a sort of halo of light about them; the creepers on the walls quite dazzled with the brilliancy of their flowers and leaves; the people lay in the cool shadows, happy and idle, with handsome solemn faces; nobody seemed to be at work; they only talked a very little, as if idleness and silence were a condition of the delightful shining atmosphere in which they lived.

123   *Days of Divine Wrath, Santorini, 1650*

SUNDAY dawning, the twenty-ninth day of this month, we saw something like smoke, but colossal and extraordinary, I dare to say, which tried to force its way beyond the sky. And on the crest of this smoke flames appeared and shot out like lances or I might say like lightning and struck the earth; and fearing lest that mystery burn us we went into the churches and held a service. Many people in their terror took communion.

But that which had risen up, my Christians, did not die down, as it had done the day before, but thickened still more. And it gathered force and raised rocks and earth on high, as we said above, and some shot up and some fell down and terrible bangings were heard and sounded as far away as the castles of Constantinople, and they thought that there were armadas fighting, as they told us afterwards. . . .

Coming here to Pyrgo they told us that the sea had risen about two miles from the great disturbance there had been and had surrounded the island. And it rooted up . . . great stones from the sea's depths and hurled them on to the earth and had not left a single ship on any shore of the island. . . .

In the other part nothing was left, as we said above. The sea swallowed acres of fields. It swallowed fig-trees, razed churches to the foundations. And it brought to light . . . Greek buildings, which none of us or of our parents ever knew existed.

And tombs were found full of human bones. And we had had fig-trees planted over them and we had sown barley and we had lived. And now it is an entire wilderness and you see nothing but walls built of lime and huge and beautiful marble. So we said that we too would suffer the same fate and would be lost like those lands, which years before had sunk and now had risen up again. . . .

Santorini

BEND if you can to the dark sea forgetting
the flute's sound on naked feet
treading your sleep in the other, the sunken life.

Write if you can on your last shell
the day the name the place
and fling it into the sea that it may sink.

Naked on the pumice-stone we stood
watching the rising islands
watching the red islands go down
into their sleep into our sleep.
Here naked we stood, holding
scales which weighed down towards
injustice.

Instep of power, unshadowed will, disciplined love
projects which ripen in the noontide sun,
avenue of fate with the beat of a new hand
on the shoulder;
to the land which was scattered, does not endure,
to the land which was once our own land
the islands—rust and ash—are sinking.

Altars destroyed
and friends forgotten:
leaves of the palmtree in the mud.

Allow your hands if you can to travel
here on the curve of time with the ship
that has touched the horizon.
When the dice has struck on the slate,

when the lance has struck on the breast-plate,
when the eye has recognized the stranger,
and love has dried up
in punctured souls;
when looking round you see
a circle, the feet harvested,
a circle, the hands dead,
a circle, the eyes darkened;
when no longer are you able to choose
the death you wish for your own,
hearing a cry,
the cry of the wolf even,
your justice:
allow your hands if you can to travel,
free yourself from the faithless time
and sink,
sinks whoever raises the big stones.

125   *Easter on Santorini*

THE Easter Passion here is a great drama, Christian and pre-Christian. The miracle of the Resurrection is well understood by a people who have suffered anxiety for the resurrection of Persephone throughout their heritage; will she be released from the Underworld? Will Adonis come to life again to fructify the Mother and all her creation? The fasting becomes more and more of a strain, tempers shorten, the people lack energy, all minds are concentrated on the Resurrection and release from privation.

Such was the condition of the body and mind in which they attended the long service of Good Friday night. Service, I have said, but drama was a more fitting word, funeral drama. At the top of the nave, just below the chancel step, stood a bier and upon it lay the figure of the Christ, all too death-like in the dim light. The congregation gaze upon him reverently and hushed, while the priests' voices rise in prayer and chant as it were in lamentation for the dead God lying there in state. Hour after hour passes. The women have kissed the dead form and are gone. The moment has come for carrying the Christ out for burial. The procession moves forward—in front the priests with candles and torches and, guarded by them, the open bier borne shoulder-high—behind a reverent, bare-headed crowd. The night is dark and gusty. It rains, and the rugged, tortuous alleys of the town are slippery. It is late but none are sleeping. Unheeding of wind and rain, the women kneel at open door or window, praying, swinging censers, sprinkling perfume on the passing bier. Slowly, haltingly, led by the dirge of priests, now in darkness, now lighted by the torches' flare and intermittent beams from cottage doorways, stumbling in unpaved by-ways the mourners follow their God to his grave. The circuit of the town is done. All have taken their last look upon the dead. The sepulchre is reached—a vault beneath the church from which the funeral started. The priests alone enter with the bier. There is a pause. The crowd waits. The silence is deep as the darkness, only broken here and there by a deep-drawn sigh. Is it the depth of anguish, or is it well-nigh relief that the long strain is over? The priests return. In silence the priests return. In silence the crowd has waited, in silence they disperse. It is finished.

But there is a sequel on the morrow. Soon after dark on Easter-eve the same weary but excited faces may be seen gathered in the church. But there is a change too; there is a feeling abroad of anxiety, of expectancy. Hours must yet pass ere midnight, and not till then is there hope of the announcement, 'Christ is risen!' The suspense seems long. Tonight there is restlessness rather than silence. Some go to and fro between the church and their homes; others join discordantly in the chants and misplace the responses, anything to cheat the long hours of waiting. Midnight draws near; from hand to hand are passed the tapers and candles which shall light the joyful procession, if only the longed-for announcement be made. What is happening there behind those curtains which veil the chancel from the expectant throng? Midnight strikes. The curtains are drawn back. Yes, there is the bier, borne but yesternight to the grave. It is empty. That is only the shroud upon it. The words of the priest ring out true 'Christ is risen!' And there behind the chancel, see, a second veil is drawn back. There in the sanctuary, on the altar steps, bright with a blaze of light stands erect the figure of the Christ who, so short and yet so long a time ago, was borne lifeless to the tomb. A miracle, a miracle! Quickly from the priest's lighted candle the flame is passed. In a moment the dim building is illuminated by a lighted taper in every hand. A procession forms, a joyful procession now. Everywhere are light and glad voices and embraces of friends, crying aloud the news 'Christ is risen!' and answering 'He is indeed'. In every home the lamb is prepared with haste, the wine flows freely; in the streets is the flash of torches, the din of firearms, and all the exuberance of simple joy. The fast is over; the dead has been restored to life before men's eyes; well may they rejoice even to ecstasy. For have they not felt the ecstasy of sorrow? This was no tableau on which they looked, no drama in which they played a part. It was all true, all real. The figure on the bier was indeed the dead Christ. In these simple folk religion has transcended reason; they have reached the heights of spiritual exaltation; they have seen as minds more calm and rational can never see or feel.

CRETE

CRETE is a land of tremendous scenic gestures, emphatic and innocent. It strikes one at once with its breadth and magnificence. It is not a peaceful landscape but a tumultuous one, fully orchestrated. We seem incapable of embracing directly the totally new, but must approach it obliquely for safety. And so I sought to relate the effect of Crete upon me to something else in my experience. Only music, I think, can translate the spirit in the same way as Crete does. The most gorgeous sound I know is a fanfare of silver trumpets sounding when an orchestra has fallen silent. But in this landscape of mountainous distances the sound of those trumpets is quite mute, their note has passed into vibrations beyond registration by our ears. Yes, broad, in its magnificent sense, is a word for Crete.

And the 'canvas'? Because it is challenging, because it is a background against which to live with special vigour and purpose, like a painter creating the new entity and a new life when he paints upon a canvas. Because, too, Crete has the integral quality of a creation, splendidly conceived and splendidly executed. One recognizes here the work of the Master of creative forces at his greatest.

I confess my incapacity to write of Crete. Even when there I knew that my ambition had outstripped my abilities. My diary gave out, my puny human capacity for registration gave out. If we are to transmit our experience to others we must encompass and understand it. Even for our own enjoyment we must do this as far as we can. But some experiences can only be encompassed by especially great men and only saints can transmit them to us. The Revelation of St John appals us in the reading alone. Had it been vouchsafed us, most of us would have been blasted by its glory. In the same way the splendour of Crete is perilous for ordinary people. When I visited Phaestos at the end of my stay I felt almost listless as the car swung into view of the southern plain fringed with mountains. I felt its loveliness was swamping my mind and overcharging my imagination.

I would be lucky to remember more than a glimpse of it, more than a pulse of the disembodying joy that sweeps the spirit clean. The impact of Crete is a sustained onslaught and stimulation. . . .

Crete offers unending vistas of excess. Deserts which can give one spiritual refreshment by their offering of inexhaustible repose, are able to compensate one for not being a hero. But Crete challenges one to attain a greater stature, it seems to promise this if, after all, one can achieve the hero's stamina. This challenge, which the landscape itself seems to throw out, is not for the visitor alone. The Cretans themselves acknowledge it and much of the visitor's pleasure is due to the spirited way in which they accept it. Generation after generation takes it up and it is the touchstone by which they live.

Though Canea is the provincial capital, Herakleion is the chief town. It is a sprawling, barren place whose history has been almost entirely defaced from its fabric. But there are corners in the town where the visitor can find solace for his disappointment at the lack of character in this heir of Knossos, founded by the Saracens. There is the great Venetian gate in the western wall and the gloomy splendour of the interior of the Gothic cathedral. The meat market is bloodshot with the crimson aprons of the butchers and there is the sweep of the seaward wall and the triangular platea where at night the cafés overflow round the Italianate fountain. The harbour, which must have been an attractive one, is now so laid waste by the bombing that it still smells like a stonemason's yard.

But immediately outside the range of the town the countryside takes control of one. The ground rises gently behind the town to fall away again more steeply. The heat of July smoulders in sunset. The colour, drained from the sea, gathers into purple in the folds of Mount Luktas and flushes the massive peaks of Ida. Drifts of blue shadow lie in the curl of the plain. Beautiful and *violent*. Always, at the back of one's mind, is the half thought that southward, behind those mountains, there is nothing but the sea until you come to the desert coasts of Africa. This is the end of Europe. And for us Europeans a special excitement lies beyond our frontiers, West from Spain, South from Crete and East from Istanbul. One is out in that landscape of possibilities which is so much more than adequate to meet one's expectations.

For Crete is a place which one inevitably expects much of. It is the land of the Minotaur and the turgid mythology of Knossos; it was conquered by the Saracens; it was the home of the most bloodthirsty mercenaries and of El Greco. It was the scene of countless heroic episodes of revolt against the Sultans. It is the birthplace and grave of Zeus. On a map it catches the eye by its resemblance to a galleon pitching in a heavy sea. And Cretans, when you meet them away from home, appear larger and more vigorous than life.

127   *Minoan Crete*

IF we give ourselves up to the naive enjoyment of what Cretan pictorial art has to offer: the passionate beauty of plants in bloom, of youth at their games, the delicate mysteries of subaqueous life, colour and movement—but movement even more than colour— seem to be the secret of our enchantment, and above all its naturalness, the beauty of its freedom. For even human beings here move with the joyous ease of creatures at play. Can it be that the faint air of unreality which so many of the figures have for us . . . is in some way related to the fact that we have lost the grace of serious play so that we look upon it charmed but doubtful as something incompatible with our maturer world?

We would be guilty of an even worse absurdity . . . if we were to overstress the playful character of Minoan culture on the basis of an uncritical experience of its art. Yet we shall find that the concept of play may be more illuminating than appears at first sight. For the content of the scenes in fresco and relief, when compared with Egyptian or Mesopotamian work, is strikingly devoid of the peculiar seriousness which is theirs. Cretan artists not only revel in the beauty of natural forms; they also avoid depicting human achievement, whether in the modest sense of manual work—as in Egyptian tombs or in the challenging one of battles won, political power asserted.

They do not even boast of slaughter made in honour of the gods, or the building of temples. In fact, the lack of 'monumental art', so often emphasized by scholars who use the term more loosely than we do, is but a symptom of the very strangeness we are trying to define: Cretan civilization is unhistorical not only in the sense that the modern historian happens to be unable to write an articulate account of its past, a record in which events and personalities have name and character, but because it lacked the desire for monumental statement, pictorial or otherwise. We find no interest in single human achievement, no need to emphasize, to rescue its significance.

But if the scenes in which humans occur are thus devoid of this peculiar seriousness, they are by no means wholly frivolous, and here the concept play may be more than a tempting metaphor. I do not want to suggest that the action depicted pertains to that irresponsible world of play which feeds on the impulse of the player and dies with that impulse, a self-willed world under self-willed rules that can be called to life, annihilated, and revived at will. The acrobatic bull-jumping and the dances are neither irresponsible nor without function, for they are ritual acts, parts of religious festivals. And what distinguishes ritual from secular play is just the character of its seriousness. We might speak here of objective, as distinct from subjective seriousness. For it is true that secular play also may be 'taken seriously', but its importance remains within the framework of a limited self-created world that can always be recognized as such. Even the values of such a play-world are fictitious, the skill and courage required never wholly valid outside the limitations of the game's concrete fantasy; a self-imposed conflict or problem, and an arbitrary solution or victory, are its scope. But for the participants of ritual games, contests, and dances, these have an objective importance, for the issue is no more, no less than the problematic relation between human and superhuman forces, a problem mimed, that is, experienced and stated at the same time. Hence the contest is not felt to be self-imposed but, as it were, forced upon the players; and victory or solution not a feat, valueless outside its own restricted sphere, but a significant achievement. . . .

What concerns us here is not the possibly negative aspect of a one-sided religious orientation but its bearing on a unique artistic development. Cretan art ignored the terrifying distance between the human and the transcendent which may tempt man to seek a refuge in abstraction and to create a form for the significant remote from space and time; it equally ignored the glory and futility of single human acts, time-bound, space-bound. In Crete artists did not give substance to the world of the dead through an abstract of the world of the living, nor did they immortalize proud deeds or state a humble claim for divine attention in the temples of the gods. Here and here alone the human bid for timelessness was disregarded in the most complete acceptance of the grace of life the world has ever known. For life means movement and the beauty of movement was woven in the intricate web of living forms which we call 'scenes of nature'; was revealed in human-bodies acting their serious games, inspired by a transcendent presence, acting in freedom and restraint, unpurposeful as cyclic time itself.

128   *The pleasant valley of Suda, Crete*

BEING here disappointed of transportation to Archipelago, I advised to visit Candy: and in my way I past by the large Haven of Suda, which hath no Towne or Village, save onely a Castle, situated on a Rocke in the Sea, at the entry of the Bay: the bounds of that Harbour may receive at one time above two thousand Shippes and Galleys, and is the onely Key of the Iland: for the which place, the King of Spaine hath oft offered an infinite deale of money to the Venetians, whereby his Navy which sometimes resort in the Levante, might have accesse and reliefe, but they would never graunt him his request; which policy of his was onely to have surprized the King-dome.

South-west from this famous harbour, lieth a pleasant plaine surnamed the Valley of Suda: It is twenty Italian Miles long, and two of breadth: And I remember, or I discended to crosse the Valley, and passe the haven, me thought the whole planure resembled to me a greene sea; and that was onely by reason of infinite Olive trees grew there, whose boughs and leaves over-toppe all other fructiferous trees in that plaine: The Villages for losse of ground are all built on the skirts of Rockes, upon the South side of the Valley; yea, and so difficile to climbe them, and so dangerous to dwell in them, that me thought their lives were in like perill, as he who was adjoyned to sit under the poynt of a two handed sword, and it hanging by the haire of a horse tayle.

Trust me, I told along these Rockes at one time, and within my sight, some 67 Villages; but when I entred the valley, I could not find a foote of ground unmanured, save a narrow passing way wherein I was: The Olives, Pomgranets, Dates, Figges, Orenges, Lemmons, and Pomi del Adamo growing all through other: And at the rootes of which trees grew Wheate, Malvasie, Muscadine, Leaticke Wines, Grenadiers, Carnobiers, Mellones, and all other sorts of fruites and hearbes, the earth can yeeld to man; that for beauty, pleasure, and profit it may easily be surnamed, the garden of the whole Universe: being the goodliest plot, the Diamond sparke, and the Honny spot of all Candy: There is no land more temperate for ayre, for it hath a double spring-tyde; no soyle more fertile, and therefore it is called the Combat of Bachus and Ceres; nor region or valley more hospitable, in regard of the sea, having such a noble haven cut through its bosome, being as it were the resting place of Neptune.

129   *The Monastery of Gonia*

THE monastery of Gonia boards and lodges seventeen monks, and has a revenue of some £468. Its site is well chosen by the anchorite who in the first century of Christianity was concerned with its foundation. The walls of it rise sheer from the rocks which skirt the coast, so that a stone drops a hundred feet from the admirable little terrace which adjoins the guest-rooms of the monastery, before it touches ground. The great Bay of Canea with the farther mountain-

ous cape of Akrotiri are before it. The town of Canea, though eight or nine miles away, is distinctly seen across the blue water, as a graceful agglomerate of snowy houses—which, of course, it is not in reality. Between Canea and Gonia, a bright edging of sand by the shore, and the dark masses of olive-woods, spotted with small villages and isolated white houses which border the sand and continue to the base of the broken hills, form a very engaging foreground to the always impressive Madara Vouna. From Gonia, these mountains are unfolded like a huge white wing, and the sight of them fairly transports one into dreamland. As for the back of the monastery, that is steep rock, vermilion where it is naked, but otherwise thickly clothed with perfumed blossoms and many an aromatic herb that an untravelled herbalist might sigh for. So steep is it, indeed, that very little of it is seen from the building, and the two or three houses that are erected between it and the monastery seem to have their foothold hewn out of the matrix. A few hundred yards to the north, a precipitous bluff falls into the sea, and shuts off the view in that direction.

I was allowed to make this mental sketch of my surroundings when a bevy of the monks had escorted us into the new wing of the monastery, and out on the terrace, with intent to charm me into a short stay with them. What a sublime honeymoon might be enjoyed here, methought! . . .

Our early ramble over the cliffs had given all three of us a vigorous appetite. The monks vouched for their hunger by patting their stomachs; and they pointed to the sheaves of herbs and roots they had picked from the rocks, so that at first I imagined we were to stay our cravings with these alone. We did not return to the monastery, but made our way to a little cottage, bowered in high shrubs, standing on a sheltered plateau above the Gonia chimneys. And here, in a tiny garden filled with blossoming orange and lemon trees, mammoth pink geraniums, tall stocks, and scarlet verbenas, we found a table prepared for us, upon which the sunlight gleamed prismatically through the brake of leafage and flowers.

Adjoining the house was a strongly-barricaded building, like a stable, with cobwebbed windows looking into the garden. We deposited our botanical collection, and approached this building, the superior with a large key in his hand, and Father Jack with a wineglass. It was the Gonia buttery that we were about to attack—nothing less. And the next minute we were in the dim dusty room, with its rows of portly barrels, and an atmosphere that made me shiver, tasting the cool pure wines of the last year's vintage, and making our choice for the breakfast that was to follow. The superior confessed that they prided themselves upon their wine: there was a mere handful of gypsum in all their hogsheads put together.

By-the-bye, the following is the benedictory prayer which the Abbots of the Cretan monasteries say over their wine when the vintage is safely stored in the casks:

'O Lord God! Who lovest mankind, turn Thine eyes upon this wine, and on those who may drink of it; bless our casks as thou didst in old times bless Jacob's Well, the Pool of Siloam, and the wine drunk by the Holy Apostles. O Lord! Who wast present at the feast of Cana, and by the changing of water into wine manifested Thy glory to the young married couple, send now Thy Holy Spirit upon this wine, and bless it in Thy name. Amen.' . . .

Well, when we had selected our liquor, we returned to the table, and the superior clapped his hands. A sound was heard overhead, and soon afterwards a burly Turkish woman appeared, and gave the fathers a very unceremonious greeting. Then a child began to cry, and the woman, who was no doubt its mother, periodically left the preparation of our greens to upbraid the youngster from the foot of the stairs. I would not slander the good monks by imputation or assertion; but it seemed odd that this lone woman (a Turk, moreover) should have upon her the keeping of the monastic buttery, and the superintendence of such mild Horatian repasts as ours in the midst of romantic perfumes and flowers. However, there she was; and when she had dressed the herbs and squeezed the lemon-juice upon them and the roots, she stood with her fists in her sides and watched us at our meal. I drank her health, moreover; and it was significant that the superior cordially seconded me: Father Jack being less eager. We ate barley-bread, beans soaked in cold water, olives, and the mountain herbs; all which, combined with the wine, glass after glass, made a most healthful and pleasant meal, totally free from dyspeptic responsibilities. The kindly fellows beamed with a goodwill that I should have supposed to have been universal in its extent, but for one little circumstance. The woman left the room for a moment, and when she returned, a hungry-looking dog, with a scared expression, came in at her heels. But at the sight of the poor animal, Father Jack became demoniacal: he rose abruptly and shouted, and eventually kicked the dog through the doorway.

The superior, in acknowledgement of my look of surprise, just moved his shoulders, and said smilingly:

'It is a woman-dog!'

I was glad to see a calm smile of strength steal over the lips of the Turkish lady. . . .

ENVOI

A YOUTH of the village of Sgourokephali, who had great skill upon the lyre, used to accompany the Nereids to their cave and play to them. One of them more especially excited his admiration, and he appealed to a wise old woman of his village to reveal to him how he might gain her for his bride. The old woman bade him seize her by the hair when the time approached at which the cock crows, and never let go, whatever forms she might assume in order to terrify him or to elude his grasp, until the cock had crowed. Accordingly, the next time the Nereids took him to their cave, he played, as was his wont, for them to dance to; but when the hour of cock-crow drew near, he flung the lyre aside and clutched his beloved by the hair. At once she changed her aspect, and turned under his hand, like Proteus, into a dog, then into a snake, a camel, and at last into the semblance of fire. Just then the cock crew, the other Nereids disappeared, and his prisoner, reassuming her natural form, followed him quietly to the village, where within the space of a year she bore him a son. But all this while she was never heard to utter a word. Again he had recourse to the wise woman to aid him in breaking this spell of silence. She instructed him to heat the oven, which stands outside every Greek cottage, and then taking their boy, to say to the Nereid wife, 'As thou wilt not speak to me, I mean to burn the child,' and to feign the action of doing so. He again took her advice, and the Nereid found her voice, but only to cry, 'You hound, let go my child!' as she tore the infant from his hands and fled. The story goes on to say that, being a mother, she could not return to her sisters, and took up her abode in a neighbouring fountain, where now and then she might be seen holding the child in her arms.

In some stories a masculine form of the word occurs, the husband of the Nereid. Such a being plays a part in an account given me by the well-known Cretan chieftain, Captain Christodoulaki, of a fellow Sphakiote, whom he had known well, who was or pretended to be a very mysterious person, and had uncanny relations with powers mystical. As a child, he had disappeared for a long while, and was sought for all over the mountains. It was only after long seeking that his brother, who was calling his name, heard his voice answered, and going to the spot, found him in a strangely dazed condition. At length, he related that he had been carried off by a man and a woman to the high point where he was found; he had heard the voices of the seekers calling, but was prevented from answering by the woman, for they were Nereids. At last, the man and the woman fell out, and he took the opportunity of their coming to blows to answer the cry, but when his brother drew near, the Nereids disappeared.

From Crete also comes another story in which such male Nereids occur, taken down by the traveller Pashley in the early part of this century, as he heard it from the lips of a Sphakiote. Two men, his informant told him, went one fine moonlight night into the mountains to hunt the Cretan wild goat. They heard a great tumult, and at first supposed it to be a company of people coming to fetch snow to take to the city; but as they drew nearer, they heard the sound of musical instruments. Soon they discovered these were not mortals, but an assemblage of goblin beings, all clothed in varied garments, 'Both men and women, on foot and on horseback, a multitude of people; and the men were white as doves, and the women beautiful as the sunbeams.' Also it was evident that they were carrying something which resembled a bier. The mountaineers determined to shoot at the aerial host as they passed along singing—

> We go, we go to fetch the lady bride
> From the steep rock, a solitary nymph.

As the shot was fired, those who were last in the procession exclaimed; 'They've murdered our bridegroom—they've murdered our bridegroom!' and as they thus exclaimed they wept, and shrieked, and fled.

There must have existed among the ancient Greeks, as there undoubtedly exists among the modern population of this land, some subtle instinct suggesting a divinity inherent in certain spots of earth

of exceptional beauty, of striking grandeur, or of solitude; some close
sympathy with nature, due rather to feeling than to a rational process, such as that which has evoked the nature-lore of Northern poets.
It is possible that this very susceptibility makes it difficult for them to
analyse the feeling, and reason upon it, and we may be quite wrong
in attributing to the Southern character a want of appreciation of
what in reality they keenly feel, as indeed they show when placed in
other surroundings. This same instinct perhaps it was that suggested
the anxious sense of the weirdness of midday, in the pause and rest of
nature in a summer land through the hottest hours of noon, which,
indeed, all who are sensitive to the impressions of nature will acknowledge has some intangible influence on man and beast, in its
stillness, its intensity, its brilliance, and which can only be compared
to the influence of the full moon on a summer night in the South.
It was this feeling which found expression in the representation of the
sleep of Pan, set in the mouth of the swain of Theocritus:

> O shepherd, not at noon, we may not pipe at noon,
> For Pan we dread, who then comes from the chase
> Weary, and takes his rest.

131 *Betrayal*

NIGHT it was, dear, when we kissed:
   Who could have seen us?
It was the night and dawn that saw,
   It was the moon and stars.
A star leant down and told the sea,
   The sea, it told the oar,
The oar spoke to the sailor, and
   The sailor went and sang it
At the window of his love.

132   *Night*

THE Moon is gone
And the Pleiads set,
Midnight is nigh;
Time passes on,
And passes, yet
Alone I lie.

133   *The Lament of the Seal*

BELOW the sea-washed cliff, where the path that begins at
Mamogianni's mill passes, with the Cemetery opposite and to the
west the low jutting-out shore called by the village-children, who all
summer from dawn to dusk bathe there, 'The Shell'—it seems that it
has this shape—down this path, at twilight, goes, a basket under her
arm, Mother Loukaina, a poor shrivelled woman, to wash her wool-
len sheets in the salt wave and to rinse them afterwards in the small
fresh-water spring that trickles from the slate rocks and falls gently
into the sea. Slowly she descended the slope of the path, singing with
quiet voice a sad lament and holding at the same time her hand to her
brow to shade her eyes from the dazzle of the sun which was going
down behind the mountain opposite, and which caressed before her
the small garden and the white-washed tombs of the dead, shining
in the last rays.

She remembered the five children she had buried in that threshing-floor of death, in that garden of decay, one after the other, many
years ago, when she was still young. Two girls and three boys—in
their childhood had insatiable death harvested them.

Recently he had taken her husband, and two sons alone were left
her, abroad now: one, they told her, had gone to Australia and for
three years he had not written; she didn't know what had become of
him; the other, the younger, travelled with ships in the Mediter-

ranean, and sometimes he still remembered her; one daughter she also had, married, with half a dozen children.

With her now in her old age Mother Loukaina worked, and for her she went down the footpath, to wash the woollens and other clothes in the salt wave and to rinse them afterwards in the fresh-water spring.

The old woman bent at the edge of the sea-eaten rock and began to wash the clothes. To her right fell sharply the smooth cliff of the hill on which the Cemetery stood and down whose slopes rolled always towards the all-welcoming sea bits of rotten wood from un-earthed coffins, relics of human skeletons, fragments of gold slippers or of gold-embroidered bodices of young women which had been buried with them, threads of blond hair and other spoils of death. Above her head, a little to the right, in a small hidden hollow beside the Cemetery, a young shepherd, returning with his flock from the fields, had sat down and, without thinking of the sorrow of the place, had taken his pipe from his bag and had begun to play a lively shepherd's song. The old woman stopped her lament at the sound of the pipe, and those who at that hour came back from the fields—the sun meanwhile had set—heard only the flute, and looked to see who the player was; but he was not visible, hidden among the bushes in the deep hollows of the cliff.

A sailing-boat had raised her sails and was circling in the harbour. But there was not enough wind for her and she never reached the west point. A seal, feeding there in the deep water close by, had heard perhaps the quiet lament of the old woman, and was drawn now by the loud piping of the young shepherd, and came out, into the shadows, spelled by the sound and rocking on the waves. A young girl, Akrivoula, the grandchild of the old woman, aged nine years, sent perhaps by her mother or more probably stealing away from her watchfulness and learning that her grandmother was down in 'The Shell', washing on the shore, came to find her, to play a little in the sea. But she did not know where the path began, by Mamogi-anni's mill, opposite the Cemetery, and when she heard the pipe she went towards it and found the hidden piper; and when she had heard him play enough and had taken pride in the young shepherd, she saw there, in the evening twilight, a small path, very abrupt and steep, and she thought that that was the path by which her grandmother had gone down; and she took that abrupt, steep path, to reach the shore, to find her. And by now it was quite dark.

The little girl went some steps down. Then she saw that the path became still more precipitous. She called out, and tried to climb up, to go back. She found herself on the brow of a projecting rock, some twelve feet above the sea. The sky darkened, clouds covered the stars, the moon was on the wane. She tried to find the way by which she had descended, but could not. She turned again and tried to go down. She slipped and fell bloomp! into the water. The water was as deep as the rock was high. Two fathoms at least. The pipe's sound hid her cry. The shepherd heard a splash, but from where he was he could not see the base of the rock and the sea-shore. Besides, he had not taken much notice of the little girl and had scarcely felt her presence.

As it became dark, Mother Loukaina had filled her basket and had begun to go up the path, on her way home. As she went, she heard a splash, turned and gazed into the darkness, towards the shepherd.

'Souravlis it will be,' she said, for she knew him. 'It's not enough that he wakes the dead with his pipe, he has to throw stones on to the shore as well. . . . Ill-starred clumsy fool that he is.'

And she went on her way.

And the sailing-boat continued to circle in the harbour, and the young shepherd to blow his pipe in the silence of the night.

And the seal, as she came up into the shallows, found the drowned body of the poor Akrivoula, and began to move round it, and to lament, before beginning her evening meal.

The lament of the seal, which the old Fisherman, skilled in the dumb language of seals, has translated into human words, goes something like this:

This was little Akrivoula
Grand-daughter of Mother Loukaina.

274

ENVOI

Sea-weed is her marriage-crown,
Shells are her dowry . . .
The old woman still laments
Her ancient child-bearing:
As if the world's pain and sorrow
Never ended, never ended.

ACKNOWLEDGEMENTS

THE compiler and publisher of this Anthology would like to thank the following authors, publishers, and literary agents for permission to include many poems and prose passages:

1. Miss M. Aravantinou, author of an unpublished work on the Meteora Monasteries.
2. The Authorised Version of the Bible is Crown Copyright and extracts printed herein appear with permission.
3. Cambridge University Press, publishers of C. Lawson's *Modern Greek Folklore and Ancient Greek Religion*.
4. Jonathan Cape Ltd., publishers of William Plomer's *Ali the Lion*.
5. Mr Odysseus Elytis, author of the poems, *Drinking the Sun of Corinth* and *Aegean Melancholy*.
6. Faber and Faber Ltd., publishers of H. A. Groenewegen-Frankfort's *Arrest and Movement*; of Lawrence Durrell's *Prospero's Cell, A Private Country*, and *Cities, Plains and People*; of Louis MacNeice's translation of Aeschylus' *Agamemnon*; and of Barry Sullivan's translation of E. Kaestner's *Mount Athos*.
7. The Faith Press Ltd., publishers of *The Undistorted Image* by the Archimandrite Sophrony, which contains the English translation of the writings of the Staretz Silouan of Mount Athos.
8. S. Fischer Verlag, publishers of Hugo von Hofmannsthal's *Griechenland*.
9. Mr Michael Hamburger, translator of Hölderlin's *Patmos*.
10. William Heinemann Ltd., and New Directions, N.Y., publishers of Henry Miller's *The Colossus of Maroussi*.
11. International Authors N.V., copyright owners of 'Ouzo Unclouded' by Robert Graves (published in *New Poems 1962*, Cassell & Co. Ltd.).
12. Professor Romilly Jenkins, translator of Kostis Palamas' *Monk of Athos*.
13. Mr N. D. Karouzos, author of the poem, *Triplets for Beautiful Mistra*.
14. Mr Christopher Kininmonth, author of *The Children of Thetis*.
15. Mr Photis Kontoglou, author of *Travels* (Athens, 1928).
16. Mr John Lehmann, the literary executor of Demetrios Capetanakis, for permission to include *The Isles of Greece*.
17. The Lutterworth Press, publishers of Sydney Loch's *Athos: The Holy Mountain*.

18. John Murray (Publishers) Ltd., publishers of Patrick Leigh Fermor's *Mani*.

19. Peter Owen Ltd., publishers of Marco Pallis' *The Way and the Mountain*.

20. A. D. Peters, literary agents for Mr Kevin Andrews, author of *The Flight of Ikaros* (Weidenfeld and Nicolson, London, 1959).

21. Librairie Plon, publishers of *Le Voyage de Sparte* by Maurice Barrès.

22. Presses Universitaires de France, publishers of *La Philosophie Byzantine* by B. Tatakis.

23. Lord Rennell of Rodd, literary executor of Rennell Rodd, translator of 'Mycenæ' by Alpheus and author of *The Customs and Lore of Modern Greece*.

24. Routledge and Kegan Paul, publishers of Robert Byron's *The Byzantine Achievement* and *The Station*, and of E. Rohde's *Psyche*, translated by W. B. Hillis.

25. Martin Secker & Warburg Ltd., publishers of 'The Old Ships' by James Elroy Flecker.

26. Mr George Seferis, author of *Delphi* (Athens, 1963) and of the poem, *Santorini*.

27. Mrs Anna Sikelianou, for Anghelos Sikelianos' *The Sacred Way* and *In the Monastery of St Luke*.

28. W. J. N. Sowels and the executors of J. M. Edmonds, translator of 'Night' by Sappho.

29. Ullstein Verlag, publishers of *Grieschischer Frühling* by Gerhart Hauptmann.

30. The Vittoriale, Gardone, Italy, executors of Gabriele D'Annunzio, author of *La Città Morta*, and Arnoldo Mondadori, his publishers.

31. Mr Rex Warner, author of *Views of Attica* (London, 1950).

LIST OF SOURCES

*(The numbering follows the order in which the prose passages
and poems appear in the Anthology. All translations unless
otherwise stated are by the compiler.)*

1. Lawrence Durrell [b. 1912], *Prospero's Cell* (London, 1945), p. 11.

2. I. Dragoumis [1878–1920], *Greek Civilization* (2nd ed. Athens, 1927), p. 230. In Greek.

3. Hugo von Hofmannsthal [1874–1929], *Griechenland* (1922).

4. Robert Byron [1905–41], *The Byzantine Achievement* (London, 1929), pp. 21-22.

5. George Gordon, 6th Lord Byron [1788–1824], Note to *Childe Harold's Pilgrimage* (London, 1812).

6. W. M. Thackeray [1811–63], *Notes of a Journey from Cornhill to Grand Cairo* (London, 1846), pp. 65 ff.

7. Anon., *Sketches in Greece and Turkey* (London, 1833), pp. 196 ff.

8. Gabriele d'Annunzio [1864–1938], *La Città Morta* (1898).

9. F. W. Nietzsche [1844–1900], *The Will to Power* [1887] (trans. by Anthony Ludovici).

10. Konstantine Mavroyannis [1816–61], *Observations on the Climate of Athens* (Athens, 1841), p. 40. In Greek.

11. Patrick Leigh Fermor [b. 1915], *Mani* (London, 1959), pp. 286-288.

12. Clement of Alexandria [b. *c.* A.D. 150], *Stromateis*, V, 104, I ff.

13. Plato [428–347 B.C.], *Phaedrus*, 249 D ff.

14. Demetrios Capetanakis [1912–44], from: *Demetrios Capetanakis: A Greek Poet in England* (London, 1947).

15. Greek Folk Song.

16. W. M. Thackeray [1811–63], *Notes of a Journey from Cornhill to Grand Cairo* (London, 1846), pp. 69 ff.

17. Pericles Yannopoulos [1869–1910], *The Greek Line* (ed. Athens, 1961), pp. 75 ff. In Greek.

18. F. R. de Chateaubriand [1768–1848], *Travels in Greece, Palestine, Egypt, and Barbary during the years 1806–1807* (trans. by Frederic Snoberl).

19. Plato [428–347 B.C.], *Socrates' Apologia*, 38 C ff.

20. The Acts of the Apostles, 17, 15–34.

21. General Makriyannis [1797–1864], *Memoirs* (2nd ed. Athens, 1947), Vol. I, pp. 288 ff. In Greek.

22. Anonymous [20th cent.].

23. Sophocles [496–405 B.C.], *Oedipus at Colonus*, 1587 ff.

24. Rex Warner [b. 1905], *Views of Attica* (London, 1950), pp. 55 ff.

25. Anghelos Sikelianos [1884–1951], from: *Lyrical Life* (Athens, 1946–1947), Vol. 3, pp. 204 ff.

26. Marco Pallis, *The Way and the Mountain* (London, 1960), pp. 30–31.

27. Herodotus [*c.* 484–425 B.C.], *The History*, VIII, 65 (trans. by G. C. Macaulay).

28. Thomas Taylor [1758–1835], *Dissertation on the Eleusinian and Bacchic Mysteries* (London, 1791), pp. 93 ff.

29. Rex Warner [b. 1905], *Views of Attica* (London, 1950), pp. 67 ff.

30. Euripides [*c.* 484–407 B.C.], *Bacchae*, 677 ff.

31. Kevin Andrews [b. 1924], *The Flight of Ikaros* (London, 1959), pp. 123–125.

32. Odysseus Elytis [b. 1911], from: *The First Sun* (Athens, 1943).

33. Maurice Barrès [1862–1923], *Le Voyage de Sparte* (ed. Paris, 1906), pp. 155 ff.

34. Lawrence Durrell [b. 1912], from: *A Private Country* (London, 1943).

35. Rex Warner [b. 1905], *Views of Attica* (London, 1950), pp. 115 ff.

36. Alpheus [2nd cent. A.D.] (trans. by Rennell Rodd).

37. Gabriele d'Annunzio [1864–1938], *La Città Morta* (1898).

38. Aeschylus [525–456 B.C.], *Agamemnon*, 1085 ff. (trans. by Louis MacNeice).

39. Photis Kontoglou [b. 1895], *Travels* (Athens, 1928), pp. 13 ff. In Greek.

40. William Lithgow [1582–?1645], *Comments upon Greece, 1609* from *The Totall Discourse of the Rare Adventures and Painefull Peregrinations of William Lithgow* (Glasgow, 1906), pp. 62 ff.

41. Pausanias [2nd cent. A.D.], *Description of Greece*, 2, 27.

42. Henry Miller [b. 1892], *The Colossus of Maroussi* (London, 1945), pp. 74 ff.

43. Robert Graves [b. 1895]. *New Poems 1962*, © International Authors N.V. (London, 1962).

44. F. R. de Chateaubriand [1768–1848], *Travels in Greece, Palestine, Egypt, and Barbary during the years 1806–1807* (trans. by Frederic Snoberl).

45. Maurice Barrès [1862–1923], *Le Voyage de Sparte* (Paris, 1906), pp. 234 ff.

46. Maurice Barrès, *Le Voyage de Sparte* (Paris, 1906), pp. 221 ff.

47. Photis Kontoglou [b. 1895], *Travels* (Athens, 1928), pp. 88 ff. In Greek.

48. Maurice Barrès, *Le Voyage de Sparte* (Paris, 1906), pp. 243 ff.

49. B. Tatakis, *La Philosophie Byzantine* (Paris, 1949), pp. 283 ff.

50. Robert Byron [1905–41], *The Station* (London, 1928), pp. 209–210.

51. N. D. Karouzos, from: *The Hind of the Stars* (Athens, 1962). In Greek.

52. Kevin Andrews [b. 1924], *The Flight of Ikaros* (London, 1959), pp. 86–90.

53. Patrick Leigh Fermor [b. 1915], *Mani* (London, 1959), pp. 66–67 and pp · 82–83.

54. John B. S. Morrit of Rokeby [1772?–1843], *Letters* (London, 1914), pp. 199 ff.

55. Anon., *Sketches in Greece and Turkey* (London, 1833), pp. 89 ff.

56. Patrick Leigh Fermor, *Mani* (London, 1959), pp. 54–55.

57. Greek Folk Song (trans. by Rennell Rodd).

58. From the Orthodox Service for the Burial of the Dead.

59. Greek Folk Song.

60. Gustave Flaubert [1821–80], *Voyage en Orient, 1849–1851*, Œuvres Complètes Illustrées, Édition du Centenaire (Paris, 1925), pp. 322 ff.

61. Gerhart Hauptmann [1862–1946], *Griechischer Frühling* (Berlin, 1921), pp. 70 ff.

62. George Gordon, 6th Lord Byron [1788–1824], *Childe Harold's Pilgrimage* (London, 1812), XLI ff.

63. Homer [?8th cent. B.C.], *Odyssey*, XIV.

64. Porphyry [b. c. A.D. 233], *On the Cave of the Nymphs* (London, 1917), pp. 5 ff. (translated by Thomas Taylor).

65. Henry Miller [b. 1892], *The Colossus of Maroussi* (London, 1945), pp. 103–105.

66. Master Thomas Dallam, *Diary 1599–1600* (Hakluyt Society, London, 1893), pp. 19 ff.

67. Edward Lear [1812–88], *Letters* (ed. by Lady Strachey, London, 1907), pp. 234 ff.

68. William Fletcher, in: The Westminster Review, 1824.

69. John L. Stephens, *Incidents of Travel in Greece, Turkey, Russia, and Poland* (Edinburgh, 1839), p. 6.

70. Dionysios Solomos [1798–1857], *The Woman of Zakynthos* (c. 1827). In Greek.

71. Nicholas Kasomoulis [1792–1872], *Military Memoirs* (Athens, 1939–1942), Vol. 2, pp. 256 ff. In Greek.

72. Gerhart Hauptmann [1862–1946], *Griechischer Frühling* (Berlin, 1921), pp. 159 ff.

73. Plato [428–347 B.C.], *Phaedrus*, 244 A–B.

74. Pindar [518–c. 438 B.C.], *Pythian I*, 1 ff.

75. Anonymous [20th cent.].

76. Heracleitus [c. 500 B.C.], fr. 93.

77. George Seferis [b. 1900], *Delphi* (Athens, 1963), pp. 13–14. In Greek.

78. Sir George Wheler [1650–1723], *A Journey into Greece* (London, 1682), pp. 321 ff.

79. Photis Kontoglou [b. 1895], *Travels* (Athens, 1928), pp. 63 ff. In Greek.

80. Anghelos Sikelianos [1884–1951], from: *Lyrical Life* (Athens, 1946–1947), Vol. 3, pp. 209 ff.

81. Greek Folk Song (trans. by Rennell Rodd).

82. Kostas Pasagianis [1872–1933], *Greek Travels* (Athens, 1931). In Greek.

83. Edward Lear [1812–88], *Journals of a Landscape Painter in Albania and Illyria* (2nd ed., London, 1852), pp. 371 ff.

84. Kostas Pasagianis [1872–1933], *Greek Travels* (Athens, 1931). In Greek.

85. William Plomer [b. 1903], *Ali the Lion* (London, 1939), pp. 58 ff., pp. 93 ff., and pp. 111 ff.

86. M. Aravantinou, from an unpublished work on the Meteora Monasteries [20th cent.].

87. St Basil the Great [329–379] (trans. by W. K. L. Clarke).

88. The Hon. Robert Curzon [1810–73], *Visits to Monasteries in the Levant* (London, 1849), pp. 243 ff.

89. Edward Lear [1812–88], *Journals of a Landscape Painter in Albania and Illyria* (2nd ed. London, 1852), pp. 391 ff.

90. Hesiod [8th cent. B.C.], *Works and Days*, 504 ff.

91. Greek Folk Song.

92. Kevin Andrews [b. 1924], *The Flight of Ikaros* (London, 1959), pp. 235–239.

93. E. Rohde [1845–98], *Psyche* (London, 1925), p. 256 ff. (trans. by W. B. Hillis).

94. *The Book of Sir John Maundeville, A.D. 1322–1356*, in *Early Travels in Palestine*, ed. by Thomas Wright (London, 1848), p. 135.

95. The Hon. Robert Curzon [1810–73], *Visits to Monasteries in the Levant* (London, 1849), p. 303 ff.

96. John Covel [1638–1722], *Account of Athos* (1677), from: *The Journal of John Covel*, printed with notes by F. W. Hasluck in the *Annual of the British School at Athens*, XVII, pp. 103–131.

97. Z. Papantoniou [1877–1940], *The Holy Mountain* (Athens, 1934), p. 78 ff. In Greek.

98. Nicephorus the Solitary of Athos (d. c. 1340), from: *The Philokalia* (Venice, 1782), p. 870. In Greek.

99. Abba Philemon, from: *The Philokalia* (Venice, 1782), p. 486. In Greek.

100. Konstantinos Dapontes, *The Garden of Graces* (Athens, 1880). In Greek.

101. Symeon the New Theologian (d. c. 1022), in *The Works of St Symeon the New Theologian*, ed. by Dionysios Zagoraios (Venice, 1790), Part 2, p. 115.

102. Sydney Loch, *Athos, The Holy Mountain* (London, 1957), pp. 81 ff.

103. Z. Papantoniou [1877–1940], *The Holy Mountain* (Athens, 1934), pp. 176 ff. In Greek.

104. Kostis Palamas [1815–1943], from: *Fatherlands* in *Life Immovable*, Vol. 4 of the Poetical Works of Kostis Palamas (Athens, 1952), p. 10 (trans. by Romilly Jenkins).

105. E. Kaestner, *Mount Athos* (London, 1961), pp. 138–140 (trans. by Barry Sullivan).

106. Silouan of the Holy Mountain (d. 1938), from: *The Undistorted Image*, by the Archimandrite Sophrony (London, 1958), pp. 162–163.

107. Robert Byron [1905–41], *The Byzantine Achievement* (London, 1929), pp. 7–8.

108. I. Dragoumis, *Samothrace* (2nd ed. Athens, 1926), pp. 5 ff. In Greek.

109. A. W. Kinglake [1809–91], *Eothen* (Leipzig, 1846), pp. 62 ff.

110. Odysseus Elytis [b. 1911], from: *Orientations* (Athens, 1940).

111. Pericles Yannopoulos [1869–1910], *The Greek Line* (Athens, 1961), pp. 101 ff. In Greek.

112. Christopher Kininmonth, *The Children of Thetis* (London, 1949), pp. 143 ff.

113. Herman Melville [1819–91], from 'Syra'. First stanza omitted.

114. J. T. Bent [1852–97], *The Cyclades* (London, 1885), pp. 242 ff.

115. J. T. Bent, *The Cyclades* (London, 1885), pp. 215 ff.

116. Lawrence Durrell [b. 1912], from: *Cities, Plains and People* (London, 1946).

117. Christopher Kininmonth, *The Children of Thetis* (London, 1949), pp. 121 ff.

118. Friedrich Hölderlin [1770–1843] (trans. by Michael Hamburger).

119. The Revelation of St John the Divine on Patmos, 21, 1 ff.

120. James Elroy Flecker [1884–1915].

121. A. W. Kinglake [1809–91], *Eothen* (Leipzig, 1846), pp. 60–61.

122. W. M. Thackeray [1811–63], *Notes of a Journey from Cornhill to Grand Cairo* (London, 1846), pp. 140 ff.

123. From an anonymous contemporary account, ed. by I. Vouros in the *Anthology of Useful Knowledge*, ed. by D. Anselmos (Athens, March 1837), pp. 50 ff. In Greek.

124. George Seferis [b. 1900], from: *Poems 1924–1946* (Athens, 1950), pp. 81 ff.

125. C. Lawson, *Modern Greek Folklore and Ancient Greek Religion* (Cambridge, 1910), pp. 574 ff.

126. Christopher Kininmonth, *The Children of Thetis* (London, 1949), pp. 176 ff.

127. H. A. Groenewegen-Frankfort, *Arrest and Movement* (London, 1951), pp. 185–187 and p. 216.

128. William Lithgow, *Comments upon Crete, 1609–1610*, from *The Totall Discourse of the Rare Adventures and Painefull Peregrinations of William Lithgow* (Glasgow, 1906), pp. 76 ff.

129. Charles Edwardes, *Letters from Crete* (London, 1887), pp. 305 ff.

130. Rennell Rodd, *The Customs and Lore of Modern Greece* (London, 1892), pp. 178 ff.

131. Greek Folk Song.

132. Attributed to Sappho [b. *c.* 612 B.C.] (trans. by J. M. Edmonds).

133. Alexander Papadiamantis [1851–1911], from: *Songs of God*. A selection of the Short Stories of Alexander Papadiamantis (Athens, 1962), pp. 217 ff. In Greek.

LIST OF AUTHORS

(Numbers refer to pages on which extracts start)

Aeschylus, 71
Alpheus, 70
Andrews, Kevin, 62, 107, 185
Anonymous, 23, 30, 42, 113, 118, 120,
    154, 167, 184, 250, 271
Aravantinou, M., 177

Barrès, Maurice, 64, 91, 93, 97
Basil, St, 179
Bent, J. T., 228, 231
Byron, George Gordon, Lord, 22, 129
Byron, Robert, 21, 102, 215

Capetanakis, Demetrios, 30
Chateaubriand, F. R. de, 36, 89
Clement of Alexandria, 28
Covel, John, 199
Curzon, Hon. Robert, 180, 197

Dallam, Master Thomas, 134
D'Annunzio, Gabriele, 24, 70
Dapontes, Konstantinos, 204
Dragoumis, I., 19, 216
Durrell, Lawrence, 19, 66, 234

Edwardes, Charles, 262
Elytis, Odysseus, 64, 222
Euripides, 61

Fermor, Patrick Leigh, 26, 110, 117
Flaubert, Gustave, 120
Flecker, James Elroy, 246
Fletcher, William, 143

Graves, Robert, 85
Groenewegen-Frankfort, H. A., 259

Hauptmann, Gerhart, 123, 150
Heracleitus, 156
Herodotus, 53
Hesiod, 183
Hofmannsthal, H. von, 20
Hölderlin, Friedrich, 236
Homer, 129

John, St (the Divine), 243

Kaestner, E., 210
Karouzos, N. D., 103
Kasomoulis, Nicholas, 148
Kinglake, A. W., 217, 247
Kininmonth, Christopher, 225, 234,
    257
Kontoglou, Photis, 74, 94, 161

Lawson, C., 252
Lear, Edward, 138, 169, 182
Lithgow, William, 79, 261
Loch, Sydney, 205
Luke, St, 20

Makriyannis, General, 40
Maundeville, Sir John, 197
Mavroyannis, Konstantine, 26
Melville, Herman, 227
Miller, Henry, 83, 132
Morrit of Rokeby, John B. S., 112

285

Nicephorus the Solitary of Athos, 202
Nietzsche, Friedrich, 24

Palamas, Kostis, 209
Pallis, Marco, 53
Papadiamantis, Alexander, 272
Papantoniou, Z., 200, 208
Pasagianis, Kostas, 168, 171
Pausanias, 82
Philemon, Abba, 203
Pindar, 153
Plato, 29, 38, 153
Plomer, William, 172
Porphyry, 131

Rodd, Rennell, 269
Rohde, E., 189

Sappho, 272
Seferis, George, 156, 251
Sikelianos, Anghelos, 50, 163
Silouan of the Holy Mountain, 211
Solomos, Dionysios, 146
Sophocles, 47
Stephens, John L., 145
Symeon, St, the New Theologian, 205

Tatakis, B., 100
Taylor, Thomas, 54
Thackeray, W. M., 23, 33, 247

Warner, Rex, 48, 56, 67
Wheler, Sir George, 156

Yannopoulos, Pericles, 34, 223

INDEX

Acheron, 173, 174
Achilles, 21
Acropolis, Athens, 2, 33, 34, 36, 37, 49, 132
—, Mycenae, 67, 68
Addison, Joseph, 8
Adonis, 36, 252
Aegaleos, Mount, 36
Aegean, the, 215, 222, 223, 224, 227
Aegisthus, 68
Aegosthena, 67
Aeneas, 81
Aeschylus, 3, 19
Agamemnon, 68
Agave, 61
Akrotiri, 263
Albania(ns), 10, 19, 37, 89, 129, 171, 174, 215
Alexander the Great, 4
Alexandria, 4
Ali Pasha, 171, 172, 175, 176
Alpheios (Alpheius), 121, 124, 125
Amyclae, 89
Anchesmus, Mount, 37
Andritzena, 120
Antioch, 4
Aphrodite, 36
Apollo, 49, 151, 153
—, priests of, 150
Arcadia, 79, 99
Ardettos, 34
Areopagus, 37, 39
Arethusa, 124
Arta, bridge of, 167–8
Asclepius, 82
Athanasius, St of Athos, 200
—, St of the Meteora, 177–8
Athene, 129

Athens, 34, 37
Athos, Mount, 177, 178, 197, 198, 201, 204, 209, 210
Atreus, 68, 69, 74
Atridae, palace of, 68
Autonoë, 61

Bacchus, 37, 56
Barlaam, monastery of, Meteora, 180
Basil the Great, St, 204
Bessarion, John, Cardinal, 101
Bessoi, the, 194
Blake, William, 12
Boniface, 75
Bulis, 159
Burne Jones, Sir Edward, 12
Byron, George Gordon, 6th Baron, 9, 22, 143–5, 174
Byron, Robert, 1, 3
Byzantium, 12, 14, 215

Calabria, 19
Canea, 258, 262, 263
Cantacuzene, Manuel, 95
Capodistrias, Count John, 114, 115
Cardamyle, 113
Cassandra, 68, 71–4, 93
Charon (Charos), 117, 118, 233
Christodoulaki, Capt., 269
Chrysobuls, 177
Cithaeron, see Kithaeron
Clytemnestra, 68, 70
Colocotronis, T., 76
Constantinople, 157, 161, 215, 250
Corfu, 19, 133, 139, 215
Corinth, 38, 63, 64, 66
Corpus Eremiticum, 210
Corydallus, Mount, 36

Crete, 215, 257–65
Cronius, 131,
Cythera, 92, 99

Dalton, O., 12
Damaris, 40
Daniel the Hesychast, 178
Daphni, 48
De Lisle, Leconte, 65
Delos, 38, 82, 224, 229, 234
Delphi, 69, 150–3, 154–5, 156, 194
Demaratos the Lacedemonian, 53, 54
Demeter, 51, 54, 55, 56
Demetrios, St, church of, Athens, 34
Dervish-Tcheleby, 122
Dicaios, 53
Dionysos (Dionysus), 24, 25, 125, 150,
    151, 189–94, 235, 236
Dionysius the Areopagite, 40
Dioscuri, the, 93
Dodona, 153, 171
Durrell, Lawrence, 14

Eleusinians, 55, 56
Eleusis, 50, 52, 53–4, 151
Eleutherae, 67
El Greco, 49, 259
Ephesus, 4, 234
Epicureans, 39
Epidaurus, 36, 82, 83–5
Epiros, 168–9, 171
Erythrae, 61
Etna, Mount, 154
Eurotas, 90, 91, 92
Evans, Sir Arthur, 11

Fallmerayer, J. Ph., 11
Fanariotes, the, 23
Faust, 98, 210, 211
Fauvel, M., 37
Finlay, G., 11
Fourmont, Abbé, 89
Frankopoulos, John, 95

Franks, 22, 74
Furies, the, 4

Garthikaki, 169
Gibbon, Edward, 8, 12
Goethe, 25, 94, 211
Gonia, monastery of, Crete, 262–5
Gregory of Sinai, St, 178
Gregory Palamas, St, 178, 179
Grosso, Cape, 107, 108
Gytheion, See Yitheion

Hades, 55, 117
Helen, 80, 93–4, 98, 100
Helikon, 63, 64, 160
Hellas, 9
Hellenika, 100
Hera, 125
Heracleitus, 28
Herakleion, 258
Hercules, 125
Herodes Atticus, 37
Hierotheos, Bishop of Koritsa, 205–7
Homer, 3, 5, 131, 132, 193
Hyacinthus, 89
Hymettos (Hymettus), Mount, 36, 37,
    224
Hysiae, 61

Iamblichus, 101
Icarus, Mount, 36
Ida, Mount, 258
Independence, Greek War of, 8, 10
Io, 61
Ioannina (Yannina), 169–71, 171, 172,
    175
Italy, 1, 8, 19
Ithaca, 129, 131

Jardanus, 121
John, St, 243, 257
—, Knights of, 248
Jourdain, Admiral, 76

Jupiter, 79
—, temple of, 37

Kakovóuni, 107
Keats, John, 14
Kierkegaard, S., 200, 201
Kifissia, 42
Kissavos, Mount, 184
Kithaeron (Cithaeron), 2, 36, 61, 63
Kitta, 111
Klephts, 28, 174
Knossos, 11, 14, 258, 259
Kronos, 123
Kunghi, 176, 177
Kybele, 190

Lacedaemon (Lacedemon), 79, 90
Laura, St, monastery of, Athos, 197, 200, 202
Lawrence, D. H., 14
Leda, 93
Lethaby, W. R., 12
Litharitza, fortress of, 170, 171
Luke Stiriotes, St, monastery of, 156, 161, 162, 163
Luktas, Mount, 258
Lycabettos(us), 34, 37
Lycurgus, 90, 92

Mani (Maina), 107, 109, 112, 113, 114, 115, 116
Mavromichaelis, George, 114, 115
—, Pietro, 113–16
Menelaeon, 92, 99
Meteora, 177, 180, 181
Minutius Felix, 54
Missolonghi, 145, 146–7, 149–50
Mistra, 94, 97–9, 100, 102, 103
Mitzikeli, Mount, 170, 171
Morea, 79
Morosini, General, 74, 75
Morris, William, 12
Mycenae, 11, 67–9, 70, 80

Mykonos, 224, 231
Mýtikas, 186, 187, 188, 189

Naiades, the (see also Nereids), 131, 132
Nauplia, 74–8
Naxos, 224, 234
Nemea, 66
Nereids, the, 269, 270
Nevison, H. W., 2
Nietzsche, F., 11
Nomia, 111

Odysseus, 129–30
Oedipus, 38, 47, 48
Olympia, 123
Olympos(us), Mount, 28, 184, 185–9, 209
Olytzika, Mount, 171
Orestes, 4, 68, 69
Orpheus, 56
Orphism, 154
Ossa, Mount, 28

Palaeologoi, palace of, 95
Paleokastrizza, 138, 139
Pan, 9, 152, 169, 235, 271
Pantanassa, monastery of, Mistra, 95, 96, 98, 102, 103
Parnassos(us), 64, 66, 154
Parnes, 2, 36
Paros, 224, 235
Parthenon, 11, 37, 48
Patmos, 236, 238, 243
Paul, St, 39, 40
Pausanias, 159, 161
Pausias, 82
Pegasus, 66
Peloponnesus (Peloponnese), 63, 120
Peneus, 183
Pentelicus, 36
Persephone (Proserpine), 54, 55, 80, 228, 247, 252

Petrarch, 6
Phaedriades, the, 150
Phaestos, 257
Pharos, 224
Phidias, 125
Philopappus, 34, 35, 37
Phrosini, 171
Phrygians, 190
Piero della Francesa, 49
Piraeus, 33, 38, 249
Plato, 2, 100, 101, 152
Plethon, Gemistos, 100–1, 155
Pluto, 54, 55
Pnyx, the, 37
Polycleitus, 82
Porphyry, 101
Porto Catena, 78
Princes' Islands, 215
Proclus, 55, 101
Psellos, 101
Pythagoras, 55
Pythia, Pythian, 152, 194

Rhea, 55
Rhodes, 215, 247–9
Romanus, Emperor, 158

Sabazios, 189, 190, 191
Sabos, 189, 191
Salamis, 10, 36, 54, 58
Sallust, 55
Samos, 235
Samuel, 'Last Judgement', 176, 177
Santorini, 250, 251, 252
Sappho, 2
Saturn, 55
Schliemann, Heinrich, 11, 68
Scott, Sir Walter, 69, 199
Sgourokephali, 269
Shelley, P. B., 9, 10, 14
Sibyl, the, 151
Sikelianos, Anghelos, 56–8, 155
Silas, 39

Skala, 186, 187, 188
Skolió, 186, 187, 189
Smyrna, 215, 247
Socrates, 23, 38
Sophia, St, 12, 161
Sophocles, 3
Sparta, 79, 92, 93, 98, 99
Staikopoulos, Staikos, 75, 76
Stepháni, peak of, 186, 188, 189
Stephen, St, 206
Stiriotes, St Luke, 156
Stoics, 39
Suda, 261
Suli, 129, 172, 173, 175, 176
Suliots, 172–7
Swainson, H., 12
Symons, Arthur, 12
Syra, 223, 227

Tainaron,107
Taygetus, 89, 90, 91–3, 94, 99, 102, 104, 107
Theocritus, 271
Theodorus, St, isle, 78
Thermopylae, 10, 90
Theseus, 47, 48
Thessalonica, 178, 182, 183
Thrace, 189–90
Thrasymedes, 82
Threspotia, 172
Thyestes, 74
Timotheus, 39
Tinos, 224, 229
Tosks, the, 11
Trebizond, George, 101
Troy, 11, 93
Tsokris, Demetrios, 75
Turk, Turks, 8, 22, 36, 40–2, 75, 76, 81, 107, 113, 145, 146, 157, 174, 248, 264

Venetians, 75, 261
Vesuvius, 99

Villehardouin, 75
Vourtzi, 74, 75, 76

Wilde, Oscar, 12
Winckelmann, J-J., 25
Woolf, Virginia, 2

Yannina, *see* Ioannina

Yeats, W. B., 14
Yerania Mountains, 62
Yitheion (Gytheion), 92, 107

Zakinthos (Zante), 134, 146
Zalongo, Mount, 177
Zeus, 49, 54, 123, 124, 125, 259